Events Management for the Infant and Youth Market

Events Management for the Infant and Youth Market

EDITED BY

HUGUES SERAPHIN

Oxford Brookes Business School, UK

emerald
PUBLISHING

United Kingdom – North America – Japan – India – Malaysia – China

Emerald Publishing Limited
Howard House, Wagon Lane, Bingley BD16 1WA, UK

First edition 2023

Reprints and permissions service
Contact: permissions@emeraldinsight.com

British Library Cataloguing in Publication Data
A catalogue record for this book is available from the British Library

ISBN: 978-1-80455-691-7 (Print)
ISBN: 978-1-80455-690-0 (Online)
ISBN: 978-1-80455-692-4 (Epub)

Printed and bound by CPI Group (UK) Ltd, Croydon, CR0 4YY

ISOQAR certified
Management System,
awarded to Emerald
for adherence to
Environmental
standard
ISO 14001:2004.

Certificate Number 1985
ISO 14001

INVESTOR IN PEOPLE

Table of Contents

About the Contributors

Yasmine Ait-Challal holds a Master's degree in Business Sciences with a marketing option. She is currently preparing a PhD in Territorial Marketing at EHEC Algiers (Business School – Kolea University Centre). She is also a member of the Marketing laboratory within the same school. Her research mainly focusses on sports events and their impact on destinations. She has participated in colloquiums and conferences. Her last one was in an international colloquium in India (ICOMBS 2022).

Kamila Ait-Yahia Ghidouche is a Professor at EHEC Algiers (Business School – Kolea University Centre). She teaches modules related to marketing, consumer behaviour and territorial marketing. She is currently Deputy Director of research programming at DGRSDT/MESRS (Directorate General for Scientific Research and Technological Development, Ministry of Higher Education and Scientific Research). Her main areas of research are marketing and its fields of application, more specifically: attractiveness and territorial marketing, the image of cities, the impact of events on cities, citizen participation and smart cities. She has moreover published several articles on the subject and has presented her work in numerous international conferences (IPBA, MTO, INTI, CIST...). In addition, she is a member of scientific committees in many conferences on marketing and tourism in North Africa.

Jan Carlyle is the Founder and Managing Director of events agency Autumn Live Ltd, who deliver live, online and hybrid events and experiences within the creative, digital, tech, health and wellbeing sectors. Jan is also the curator and licensee for TEDxWinchester (which ran in 2020, 2022 and is licenced for 2023). She is an award winner with BIMA, recognised as a Champion for Change as part of BIMA100. Jan chairs Be One Percent, a charity dedicated to alleviating poverty through collective giving, and is a trustee of The Cowrie Scholarship Foundation, which funds Black British students to attend university in the United Kingdom.

Karen Cripps is a Senior Lecturer in Leadership at Oxford Brookes Business School, UK. She holds a PhD in Sustainable Supply Chain Management in UK Tour Operations, and her research focusses on the application of responsible management in education. She is an active member of the United Nations 'Principles of Responsible Management' (PRME) network, with a particular interest in the 'sustainability mindset'. She acts as a 'sustainability leader' mentor for the World Economic Forum 'Global Shaper' programme, and combined with her extensive background in sustainability management and education, Karen is now focussed on maximising student empowerment for sustainability careers.

Emma Delaney has 25 years' experience as an event management practitioner and an academic. This includes working in visitor attractions, theatres and local authorities and delivering events for a variety of clients including political parties, the Trades Union Congress (TUC) and the National Health Service (NHS). Emma has a first degree in languages, from The University of Wales, Trinity St David, and both her MA in Education (with distinction) and PhD were awarded from the University of Chichester. Emma is a Senior Lecturer at the University of Surrey within the School of Tourism and Hospitality Management. Emma's publications include *Working with Venues for Events* (under the name Emma Nolan, Routledge, 2018), and her current research interests are centred on the MICE sector. She is particularly interested in destination competitiveness for MICE events and the site selection process in the organisation of international association conferences.

Souad Djedi-Birady is a Lecturer in Marketing in the School of Higher Commercial Studies (EHEC Algiers). She has worked for prestigious food brands at her early career before turning to academia. Dr Souad DJEDI holds a PhD in the field of Marketing (2021), her thesis exploring how children interact with food brands. Her current work focusses on consumer studies with a keen interest for children as current and future consumers. Her interest in researching children is now directed more towards issues of responsible and sustainable consumption in this target group.

Fatemeh Fehrest is a PhD candidate in Tourism at James Cook University. Her thesis topic is on humourous interpretation for children in tourism settings. She is particularly interested in working with children and enhancing their learning experience in the context of tourism through engaging them in fun activities.

Faouzi Ghidouche is a Professor at EHEC Algiers (Business School – Kolea University Centre) and member of the Thematic Interest Group 'Retailing in emergent countries' of the French Association of Marketing (AFM). He has also served as Head of HEC Algiers. His primary research subject focusses on studying large-scale trade and retailing. He presented his work and his contributions in many international conferences (CIST, IPBA, INTI) related to trade and services in emerging countries.

Vanessa G. B. Gowreesunkar is an Associate Professor with varied research interests in tourism. She is a citizen of Mauritius with a PhD cutting across three disciplines, namely Tourism Management, Communication and Marketing. Vanessa is the Associate Editor of the Emerald *International Journal of Tourism Cities*. With over a decade of experience in teaching, training and research, Vanessa has brought her contributions in various international universities and educational institutions. She currently serves as Associate Professor at the Anant National University in India. Previously, she was assuming the role of Head of Department for Hospitality and Tourism at the University of Africa. Vanessa is an editorial board member of several scientific journals and has a number of publications in Scopus-indexed journals. Vanessa is the main editor of a number of international textbooks, and she has authored/co-authored several research articles and book chapters.

Sarah Green is a Senior Lecturer in Digital Marketing at the University of Winchester. During her 30-year career in design branding and communications she has worked on a multitude of projects and events in the United Kingdom and abroad. With expertise in art and design she has formulated original and unique learning experiences for young children and students. In 2014 Sarah established Birdhouse Studio, a design education company with a specialism in teaching young children the principles of design in a high-quality, fun and engaging way. This included the planning, content and management of many workshops, after-school clubs, parties and other events that focussed on embracing the practices and approaches of 'grown-up' design and creative industries. Sarah is currently undertaking a Doctoral study on the impact of the design of spaces on the user experience.

Marie Haverly is an experienced wedding and event planner who currently leads the BA (Hons) Event Management UG programme at the University of Winchester. She has recently published a wedding planners guide and strives for excellence in event management study and employability skills within the event industry. Marie has a keen interest managing visitor expectations at weddings and events, and this includes ensuring children are well cared for and entertained. Marie has been an academic since 2015, prior to which she ran a successful wedding planning business in Hampshire, UK, and worked with over 600 couples over this time. She now enjoys sharing her knowledge and skills with students and fellow event planners.

Ricardo Jorge da Costa Guerra holds a PhD in Tourism, Leisure and Culture from the University of Coimbra, under the subject of health and wellness tourism and local development strategies. He completed an MSc in Tourism Management and Development and a degree in Tourism Management and Planning both at the University of Aveiro. Recently, he obtained the title of Specialist in Hospitality and Catering. Currently, he is an Assistant Professor and Subdirector of the Higher School of Tourism and Hospitality of the Polytechnic Institute of Guarda, where he coordinates the Degree in Hotel Management. He is also the representative of the Polytechnic Institute of Guarda in the Network of Higher Education Institutions for the Preservation of the Mediterranean Diet. He is an integrated researcher at CEGOT and also collaborates with CiTUR and UDI/IPG and has published several peer-reviewed articles, books, book chapters and participated in investigation projects.

Abi Knapton is an events manager at ReesLeisure, a sports event management company based in Hampshire. She leads on the operations of many sporting events including the ABP Southampton Marathon, Winchester Marafun and TryTri Events. She graduated with a degree in Events Management from the University of Winchester in 2020.

Tamas Lestar holds a PhD in Management and Sustainability from the University of Essex. He is a Senior Lecturer in Responsible Management and Leadership, University of Winchester. For several years, he has been studying spiritual communities and practices in the context of dietary change and sustainability transitions. Tamas investigates how religion enables or disables health and well-being, prosperity (without growth) and pro-environmental behaviour.

Luísa Lopes has been since 1999 an Assistant Professor at the Polytechnic Institute of Bragança. She holds a PhD in Business and Management Studies with a focus on Marketing and Strategic Management awarded by the University of Porto. She has a long curriculum in the private sector in functions linked with management and marketing. Her research interests include Relationship Marketing; Public and Nonprofit Marketing; Services Marketing; Higher Education Teaching; Tourism Marketing and Consumer Marketing. At the Polytechnic Institute of Bragança she holds various organisational positions and has promoted innumerous academic events. She attended several academic conferences both as an author and as a speaker. As a researcher she also collaborates with the Center of Tourism Research, Development and Innovation (CiTUR).

Charlie Mansfield has been a university lecturer since 1995 and taught at the University of Plymouth in Tourism Management and French, where he was also co-director of the heritage research centre. He completed a major, funded research project for the CNRS with the University of Paris 1 Panthéon-Sorbonne in digital heritage management and was a research academic with the University of Edinburgh from January 2005 until July 2009 where he successfully completed an AHRC-funded research project to digitise medieval texts. He is an independent researcher and travel writer, regularly running summer schools for literary travel writers and DMOs.

Marco Martins began his academic studies with a BA in Marketing and Advertising at the Higher Institute of Business and Tourism (ISCET). In 2012 he was awarded with a PhD in Tourism Sciences by the Université de Perpignan Via Domitia (France). Now he is an independent researcher, but he was an invited lecturer in several higher education institutions in Portugal, of which were ESACT of the Polytechnical Institute of Bragança, ESTH of the polytechnic Institute of Guarda; ISCET – Higher Institute of Business and Tourism – ISCET, among others. He is an editorial board member in the *Journal of Advanced Research*, a published author and reviewer for several leading journals.

Zohre Mohammadi is a Lecturer at University of Greenwich and a Senior Research Fellow in Tourism at James Cook University, Singapore. She received her PhD in Tourism in 2019 with her qualitative study on Childhood Travel Experiences and Motivations. Her research focus is on tourism behaviour and experience, tourism marketing and events, activities and amenities for children in order to introduce new emerging markets.

Giuseppe Pellegrini Masini is an Associate Professor at the Norwegian University of Science and Technology NTNU and an environmental social scientist working on the drivers and barriers affecting the development of bottom-up initiatives and social innovations involving renewables, sustainable transportation and energy consumption in buildings. His specific focus is on energy justice, climate justice and related policies. Currently, he is a principal investigator and WP leader in the H2020 ACCTING project, while in the recent past, he worked on the H2020 ENTRANCES and SMARTEES projects. In 2017, he gained his PhD at Heriot-Watt University (School of Energy, Geoscience, Infrastructure and Society), where he researched social acceptability of onshore wind farms. He has published with Routledge a monograph titled 'Wind Power and Public Engagement: Co-operatives and Community Ownership', and several of his papers were cited in official reports of the IPCC Intergovernmental Panel on Climate Change.

Chris Powell is the Director of The Event Expert provides event management courses and event consultancy services covering all types of business, public and virtual events. As a 25-year career event professional, he has been helping his clients from the United Kingdom, Europe and the Middle East develop the ideas, skills and confidence to run successful and rewarding events. He is a self-confessed live and virtual event groupie...a lover of all thing's events, speaker, blogger and author. With over 500 events delivered and 6,000+ event managers trained he is above all else, an events practitioner.

Lara Santos hold a PhD in Marketing and Strategy (2019) awarded by a consortium formed by University of Minho, University of Aveiro and University of Beira Interior, a Master's in Social Economy (2009) awarded by University of Minho and a degree in Social Service (2006) awarded by the Portuguese Catholic University.

At the moment she is an Assistant Professor at School of Communication, Architecture, Ars and Technologies of the Lusófona University. She is also invited Assistant Professor at the School of Communication, Administration and Tourism of the Polytechnical Insitute of Bragança. Furthermore, she is a researcher at TRIE – Transdisciplinary Research Center for Entrepreneurship and Ecosystem Innovation, and has published some peer-reviewed articles, participated in research projects and is reviewer for the *Cross Cultural and Strategic Management* journal.

Hugues Seraphin is a Senior Lecturer in Tourism, Hospitality and Events Management at the Oxford Brookes University. Hugues Seraphin holds a PhD from the Université de Perpignan Via Domitia (France). He has 20 years of teaching experience (including 12 years at The University of Winchester Business School, UK).

Shem Wambugu Maingi is a Lecturer within the Department of Hospitality and Tourism Management, Kenyatta University. He is an African researcher on sustainable tourism development in Africa and currently co-editing books in the area. He is an expert member of the International Scientific Committee on Cultural Tourism of ICOMOS (ICTC) as well as a member of the IUCN WCPA Tourism and Protected Areas Specialist Group TAPAS.

List of Contributors

Yasmine Ait-Challal	Marketic, Ecole des Hautes Etudes Commerciales, Algeria, yasmine.aitchallal@gmail.com
Kamila Ait-Yahia Ghidouche	Marketic, Ecole des Hautes Etudes Commerciales, Algeria, kamilaghidouche@gmail.com
Jan Carlyle	Autumn Live Ltd, UK, jan@autumnlive.co.uk
Karen Cripps	Oxford Brookes Business School, UK, kcripps@brookes.ac.uk
Emma Delaney	University of Surrey, UK, e.delaney@surrey.ac.uk
Souad Djedi-Birady	Marketic, Ecole des Hautes Etudes Commerciales, Algeria, s.djedi@hec.dz
Fatemeh Fehrest	James Cook University, Australia, Farima.fehrest@my.jcu.edu.au
Faouzi Ghidouche	Marketic, Ecole des Hautes Etudes Commerciales, Algeria, f.ghidouche@hec.dz
Vanessa G. B. Gowreesunkar	Anant International National University, India, gaitree.gowreesunkar@anu.edu.in
Sarah Green	The University of Winchester, UK, sarah.green@winchester.ac.uk
Marie Haverly	The University of Winchester, UK, marie.haverly@winchester.ac.uk
Abi Knapton	ReesLeisure, UK, abi@reesleisure.co.uk
Tamas Lestar	The University of Winchester, UK, tasmas.lestar@winchester.ac.uk
Charlie Mansfield	University of Plymouth, UK, cmeserveorg@gmail.com

Marco Martins	Instituto Politécnico de Tomar and centro de Geociências (CGEO), Portugal, marco.mpm@gmail.com
Zohre Mohammadi	University of Greenwich, UK; James Cook University, Singapore, z.mohammadi@gre.ac.uk
Giuseppe Pellegrini Masini	Norwegian University of Science and Technology NTNU, Norway, giuseppe.p.masini@ntnu.no
Chris Powell	The Event Expert, UK, chris.powell@theeventexpert.co.uk
Hugues Seraphin	Oxford Brookes Business School, UK, hugueser.tourism@gmail.com
Shem Wambugu Maingi	Kenyatta University, Kenya, MAINGI.SHEM@ku.ac.ke

Acknowledgements

The emerging topic of childism in Events Management (and related topics) has been addressed in this book from different perspectives by both academics and practitioners. As editor of this book, I would therefore like to thank all the contributors for sharing their experience and expertise through the chapters they have submitted. I would also like to thank them for the quick turn-around of their chapter after receiving feedback from me. Finally, I would like to thank *Emerald Publishing* for its support with this project.

Introduction

Hugues Seraphin

Overview

Existing research on events have highlighted how important they are for communities and individuals (Andrews & Leopold, 2013; Fox, Gouthro, Morakabati, & Brackstone, 2014; Mallen & Adams, 2013; Yeoman, Robertson, Ali-Knight, Drummond, & McMahon-Beattie, 2009). To do so, Andrews and Leopold (2013), for instance, have used a variety of arguments. Amongst these are: (1) History. They have indeed highlighted the fact events, and, more specifically, festivals and cultural events, have always been prominent whether in pre-modern society, modern society and post-modern society.

This view is also shared by Fox et al. (2014, p. 4), who argued that 'special events have been part of human society ever since there have been people to get together for a short time to do something different'. Andrews and Leopold (2013) have also highlighted the (2) social aspect of events, which is playing a significant role in developing social capital amongst individuals within a community. To play this cement role, Mallen and Adams (2013) have explained that events are evolving at the same pace of individuals within the community. The term 'event-based tourism', for instance, has appeared because of the growing tourism and economic impact of events for some communities (Yeoman et al., 2009). Finally, Andrews and Leopold (2013) emphasised on the (3) legacy aspect of events, through the concept of *habitus*, meaning that the type of events individuals tends to like are often inherited from their parents.

Even though literature in the field of event management has evolved since the first ever publication in 1922 (Getz & Page, 2020), the fact remains that no existing literature has considered examining events management from the perspective of infants and young adults. Additionally, existing research has offered a variety of typology of events (Getz, 2008; Getz & Page, 2020), but none of them have considered infants and young adults. This study is therefore arguing that investigating events management from an infant and young adult perspective is an opportunity to review grounded theories in events management. The same could be said for other leisure activities and industries closely connected with events such as tourism (Yeoman et al., 2009) and hospitality (Getz & Page, 2020; Yeoman, 2013).

Events Management for the Infant and Youth Market, 1–6
Copyright © 2023 Hugues Seraphin
Published under exclusive licence by Emerald Publishing Limited
doi:10.1108/978-1-80455-690-020231002

Investigating events management studies without considering infants and young adults is unethical. Indeed, it is unlawful to deny minors and young adults access to certain types of products and services because of their age alone (Enghagen & Wilson, 1995). This view is further supported by Lovelock and Lovelock (2013), who argue that leaving out a group less well off than another is unethical. Additionally, the United Nations Convention on the Rights of the Child (articles 3 and 12 UNCRC) also states that it is part of the legal right of children to have their say in matters which have impacts on their wellbeing (Nottingham, 2022). The current lack of interest for children in events management studies could be explained according to Nottingham (2022) by the fact children are not allowed to vote (and therefore rely on others to represent their interests), what puts them in a weak position, hence the reason the dogma of ethics is not systematically applied to them.

Having said that, recent research has emphasised on the fact that the voice of individuals under-age ought to be heard (Canosa & Graham, 2016; Canosa, Wilson, & Graham, 2017; Poria & Timothy, 2014; Shiraani & Carr, 2021). Indeed, in tourism, which is a field of research directly connected with events management, there is a growing number of publications focussing on under-age members of the society (Canosa & Graham, 2016; Canosa & Schanzel, 2021). These publications are covering a wide range of topics, such as sustainability (Séraphin, 2022), marketing (Séraphin & Gowreesunkar, 2020), ethics (Canosa & Graham, 2016; Shiraani & Carr, 2021), entrepreneurship (Canosa & Schanzel, 2021) perspectives, etc.

The discrepancy between considering children as important stakeholders of a community and children considered as not being that important is pushing towards the more balanced view adopted by Séraphin and Green (2019) who are arguing that children are important stakeholders for a community because they have ideas which are worth being heard, but their view should be considered with extreme care due to the fact they sometimes have a metaphorical perception of the world, as opposed to objective. To address the gap in literature in events management, this edited book is focussing on infants (0–12) and young adults (13–24).

The life course framework of Zacher and Froidevaux (2021) presents the different stages of life, namely childhood (0–12) and adolescence/youth (13–24), which are the period where individuals go to school and develop their career interests and their personal agency. The period of early adulthood (25–39) and middle adulthood (40–60) is the period where individuals find their partners, start a family (children), build their career and increase their consciousness. Finally, the period of later adulthood (61–84) and very old age (85+), which is the period of transition from work to retirement, is also the period when family holidays are used for intergeneration or transmission of values (Gram, O'Donohoe, Schänzel, Marchant, & Kastarinen, 2019; Kemper, Ballantine, & Hall, 2019).

Structure of the Book

The book is articulated around four main sections, namely – Events for infants and young adults: Theoretical Frameworks (section 1); A Youth and Childism

Perspective of Events (section 2); Planning and delivering events: A Practical guideline (section 3) and Case studies (section 4).

Events for Infants and Young Adults: Theoretical Frameworks is articulated around three chapters. The first chapter 'Children's Engagement in Event Tourism: A Conceptual Framework' proposes a framework for understanding children's engagement in events. The proposed framework incorporates a variety of theories and models to conceptualise the engaging experience of children. This framework can enhance and deepen the understanding of children's experience of events and their complexity to enhance children's wellbeing and assist with policy and event practices. As the framework emphasises the significance of the level of engagement, it is specified that children's event profiles should be unique and tailored to their needs and interests.

The second chapter, 'Childhood Family Events, Memories, Nostalgia and Sustainability Discourse: Conceptual and Theoretical Perspectives', provides a conceptual and theoretical perspective on the roles and impacts of childhood research in sustainability discourse. Family events are integral towards developing inclusive and integrated societies and in realising SDG 16. Childhood is always eco-socialised, i.e. socially, economically and ecologically integrated with other forms of life, to the extent that childhood nostalgia forms the basis for future sustainable events and tourism choices.

The third chapter, 'Marketing Sustainable Events for Children', is aiming at developing a framework to make awareness, engagement and empowerment strategies central when developing events for children. In today's world events are used as a means to achieve an array of objectives including changing behaviours.

A Youth and Childism Perspective of Events is articulated around four chapters. Chapter 4, 'University Sustainability Career Information Events for Future Leaders', explores the nexus of sustainability and employability, within the context of Higher Education career events. It provides insights into how sustainability-related career information events can be managed to support the personal and professional development of graduates most effectively.

Chapter 5, 'How Children Experience Major Sports Events: Narratives of the Mediterranean Games Oran, Algeria, 2022', explores children's experiences of major sporting events. So doing, the chapter proposes to explore both the perception of children's experiences as spectators of an event; the trace of emotions and memories left in the mind of the events and finally, the implications of children's experiences on future sports practice.

Chapter 6, 'The Agency of Children and Young People in Sustainability Transitions Eco-Spiritual Events on Hare Krishna Eco-Farms in Europe', discusses how two Hare Krishna eco-farms and their eco-spiritual events are experienced by children. More specifically, the chapter is based on the attendance of infants to an annual fair that takes place in two different Hare Krishna communities.

The final chapter of this section, 'Turning Winchester (UK) Into an Eventful Children City: Investigating the Creation of a Webtoon Festival', provides a methodological approach to assess the importance of children events within a local community. From a practical point of view, it highlights to organisers of events in Winchester gaps that need to be addressed.

As for *Planning and Delivering Events: A Practical Guideline*, it is articulated around three main chapters. Indeed, '7 Steps to the Perfect Children's Event' (Chapter 8), gives an overview of the seven steps event managers should take to ensure they deliver successful children's events. The advice shared in this chapter is for all types of events for children.

Chapter 9, 'Venue Considerations When Planning Child Centric Events', provides a detailed and practical assessment of key venue considerations for event managers, when planning child-centric events. This is all the more important as events that are designed around the needs of children are particularly challenging to plan, and thus choosing the right venue to stage such an event is a substantial task.

Chapter 10, 'Sports Events and Children: ReesLeisure Management Approach', is about the management of sports event for children. So doing, the sport events company, ReesLeisure which operates the ABP Southampton Fun Run, Winchester Children's Triathlon, Southampton Sporterium (Cycling) Youth Races and Family Ride is used as a case study. The chapter explores some of the key operational steps and marketing activity required to organise children's sports events.

The final section of the book, namely: *Case Studies*, is structured around the following chapters. Chapter 11, 'Children at Weddings: How to Manage Parents and Children Before, During and After the Wedding', discusses whether children should be invited to weddings and wedding receptions and how to ensure their presence is enjoyable for all including the young persons themselves.

Chapter 12, 'Creating Unique Workshops and Events for Children – The Case of Birdhouse Studio', provides an overview of lessons learnt by an entrepreneur on both on how to plan events for children and on how to run a business focussing on after-school leisure activities for children. Whilst there is a wealth of theory and academic models on the management of businesses and events, the focus of the chapter is primarily practical with lessons learnt from direct, and sometimes hard-earned experience.

Chapter 13, 'Organising Events With Children With Disabilities at ANPRAS (Mauritius): Insights and Implications', chooses to focus on children with disabilities and seeks to demonstrate that children with disability have a louder voice than other children. Children with disabilities are an integral part of the society, but they often confront challenges due to barriers that people throw in their way. As a result, their participations in public events are often limited. Despite several treaties and conventions, children with disabilities still face discrimination that spreads into all spheres of life and not much is done to empower them to become resilient.

Finally Chapter 14, 'Kids TEDx: Handing Over the Microphone to Children to Bring us all Inspiration, Learning and Wonder', focuses on TEDYouth, a day-long event for middle and high school students, with live speakers, hands-on activities and great conversations. Scientists, designers, technologists, explorers, artists, performers, etc share short talks, serving both as a source of knowledge and inspiration for youth around the globe.

References

Andrews, H., & Leopold, T. (2013). *Events and the social sciences*. Abingdon: Routledge.

Canosa, A., & Graham, A. (2016). Ethical tourism research involving children. *Annals of Tourism Research, 61*(15), 1–6.

Canosa, A., & Schanzel, H. (2021). The role of children in tourism and hospitality family entrepreneurship. *Sustainability*. doi:10.3390/su132212801

Canosa, A., Wilson, E., & Graham, A. (2017). Empowering young people through participatory film: A post methodological approach. *Current Issues in Tourism, 20*(8), 894–907.

Enghagen, L. K., & Wilson, R. H. (1995). Keeping it legal: Refusing to minors and young adults. *Cornell Hospitality Quarterly, 36*(1), 70–74.

Fox, D., Gouthro, M. B., Morakabati, Y., & Brackstone, J. (2014). *Doing events research. From theory to practice*. Abingdon: Routledge.

Getz, D. (2008). *Event studies: Theory, research and policy for planned events* (2nd ed.). London: Routledge.

Getz, D., & Page, S. J. (2020). *Event studies: Theory, research and policy for planned events* (4th ed.). London: Routledge.

Gram, M., O'Donohoe, S., Schänzel, H., Marchant, C., & Kastarinen, A. (2019). Fun time, finite time: Temporal and emotional dimensions of grandtravel experiences. *Annals of Tourism Research, 79*. doi:10.1016/j.annals.2019.102769

Kemper, J. A., Ballantine, P. W., & Hall, C. M. (2019). Combining the 'why' and 'how' of teaching sustainability": The case of the business school academics. *Environmental Education Research, 25*(12), 1751–1774.

Lovelock, B., & Lovelock, M. (2013). *The ethics of tourism*. London: Routledge.

Mallen, C., & Adams, L. J. (2013). *Event management in sport, recreation and tourism: Theoretical and practical dimensions* (3rd ed.). London and New York, NY: Routledge.

Nottingham, E. (2022). Securing sustainable tourism: Children's right and adults' responsibilities. In H. Séraphin (Ed.), *Children in sustainable and responsible tourism* (pp. 159–170). Bingley: Emerald Publishing Limited.

Poria, Y., & Timothy, D. J. (2014). Where are the children in tourism research? *Annals of Tourism Research, 47*, 93–95.

Séraphin, H. (Ed.). (2022). *Children in sustainable and responsible tourism*. Bingley: Emerald Publishing Limited.

Séraphin, H., & Gowreesunkar, V. (Eds.). (2020). *Children in hospitality and tourism: Marketing and managing experiences*. Berlin: De Gruyter.

Séraphin, H., & Green, S. (2019). The significance of the contribution of children to conceptualising and branding the smart destination of the future. *International Journal of Tourism Cities, 5*(4), 544–559.

Shiraani, F., & Carr, N. (2021). Disabled children are not voiceless beings. *Annals of Tourism Research*. doi:10.1016/j.annals.2021.103257

Yeoman, I. (2013). A futurist's thoughts on consumer trends shaping future festivals and events. *International Journal of Event and Festival Management, 4*(3), 249–260.

Yeoman, R., Ali-Knight, J., Drummond, S., & McMahon-Beattie, U. (2009). *Festival and events management: An international arts and culture perspective.* Oxford: Butterworth-Heinemann.

Zacher, H., & Froidevaux, A. (2021). Life stage, lifespan, and life course perspectives on vocational behaviour and development: A theoretical framework, review, and research agenda. *Journal of Vocational Behaviour, 126*, 1–22.

Section 1
Events for Infants and Young Adults:
Theoretical Frameworks

Chapter 1

Children's Engagement in Event Tourism: A Conceptual Framework

Zohre Mohammadi and Fatemeh Fehrest

Abstract

In recent years, research on children's tourism experiences has gained prominence, as children are becoming an increasingly vital market for the tourism industry. While events are a main sector of the industry and host millions of children every year, there is a lack of research specifically focussed on children's experiences in events. This chapter focusses on children's entertainment events which can provide children with a satisfying, memorable and educational experience. This study has developed a framework to facilitate deeper mixed studies on children's experiences in event tourism. The framework is composed of four pillars based on various social, tourism and event theories and models, including the Cognition–Affect–Behaviour (CAB) theoretical framework, the Orchestra Model of Experience, the Event Experience Scales (EES), the Theory of Child Well-being and the Transtheoretical Model of Behaviour Change (TTM). The framework can be used by future researchers as an analytical evaluation tool to study children's experiences in different types of events and understand the mechanisms of behaviour change in this context.

Keywords: Children; events; experience; Cognition–Affect–Behaviour; well-being; framework

Introduction

Children's experiences are gaining prominence in contemporary tourism literature. Children are becoming an increasingly important market. They are considered active consumers and decision-makers (Seraphin & Yallop, 2020). Cullingford (1995, p. 126) expressed children's significant role in the industry as 'tourists of the future' which establishes a rationale to cherish them as significant stakeholders of the industry. Over the past few years, they could attain more

Events Management for the Infant and Youth Market, 9–23
Copyright © 2023 Zohre Mohammadi and Fatemeh Fehrest
Published under exclusive licence by Emerald Publishing Limited
doi:10.1108/978-1-80455-690-020231003

attention from both industry and researchers (e.g. Israfilova & Khoo-Lattimore, 2019; Khoo-Lattimore, 2015; Koscak et al., 2021; Séraphin & Gowreesunkar, 2020). Although, research with/for children in tourism is at its initial stages (Mohammadi & Pearce, 2020) and there are still many areas of tourism research considered to be lacking in terms of children, with events being one of them. Events as one of the main sectors of tourism industry are also the hosts of millions of children every year which emphasises the significance of children's experience in events. However, there is still a huge gap studying event tourism specifically for children (Potwarka, Snelgrove, Wood, Teare, & Wigfield, 2020) since studies are limited to considering children as a group of participants (e.g. Kim, Choi, Agrusa, Wang, & Kim, 2010; Li, Kim, & Lee, 2021). Even, adult-centric event studies focussed primarily on the economic effects of events or the motivations of attendees, rather than the participants' experiences (Geus, Richards, & Toepoel, 2016).

Dolasinski, Roberts, Reynolds, and Johanson (2021) defined an event as a temporary, planned, one-of-a-kind occasion involving two or more participants. They proposed a taxonomy of four primary types of events, namely professional, entertainment, social and common cause (Dolasinski et al., 2021). This chapter focusses on children's entertainment events associated with amusement, fun and enjoyment for attendees, such as exhibitions, festivals, sports and concert events, and live performances. Festivals have been quite popular due to cultural, social and economic conditions, and also people's interest in outdoor recreations and travel (Geus et al., 2016), and they are usually planned to achieve destination marketing tools (Marković, 2019). In general, events are an effective strategy to promote a location, facility or organisation and attract tourists (Etiosa, 2012). Festivals appear to be among the most popular activities for children which can provide participants with a satisfying, joyful and memorable experience (Yolal, Gursoy, Uysal, Kim, & Karacaoğlu, 2016). Event attendees value their subjective experience; consequently, event managers must have a thorough comprehension of their experience to meet their expectations (Geus et al., 2016).

Children's participation in events is under-represented (e.g. Idema & Patrick, 2019; Li et al., 2021; Liu & Draper, 2022; Potwarka et al., 2020; van Beynen & Burress, 2018). A study conducted by Idema and Patrick (2019) on families taking part in science festivals revealed that unlike parents, children are active participants of such festivals. In another study van Beynen and Burress (2018) studied how, when and where children are engaged in science festivals through observation, and they mostly focussed on children's interaction with others particularly their parents. Similarly, Van Winkle and Bueddefeld (2016) highlighted family bonding as a result of participating in such festivals while Cole and Chancellor (2009) emphasised on participants' satisfaction that can improve the attitudes towards family life.

The lack of children's voice in tourism and event literature has been justified (see Mohammadi, 2020; Poria & Timothy, 2014, Potwarka et al., 2020; Schlemmer, Stickdorn, Kristiansen, & Schnitzer, 2022) mainly as a result of ethic approval process, children's limited ability to express themselves as target group, special expertise required to collect data from children and lack of theoretical frameworks to be used in children's studies (Poria & Timothy, 2014). However, children in events have been studied in bond with family in a few studies but children's perspective regarding their engagement is less known in tourism literature. There are several significant unanswered questions regarding children's engaging experience in events: How do children experience and perceive events? How do children's perception of the events differ from adults? How do event experiences affect children's behaviour and well-being? Studying the core of the event experience of children is not easy, which adds more complexity to study the 'black box' of event experience as Geus et al. (2016) call it. In addition, a review of the relevant literature reveals that there is no experiential processing model to systematically examine children's experience and perception of the events and determine the relationship between the experience and subsequent outcomes. Considering the research gap of children's voices in event tourism, the explained complexity and lack of theoretical frameworks prompted us to devise a framework to facilitate deeper mixed studies with and for children in event context. This framework is designed based on different social, tourism and event theories and models including Cognition–Affect–Behaviour (CAB) theoretical framework (Potwarka et al., 2020; Zheng, Qiu, Morrison, Wei, & Zhang, 2022), Orchestra Model of Experience (Pearce & Mohammadi, 2021), Event Experience Scale (EES) (Geus et al., 2016), Event Social Interaction Scale (ESIS) (Marques, Borba, & Michael, 2021), Theory of Child Well-being (Raghavan & Alexandrova, 2015) and Transtheoretical Model of Behaviour Change (TTM) (Prochaska & DiClemente, 1983) to understand how an event is experienced by children and what is the mechanism of change of behaviour. This framework can be used and tested by future researchers as an analytical evaluation tool to study children's experiences in different event types.

Framework Development

Four pillars serve as the basis for the proposed framework. The first pillar is the CAB theoretical framework (see Potwarka et al., 2020; Zheng et al., 2022) which is used as the backbone of the framework. As one of the demonstration effects models, CAB is a linear theory illustrates how behaviour is formed with the main premise that cognition of stimuli, what people think, and how they think about the experience and stimuli will lead to affection, and affection will lead to behaviour (Huang, Korfiatis, & Chang, 2018; Potwarka et al., 2020). The CAB model has been used by many researchers of various fields particularly consumer behaviour including fast food service (Chebat, Kerzazi, & Zourrig, 2010), e-service (Kao & Lin, 2016), e-commerce (Chang & Chen, 2009), e-commerce recommendation system (Abumalloh, Ibrahim, & Nilashi, 2020), destination image (Zheng et al., 2022) and intangible cultural heritage (Qiu, Zheng, Xiang, & Zhang, 2019).The extensive application of the CAB model across various areas delineates its potential to predict attitude change and behavioural intentions. CAB has been used in tourism research in the past two decades, particularly within the context of sustainability and developing pro-environmental behaviour (Chou, Horng, Liu, & Lin, 2020; Zheng et al., 2022).

The concept of *cognition* refers to tourists' reaction to the information received from surrounding environment which can lead to future expectations (Pearce & Mohammadi, 2021). Cognition was recognised as information processing taking place in human brain while handling the information which constitutes the basis of CAB framework (Newell & Simon, 1972 cited in Qiu et al., 2019). Any response related to tourists' consciousness, memory, understanding and learning is considered a cognitive experience (Pearce & Mohammadi, 2021). Therefore, it is significant what children are attracted to and what they focus on during an event, as it contributes to their cognitive development.

The concept of *affection* in tourism literature refers to the favourable or unfavourable impressions tourists have of a destination or event (Pearce & Mohammadi, 2021). Individuals can experience high levels of emotions through their experiences (Bigne, Mattila & Andreu, 2008) which are exactly what events aim to offer (Geus et al., 2016). Zheng et al. (2022) connect this concept with 'delight', the positive surprise and joy that can potentially lead to a change in behaviour. They argue that emotions can be awakened by many factors including novelty (Zheng et al., 2022). Therefore, any aspect of the event that children perceive as novel can elicit their emotions or affection. Tourism literature claims that emotions are powerful enough to shape a special behaviour (Gezhi & Xiang, 2022) including satisfaction, attachment and loyalty (Faullant, Matzler, & Mooradian, 2011; Yuksel, Yuksel, & Bilim, 2010) or responsible behaviour and pro-environmental actions (Su, Hsu, & Boostrom, 2020; Zheng et al., 2022). Based on the previous research, event planners should think about evoking positive feelings in children when organising and running events.

The third dimension of the CAB model, *behaviour*, refers to a predicted future behaviour which represents one of the most significant drivers of behaviour (Lin & Roberts, 2020). In event tourism literature, behavioural intention refers to the loyalty of visitors which is delineated through revisits in the future and recommending the event to others (Chen & Tsai, 2007; Yang, Gu, & Cen, 2011). Some researchers have gone further to extend this concept to enhancing visitors' or their companion's awareness, influencing their purchasing behaviour and facilitating tourism (Kruger & Viljoen, 2021).

The second pillar is tourism experience. Packer and Ballantyne (2016) defined the experience as 'an individual's immediate and ongoing, subjective and personal response to an activity, setting, or event outside their usual environment'. Experience plays a significant role in tourism studies as many studies have stated its relationship with behavioural intentions (Liu, Sparks, & Coghlan, 2017). Children are distinct from adults, and their experiences may be influenced by different or the same elements but in a different way. Consequently, a combination of emic and etic perspectives is necessary to comprehend children's experiences at events from their point of view.

Pine, Pine, and Gilmore (1999, p. 31) proposed the experience economy framework which illustrates the participation or engagement of the tourists in an event, or a tourism experience based on four experiential domains: entertainment, education, aesthetic, escapist. Other researchers, building on their study, have identified a variety of aspects of tourist experiences (Packer & Ballantyne, 2016; Richards, 2020). It is generally acknowledged that developing a holistic approach to the customer experience is necessary for gaining a more in-depth comprehension of customer behaviour. As a comprehensive model for this pillar, the Orchestra Model of Experience is adapted. Pearce (2011) utilised the metaphor of an orchestra to illustrate how various elements contribute to the overall quality of an experience. The performance of an orchestra depends on the coordination of a large number of distinct but essential components. The experience of visitors is compared to the piece of music in this model to show how each component play an important role. There are five different aspects that contribute to it. The visitors' experience is composed of these five contributing components (Pearce & Mohammadi, 2021). The five factors that shape the context of the visitors' experience are their sensory inputs, emotive reactions, cognitive abilities to comprehend their surroundings, behaviour and relationship.

The third pillar is children's engagement in events. Experience economy explains the significance of visitor's engagement. Engagement has been defined as a behavioural action which involves an interactive experience for customers (Brodie, Ilic, Juric, & Hollebeek, 2011). Unlike involvement, which is a passive mental state of being only interested, engagement has a behavioural aspect (Organ, Koenig-Lewis, Palmer, & Probert, 2015). It is claimed that greater engagement can lead to loyalty and behavioural intention (Brodie, Hollebeek, Juric, & Ilic, 2011) which will be applied to this chapter's conceptual framework. Even though the majority of the event literature was not conducted with children, it is still significant because it focusses on events as agents of behaviour change. van Beynen and Burress (2018) examined factors influencing elementary-school children's engagement in public science festivals in Florida. According to this study, children would prefer to actively get involved by *doing* and *talking*. The authors highlight the idea that in order to understand the festival visitor experience comprehensively and to encourage engagement, interaction and learning both visitor and setting factors should be considered (van Beynen & Burress, 2018).

The literature on children's engagement in events proposes different aspects including cognitive, affective and social (Geus et al., 2016; Richards, 2020). In behaviour studies, cognition and rationality are prominent and significant factors, and this assertion has been thoroughly examined (Cohen, Prayag, & Moital, 2014). In addition to cognitive factors, the importance of hedonic factors increases over time in studies of customer behaviour (Coetzee & Pourfakhimi, 2020). According to Coetzee and Pourfakhimi (2020), affective stimuli directly influence the decisions, beliefs and behaviours of customers. In the new context, emotions are no longer considered in the evaluation of the cognitive state but are instead recognised as stable behavioural constructs (Cohen et al., 2014). Understanding how children feel about an experience will help us assess it, enhance happy memories, create a brand image and create behavioural intentions (Coetzee & Pourfakhimi, 2020).

To expand the framework around the engaging event experience of children, besides the Orchestra Model of Experience, two other models were used. There is a well-known event-specific scale (Lee, Coetzee, Hermann, & du Plessis, 2018) known as EES (Geus et al., 2016). They view the event experience as a process that begins with the setting and conditions, continues to the experience's core and concludes with experience outcomes. Coetzee and Pourfakhimi (2020) explained that the core of the framework considers the experience as a set of interactions and engagements. These interactions are influenced by motivations or expectations. The model focusses on three types of engagements, cognitive, affective and physical. Consumers' cognitive engagement is tied to their level of self-awareness, perception, memory, learning, judgement and understanding of the experience. Affective engagement is tied to their excitement, emotional energy, intimacy, adventure, personal values and personal recollection. Excitement had the most significant relationship to loyalty to the events. Physical engagement is concerned with their actual behaviour and physical activities (Coetzee & Pourfakhimi, 2020). Behavioural outcomes of the experience are another part of the model which focusses on satisfaction which is a very well-studied topic in tourism studies.

The model is tested on different locations and cultural contexts (Richards, 2020); therefore, the scale has general validity to be used for better understanding of children's engaging experience in events. Previously, it was believed that experiences are self-directed and personalised and that they depend solely on personal characteristics. However, EES testing revealed that cultural context, age, gender, level of education, the type of event and the stage of the experience are also significant (Richards, 2020).The stage of the experience can result in different levels of engagement in each aspect, as stated by Richards (2020), cognitive engagement remained of the same importance to visitors, but affective engagement begins with anticipation in the pre-event, progresses to excitement during the event and concludes with memorable and recollection after the event.

One significant aspect of events is socialisation and networking (Getz, 2008), whereas the EES model ignores social interaction. In line with the orchestra model, we adopted another event experience scale with the focus on social interaction, ESIS by Marques et al. (2021). They believe that social interactions are not only a part of the experience but also contribute to the subjective experience; hence, they refer to events as 'social interaction platforms' (Marques et al., 2021). The ESIS focusses exclusively on visitor interactions, whereas the Orchestra Model of Experience encompasses all types. These social interactions should not be limited to those within the event but should also include those with the outside world (Simons, 2019), as even these interactions can influence the children's experience and its outcomes. ESIS also introduces social practices in two domains, private and public. Private domains happen between known and includes belonging, bonding and detaching. Public domain including communing, connecting and amiability happens with new unknown visitors (Marques et al., 2021).

The fourth pillar is concerned with the outcomes of events for children. In addition to the well-observed and studied effects on behaviour, events may also influence one's well-being. Geus et al. (2016) believe that by understanding the event experience, it is possible to comprehend how we can contribute to life quality and well-being. Therefore, the proposed framework targets both the well-being and behavioural effects of events on children. The Theory of Child Well-Being is applied to comprehend children's well-being as a result of engaging in events. Martin Seligman (2011), a positive psychologist, developed the PERMA model which defines key elements of well-being. This model elaborates that happiness may happen through *Positive emotions* such as pleasure, satisfaction, and hope; active *Engagement*; positive, meaningful *Relationships*; and a sense of *Meaningful Achievement* (Seligman, 2011) and accomplishment (Seligman, 2011). This model illustrates the relationship between various forms of engagement and well-being as the outcome.

Well-being is viewed in three categories of present feeling of happiness, past feeling of the satisfaction and future evaluation (Mannell & Kleiber, 1997, p. 86). There are three major theories of well-being, including hedonism with its emphasis on happiness, desire theories with the emphasis on the satisfaction of desires and preferences, and objective list theories, which are pluralist in contrast to the other two with the emphasis on a variety of objectively valuable things (Lin, 2014). The need for a theory of well-being tailored to children prompted Raghavan and Alexandrova (2015) to create their Theory of Child Well-Being. They examined the hedonic, desire, and objective list theories of well-being to obtain a holistic view of children's well-being. According to them, children's happiness and desire satisfaction are not the only components of well-being. This theory is not concerned with children's well-being as future adults, but rather as they are now. They explain that the theory of well-being can be articulated if the child develops stage- and environment-appropriate skills, which could set her up for a successful future and allow the child to engage with the environment in an age-appropriate manner (Raghavan & Alexandrova, 2015). Therefore, well-being for children is considered multi-dimensional including physical, psychological (mental and emotional), social and cognitive development (Moore, Murphey, & Bandy, 2012). Events can play a role in children's physical well-being by influencing new eating, health or safety habits; in psychological well-being through an increase in hope and life satisfaction; in social well-being by enhancing civic engagement and volunteering; and in cognitive well-being through improvement of critical thinking.

Behaviour change can happen through the continued involvement or marketing elements such as satisfaction, attachment, and loyalty. We adopted the TTM to understand children's behavioural change in a more qualitative manner. This model demonstrates how to encourage continued involvement with a leveraging initiative after initial engagement (Teare, Potwarka, Wigfield, & Chard, 2022). The model was initially developed by Prochaska and DiClemente (1983) in the context of health, but more recently, it has been applied to the social sciences. There have been studies on how this model might be used to assess changes in spectator behaviour at sport events (Teare et al., 2022) and sustainable tourism events (Mair & Laing, 2013). Mair and Laing (2013) used TTM to demonstrate how a sustainability-focussed event can encourage attendees' behaviour change. In the original model (Prochaska & DiClemente, 1983), there are four stages: pre-contemplation, contemplation, action and maintenance which tell us when changes happen, and 10 processes which helps to understand how change happens in each stage. TTM is a dynamic model, and individuals may progress or regress through stages (Mair & Laing, 2013). The adaptation to TTM facilitates an understanding of when, why and how a change occurs as a result of children's exposure to events. As we all know, tourism is an ideal setting for sustainability education and learning, particularly when children are the target audience. One way to achieve this is to prioritise sustainability and provide such content at events. For adults, participation in such events can indicate their initial choice of sustainable topics, whereas for children, who may have participated in such events as part of their required school or parental programmes, they can serve as a teaching tool.

The economic outcomes of events can be evaluated based on customer satisfaction and loyalty, which have not been studied with children. Consumer satisfaction has been defined as a positive emotional response or a sense of accomplishment resulting from a desired leisure experience (Geus et al., 2016; Kim, Suh, & Eves, 2010). Satisfaction with an event is influenced by how event is perceived at all different stages of the experience and may lead to loyalty, future return, purchase or participation (Chen & Tsai, 2007; Hubbard, Mandabach, McDowall, & VanLeeuwen, 2012). That is why measuring visitors' satisfaction at festivals and events has been recognised as significant in tourism literature. Aside from the importance of satisfaction in and of itself, children's satisfaction with the event in which they participate is quite important not only because it affects the holiday satisfaction of parents (Mikkelsen & Stilling Blichfeldt, 2015) and makes them recommend the experience to other families (Kozak & Duman, 2012) but also because they are an emerging market for events. Lugosi, Robinson, Golubovskaya, and Foley (2016) have considered children's satisfaction even more important than adults' satisfaction. Mohammadi and Pearce (2020) argued that childhood experiences and positive memories can be considered as an important factor to become a loyal adult. Gaines, Hubbard, Witte, and O'Neill (2004) held the opinion that offering children's programming of a top quality would result in customer satisfaction, loyalty and word-of-mouth promotion. According to the tourism literature, it has been acknowledged that children's satisfaction of events is important for them, their parents and guardians, as well as for destinations managers.

Providing a satisfactory event experience for children requires an integrated approach (Seraphin & Yallop, 2020) while addressing children's needs. However, children's explanation of satisfaction is much simpler than adults: it is *fun* (Read, MacFarlane, & Casey, 2002). Therefore, to satisfy children, it is sufficient to provide them with a fun event experience. Read et al. (2002) proposed three dimensions of fun for children including expectation, engagement and endurability. The more engaged children are during an event, the more joyful experience they will remember, which is deemed satisfactory for this age group. As children's literature suggests, play is what can make the event experience unique and rich for children and engage them in a desired way. Tourism play is defined by children under a study as a range of activities done in a new touristic place, such as seeing, tasting, buying new things, taking photos etc. (Zhong & Peng, 2021). This definition implies that play is a combination of engagements ranging from physical and sensory engagements to cognitive and social ones. There are five main approaches to children's play including: 'play as behaviour or activity', 'play as motive, attitude or state of mind', 'play as meaningful experience', 'play as form and structure', and 'play as ontologically distinctive phenomenon' (Feezell, 2010). As these approaches imply, play is more than just an activity; it can engage the child from multiple perspectives and create a meaningful experience for them, which is a goal in tourism.

To respond to the main aim of the chapter, we employed and adapted various theories based on the four pillars to develop an evaluative framework for children's engagement in events. This framework (Fig. 1) facilitates the in-depth study of children's engagement at an event and the evaluation of how the level of engagement in various aspects can affect the well-being, and behaviour changes as outcomes. Each type of engagement has the potential to predict a different outcome, such as affective engagement, which can predict emotional judgement and satisfaction; cognitive engagement, which can predict future learning effects and physical engagement, which can predict active participation during events. The rationale of this framework lies in the lack of evaluative tools and frameworks to study and understand children's role in events. This rationale involves the systematic identification of potentially relevant variables prior to the examination of specific cases.

Conclusion

This chapter proposes a framework for understanding children's engagement in events. The proposed framework incorporates a variety of theories and models to conceptualise the engaging experience of children. The CAB model serves as the backbone of the framework. The extensive use of CAB model in tourism to study environmental and sustainability concerns and attitude change among visitors (Kim, Choi, Agrusa, Wang, & Kim, 2010; Kuo, Cheng, Chang, & Hu, 2021; Qiu et al., 2019) highlight that visitors' attitudes and behavioural intentions are influenced by cognitive and affective factors during their visits. Through the Orchestra Model of Experience, EES and ESIS, the cognitive, affective, social, physical and sensory engagement are conceptualised. This framework can enhance and deepen the understanding of children's experience of events and their complexity to enhance children's well-being and assist with policy and event practices. As the framework emphasises the significance of the level of engagement, it is specified that children's event profiles should be unique and tailored to their needs and interests. Attempts should be made to engage children in relevant active and engaging experiences throughout all three stages of an event experience, based on the expected outcomes and consequences both for children's well-being and event managers' benefit. Such a diverse and well-designed profile can benefit us by attracting children, increasing their level of engagement, elevating their level of learning, promoting the event's image and producing

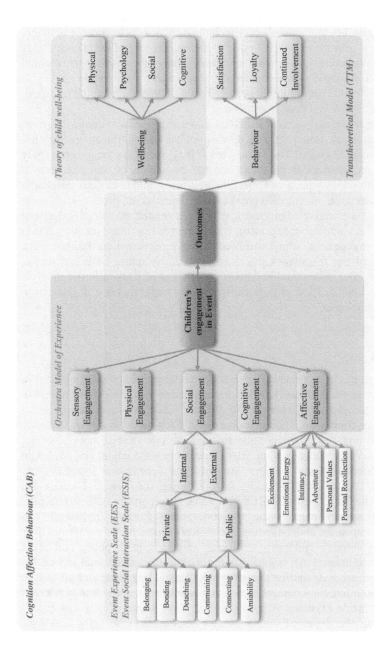

Fig. 1.   Conceptual Framework of Children's Engagement in Events. *Source:* Authors.

economic outcomes such as loyalty. The promotion of an event through children as a result of Generation Z's access to and use of the internet and social media is a free benefit for social, environmental and economic outcomes. By understanding social engagement and effectively managing it, we can facilitate and promote social bonding, value and ultimately the event's impact in numerous ways.

According to the framework, children benefit from memorable experiences, socialising, and feelings of well-being when events include physical, collaborative creative activities as well as active play and repetitively awakened emotions. Therefore, a simple answer to the complexity of children experience in events is to have fun. Children's play is not merely a physical activity, but rather a multidimensional engagement. Such an engagement can range from low cognitive level to high cognitive level, depending on whether the child is fully concentrating in an active mental state. There are different ways that how play can have a role in children's experiences in events which later may lead to positive outcomes. Therefore, play is one of the simple and perfect solutions to get children actively engaged in events and provide a meaningful and memorable experience for them.

References

Abumalloh, R. A., Ibrahim, O., & Nilashi, M. (2020). Loyalty of young female Arabic customers towards recommendation agents: A new model for B2C E-commerce. *Technology in Society, 61*. doi:10.1016/j.techsoc.2020.101253

Bigne, J. E., Mattila, A. S., & Andreu, L. (2008). The impact of experiential consumption cognitions and emotions on behavioural intentions. *Journal of Services Marketing, 22*(4), 303–315. doi:10.1108/08876040810881704

Brodie, R. J., Hollebeek, L. D., Juric, B., & Ilic, A. (2011). Customer engagement: Conceptual domain, fundamental propositions, and implications for research. *Journal of Service Research, 14*(3), 252–271. doi:10.1177/1094670511411703

Chang, H. H., & Chen, S. W. (2009). Consumer perception of interface quality, security, and loyalty in electronic commerce. *Information & Management, 46*(7), 411–417.

Chebat, J. C., Kerzazi, L., & Zourrig, H. (2010). Impact of culture on dissatisfied customers: An empirical study. *City, Culture and Society, 1*(1), 37–44.

Chen, C. F., & Tsai, D. (2007). How destination image and evaluative factors affect behavioural intentions? *Tourism Management, 28*(14), 1115–1122.

Chou, S. F., Horng, J. S., Liu, C. H. S., & Lin, J. Y. (2020). Identifying the critical factors of customer behaviour: An integration perspective of marketing strategy and components of attitudes. *Journal of Retailing and Consumer Services, 55*. doi: 10.1016/j.jretconser.2020.102113

Coetzee, W. J., & Pourfakhimi, S. (2020). Affective engagement as a contextual dimension for predicting intentions to revisit and recommend events–a multinational comparison. *Journal of Policy Research in Tourism, Leisure and Events, 12*(3), 401–421.

Cohen, S. A., Prayag, G., & Moital, M. (2014). Consumer behaviour in tourism: Concepts, influences and opportunities. *Current issues in Tourism, 17*(10), 872–909.

Cole, S. T., & Chancellor, H. C. (2009). Examining the festival attributes that impact visitor experience, satisfaction and re-visit intention. *Journal of Vacation Marketing, 15*(4), 323–333.

Cullingford, C. (1995). Children's attitudes to holidays overseas. *Tourism Management, 16*(2), 121–127.

Dolasinski, M. J., Roberts, C., Reynolds, J., & Johanson, M. (2021). Defining the field of events. *Journal of Hospitality & Tourism Research, 45*(3), 553–572.

Etiosa, O. (2012). *The impacts of event tourism on host communities. Case: The city of Pietarsaari.* Degree programme thesis. Central Ostrobothnia University of Applied Sciences, Pietarsaari, Finland.

Faullant, R., Matzler, K., & Mooradian, T. A. (2011). Personality, basic emotions, and satisfaction: Primary emotions in the mountaineering experience. *Tourism Management, 32*(6), 1423–1430.

Feezell, R. (2010). A pluralist conception of play. *Journal of the Philosophy of Sport, 37*(2), 147–165.

Gaines, B. L., Hubbard, S. S., Witte, J. E., & O'Neill, M. A. (2004). An analysis of children's programs in the hotel and resort industry market segment. *International Journal of Hospitality & Tourism Administration, 5*(4), 85–99.

Getz, D. (2008). Event tourism: Definition, evolution, and research. *Tourism Management, 29*(3), 403–428.

Geus, S. D., Richards, G., & Toepoel, V. (2016). Conceptualisation and operationalisation of event and festival experiences: Creation of an event experience scale. *Scandinavian Journal of Hospitality and Tourism, 16*(3), 274–296.

Gezhi, C., & Xiang, H. (2022). From good feelings to good behavior: Exploring the impacts of positive emotions on tourist environmentally responsible behavior. *Journal of Hospitality and Tourism Management, 50*, 1–9.

Huang, G. H., Korfiatis, N., & Chang, C. T. (2018). Mobile shopping cart abandonment: The roles of conflicts, ambivalence, and hesitation. *Journal of Business Research, 85*, 165–174.

Hubbard, K. W., Mandabach, K. H., McDowall, S., & VanLeeuwen, D. M. (2012). Perceptions of quality, satisfaction, loyalty, and approximate spending at an American wine festival. *Journal of Culinary Science & Technology, 10*(4), 337–351.

Idema, J., & Patrick, P. G. (2019). Experiential learning theory: Identifying the impact of an Ocean Science Festival on family members and defining characteristics of successful activities. *International Journal of Science Education, Part B, 9*(3), 214–232.

Israfilova, F., & Khoo-Lattimore, C. (2019). Sad and violent but I enjoy it: Children's engagement with dark tourism as an educational tool. *Tourism and Hospitality Research, 19*(4), 478–487.

Kao, T. W. D., & Lin, W. T. (2016). The relationship between perceived e-service quality and brand equity: A simultaneous equations system approach. *Computers in Human Behavior, 57*, 208–218.

Khoo-Lattimore, C. (2015). Kids on board: Methodological challenges, concerns and clarifications when including young children's voices in tourism research. *Current Issues in Tourism, 18*(9), 845–858.

Kim, S. S., Choi, S., Agrusa, J., Wang, K. C., & Kim, Y. (2010). The role of family decision makers in festival tourism. *International Journal of Hospitality Management, 29*(2), 308–318.

Kim, Y. G., Suh, B. W., & Eves, A. (2010). The relationship between food related personality traits, satisfaction, and loyalty among visitors attending food events and festivals. *International Journal of Hospitality Management, 29*, 216–226.

Koscak, M., Knežević, M., Binder, D., Pelaez-Verdet, A., Işik, C., Mićić, V., ... Šegota, T. (2021). Exploring the neglected voices of children in sustainable tourism development: A comparative study in six European tourist destinations. *Journal of Sustainable Tourism*, 1–20.

Kozak, M., & Duman, T. (2012). Family members and vacation satisfaction: Proposal of a conceptual framework. *International Journal of Tourism Research, 14*(2), 192–204.

Kruger, M., & Viljoen, A. (2021). Terroir wine festival visitors: Uncorking the origin of behavioural intentions. *Current Issues in Tourism, 24*(5), 616–636.

Kuo, N. T., Cheng, Y. S., Chang, K. C., & Hu, S. M. (2021). How social capital affects support intention: The mediating role of place identity. *Journal of Hospitality and Tourism Management, 46*, 40–49.

Lee, C., Coetzee, W., Hermann, U., & du Plessis, L. (2018). Why should I come back?: Predicting behavioural intentions of beer festival attendees by their event experience. In *CAUTHE 2018: Get smart: Paradoxes and possibilities in tourism, hospitality and events education and research* (pp. 612–616). Newcastle, NSW: Newcastle Business School, The University of Newcastle.

Li, X., Kim, J. S., & Lee, T. J. (2021). Contribution of supportive local communities to sustainable event tourism. *Sustainability, 13*(14). doi:10.3390/su13147853

Lin, E. (2014). Pluralism about well-being. *Philosophical Perspectives, 28*, 127–154.

Lin, N., & Roberts, K. R. (2020). Using the theory of planned behavior to predict food safety behavioral intention: A systematic review and meta-analysis. *International Journal of Hospitality Management, 90*. doi:10.1016/j.ijhm.2020.102612

Liu, Y., & Draper, J. (2022). The influence of attending festivals with children on family quality of life, subjective well-being, and event experience. *Event Management, 26*(1), 25–40.

Liu, W., Sparks, B., & Coghlan, A. (2017). Event experiences through the lens of attendees. *Event Management, 21*(4), 463–479.

Lugosi, P., Robinson, R. N., Golubovskaya, M., & Foley, L. (2016). The hospitality consumption experiences of parents and carers with children: A qualitative study of foodservice settings. *International Journal of Hospitality Management, 54*, 84–94.

Mair, J., & Laing, J. H. (2013). Encouraging pro-environmental behaviour: The role of sustainability-focused events. *Journal of Sustainable Tourism, 21*(8), 1113–1128.

Mannell, R., & Kleiber, D. (1997). *A social psychology of leisure*. State College, PA: Venture Publishing.

Marković, S. (2019). How festival experience quality influence visitor satisfaction? A quantitative approach. *Naše gospodarstvo (Our Economy), 65*(4), 47–56.

Marques, L., Borba, C., & Michael, J. (2021). Grasping the social dimensions of event experiences: Introducing the event social interaction scale (ESIS). *Event Management, 25*(1), 9–26.

Mikkelsen, M. V., & Stilling Blichfeldt, B. (2015). 'We have not seen the kids for hours': The case of family holidays and free-range children. *Annals of Leisure Research, 18*(2), 252–271.

Mohammadi, Z. (2020). Listening to children as a tourism market: The Asian context. In *Tourism's new markets: Drivers, details and directions* (pp. 176–190). Oxford: Goodfellow.

Mohammadi, Z., & Pearce, P. (2020). Making memories: An empirical study of children's enduring loyalty to holiday places. In *Children in hospitality and tourism* (pp. 137–156). Oldenbourg: De Gruyter.

Moore, K. A., Murphey, D., & Bandy, T. (2012). Positive child well-being: An index based on data for individual children. *Maternal and Child Health Journal, 16*(1), 119–128.

Newell, A., & Simon, H. A. (1972). *Human problem solving* (Vol. 104, No. 9). Englewood Cliffs, NJ: Prentice-Hall.

Organ, K., Koenig-Lewis, N., Palmer, A., & Probert, J. (2015). Festivals as agents for behaviour change: A study of food festival engagement and subsequent food choices. *Tourism Management, 48*, 84–99.

Packer, J., & Ballantyne, R. (2016). Conceptualizing the visitor experience: A review of literature and development of a multifaceted model. *Visitor Studies, 19*(2), 128–143.

Pearce, P. L. (2011). Tourist behaviour and the contemporary world. In *Tourist behaviour and the contemporary world*. Bristol: Channel View Publications.

Pearce, P. L., & Mohammadi, Z. (2021). Building the orchestra model of tourist experience, integration and examples. In *Routledge handbook of the tourist experience* (pp. 50–63). London: Routledge.

Pine, B. J., Pine, J., & Gilmore, J. H. (1999). *The experience economy: Work is theatre & every business a stage*. Boston: Harvard Business Press.

Poria, Y., & Timothy, D. J. (2014). Where are the children in tourism research. *Annals of Tourism Research, 47*, 93–95.

Potwarka, L. R., Snelgrove, R., Wood, L., Teare, G., & Wigfield, D. (2020). Understanding demonstration effects among youth sport spectators: Cognitive and affective explanations. *Sport, Business and Management: An International Journal, 10*(2), 187–206.

Prochaska, J. O., & DiClemente, C. C. (1983). Stages and processes of self-change of smoking: Toward an integrative model of change. *Journal of Consulting and Clinical Psychology, 51*(3), 390.

Qiu, Q., Zheng, T., Xiang, Z., & Zhang, M. (2019). Visiting intangible cultural heritage tourism sites: From value cognition to attitude and intention. *Sustainability, 12*(1), 132.

Raghavan, R., & Alexandrova, A. (2015). Toward a theory of child well-being. *Social Indicators Research, 121*(3), 887–902.

Read, J. C., MacFarlane, S., & Casey, C. (2002, August). Endurability, engagement and expectations: Measuring children's fun. In *Interaction design and children* (Vol. 2, pp. 1–23). Eindhoven: Shaker Publishing.

Richards, G. (2020). Measuring the dimensions of event experiences: Applying the event experience scale to cultural events. *Journal of Policy Research in Tourism, Leisure and Events, 12*(3), 422–436.

Schlemmer, P., Stickdorn, M., Kristiansen, E., & Schnitzer, M. (2022, January). A mixed methods stakeholder satisfaction study of sports events based on the case of the 2016 international children's games. *Journal of Convention & Event Tourism, 23*(1), 41–62.

Seligman, M. E. (2011). *Flourish: A visionary new understanding of happiness and well-being*. New York: Simon and Schuster.

Séraphin, H., & Gowreesunkar, V. (Eds.). (2020). *Children in hospitality and tourism: Marketing and managing experiences* (Vol. 4). Oldenbourg: Walter de Gruyter GmbH & Co KG.

Seraphin, H., & Yallop, A. (2020). An analysis of children's play in resort mini-clubs: Potential strategic implications for the hospitality and tourism industry. *World Leisure Journal, 62*(2), 114–131.

Simons, I. (2019). Events and online interaction: The construction of hybrid event communities. *Leisure Studies, 38*(2), 145–159.

Su, L., Hsu, M. K., & Boostrom, R. E., Jr. (2020). From recreation to responsibility: Increasing environmentally responsible behavior in tourism. *Journal of Business Research, 109*, 557–573.

Teare, G., Potwarka, L. R., Wigfield, D., & Chard, C. (2022). Here today, gone tomorrow: Experiences of youth who responded to an event leveraging initiative. *Managing Sport and Leisure*, 1–14.

van Beynen, K., & Burress, T. (2018). Debris, diatoms, and dolphins: Tracking child engagement at a public science festival. *International Journal of Science Education, Part B, 8*(4), 355–365.

Van Winkle, C. M., & Bueddefeld, J. N. (2016). Service-dominant logic and the festival experience. *International Journal of Event and Festival Management*.

Yang, J., Gu, Y., & Cen, J. (2011). Festival tourists' emotion, perceived value, and behavioural intentions: A test of the moderating effect of festivals cape. *Journal of Convention & Event Tourism, 12*(1), 25–44.

Yolal, M., Gursoy, D., Uysal, M., Kim, H. L., & Karacaoğlu, S. (2016). Impacts of festivals and events on residents' well-being. *Annals of Tourism Research, 61*, 1–18. doi:10.1016/j.annals.2016.07.008

Yuksel, A., Yuksel, F., & Bilim, Y. (2010). Destination attachment: Effects on customer satisfaction and cognitive, affective and conative loyalty. *Tourism Management, 31*(2), 274–284.

Zheng, W., Qiu, H., Morrison, A. M., Wei, W., & Zhang, X. (2022). Landscape and unique fascination: A dual-case study on the antecedents of tourist pro-environmental behavioral intentions. *Land, 11*(4), 479.

Zhong, S., & Peng, H. (2021). Children's tourist world: Two scenarios. *Tourism Management Perspectives, 38*. doi:10.1016/j.tmp.2021.100824

Chapter 2

Childhood Family Events, Memories, Nostalgia and Sustainability Discourse: Conceptual and Theoretical Perspectives

Shem Wambugu Maingi and Vanessa G. B. Gowreesunkar

Abstract

Family events have unique significance on children as well as long-lasting impacts on them during their adulthood. A review of conceptual and theoretical literature on the subject was conducted to identify underlying trends and best practices in engaging children in the events industry. Societies are in transition from industrialised societies into risk societies and are increasingly becoming eco-socialised. Family events are integral towards developing inclusive and integrated societies and in realising Sustainable Development Goal 16 (SDG 16). Childhood is always eco-socialised, i.e. socially, economically and ecologically integrated with other forms of life. To the extent that childhood nostalgia forms the basis for future sustainable events and tourism choices. Family events are, therefore, increasingly becoming fundamental towards developing sustainability discourse. This viewpoint chapter provides conceptual and theoretical perspective on the roles and impacts of childhood research in sustainability discourse.

Keywords: Childhood; children events; family events; sustainable tourism; family tourism; nostalgia

Introduction

Family events have unique significance on children as well as long lasting impacts on them during their adulthood. Most often than not, these events have social, emotional and behavioural effects that have not been well documented in events management research, (Bartolett, 2010; Pomfret, 2020; Seraphin, 2020; Stadler & Jepson, 2017; Stone, 2022). The ideographic and cognitive value of family events have made these events quite attractive to the visitor market. These events range

Events Management for the Infant and Youth Market, 25–38
Copyright © 2023 Shem Wambugu Maingi and Vanessa G. B. Gowreesunkar
Published under exclusive licence by Emerald Publishing Limited
doi:10.1108/978-1-80455-690-020231006

from annual festivals, spectacles, exhibitions, cultural, heritage, sports and celebration events. Swarbrooke (2002) classified events as a unique component of the
visitor attraction landscape as the marker, the nucleus and (or) as an additional
complementary activity. However, most often than not, the events sector has been
a separate sector and not entirely a sub-sector of the attractions sector,
(Weidenfield, Butler, & Williams, 2016). The events industry further attracts a
wide range of consumers in terms of age, gender, social class etc. Events management research has also been biased and focussed on an 'adult-only' population
and therefore ignoring the children population who are equally attracted to and
attend events. In an adult-centred world, the need for the event industry to
address the needs and effects of social events on children has been an issue that
need to be addressed from a research perspective. Family events and trips play
important roles in the children's happiness, appeal, cognitive and social development (Gowresunkaar, Mohanty, & Maingi, 2022; Huang, Zhang, &
Ihnatoliova, 2020; Park, Pan, & Ahn, 2020). Lin (2009) notes that children
events play a significant role in shaping future autobiographical memory bias and
therefore influence future consumption. Social events have also been used to plant
scripted childhood memories on children, therefore creating unique memories on
children (Pezdek, Finger, & Hodge, 1997). Childhood memories become their
life's future souvenirs and form the children's perceptions of the world thereafter.
Memories have been connected to adults searching for identity, retracing earlier
journeys and emotional experiences, as well as favourite holiday hotspots for the
visitors. According to Marschall (2015), memories of events have triggered new
forms of tourism and popular niche phenomena called roots tourism where
African-Americans visited their roots in West Africa, birth-right tourism under-
taken by Jewish Americans and homesick tourism where tourists visit their
ancestry. These memorable experiences eventually contribute to four key
dimensions of memory, i.e. affect, expectations, consequentiality and recollection.
Extant literature has considered tourists memories as an integral aspect in their
destination choices and preferences (Martin, 2010; Trdina & Pusnik, 2022; Tung
& Ritchie, 2011). Memories form at early stages in life and they are evidenced by
the autobiographical narratives and memories of visitors in their later life. These
memories are associated with the personal identities and recalled childhood events
that influence a greater part of a person's future preferences. Xu, Zhong, Li, and
Xiao (2021) note that childhood memories have ideally challenged the traditional
views of the passive roles of childhood in tourism discourse. Memories have a
significant role to play in tourism. Bartoletti (2010) notes that childhood memories play a critical role in building heritage tourism as well as commodifying
nostalgia as a stimulator or incentive for travel. Nostalgia and memory have
become, to a particular extent, tourism products as more destinations seek to
recreate historical and cultural environments that relate to the memories of the
visitors. Studies have further shown that tourism experiences are remedy to
nostalgia and a means of recounting childhood memories for the visitors, (Dann,
1995; Shi, Bettache, Zhang, & Xue, 2021; Vesey & Dimanche, 2003). Tourism
experiences are critical towards developing memorable and future behavioural
outcomes, and various authors have documented this fact (Seyfi, Hall, &

Rasoolimanesh, 2019). Further, studies have confirmed that the family life events have significant impacts on adult behaviour (Rydell, 2010).

Socially, family events have nostalgic effects on host community quality of life (QOL), (Stadler & Jepson, 2017). The impacts of family events on children QOL have been well researched with the development of the impacts of events scale (IES), (Horowitz, Wilner, & Alvarez, 1979). These impacts extend beyond QOL but also towards improving the mental health of the children. Family events can either have positive or traumatic impact on the children and they play a very important role in guaranteeing positive or negative emotions of the children in later life. In a study by Liu and Draper (2022), children attending festivals with the parents had a higher family quality of life (FQOL), subjective well-being, and experience as compared to children who never attended such events with their parents. Similarly, Villalonga-Olives et al. (2010) examined other health related QOL dimensions and noted five major dimensions, i.e. physical well-being, psychological well-being, parent relations, social support and school environment. From an environmental perspective, family events influence children's emotional and physical development. Sebba (1991) and Wagner (1978) investigated the environmental preferences of adults and noted that they are greatly influenced by childhood experiences. A multi-cultural survey conducted by Lohr, Pearson-Mims, Tarnai, and Dillman (2000) further indicated that childhood environmental experiences significantly influenced the adult's sensitivities in terms of values and pro-environmental behaviours as well as participation in conservation programmes in adulthood. To a particular extent the childhood family events and experiences have an influence on the child's life trajectories and future choices, preferences and satisfaction levels. Childhood experiences during family events and vacations play a very important role in influencing future consumption choices. Despite this well-documented fact, there has been a dearth of research on childhood experiences as a way of examining future preferences with the 'Adults only' focus on tourism and events research. Studies have also documented the need to research on understanding children's events and experiences in order to understand the children's preferences in terms of products and services (Lugosi, Robinson, Golubovskaya, & Foley, 2016; Radic, 2017). Despite the fact that there has been documented research on nostalgia studies, the study of events has ignored research on exploring the roles of children in events. Much of the research on children in events have been conducted from a child right in tourism perspective (Canosa & Graham, 2022; Maingi & Gowreesunkar, 2022; Ursin & Skålevik, 2018) and familism (Shanzel, 2013). Memorable experiences have become key for the events industry (Kim, Ritchie, & McCormick, 2012), and despite the fact that a lot of research has focussed on that, childhood memories research is still in infancy stages and only a limited number of studies on this topic exist. The main purpose of this study is to provide a theoretical context to the interrelationships between family events, childhood memories, nostalgia and sustainability discourse and research.

The Concept of Family Events

The earliest attempts to define events came from Donald Getz idealised events as: 'An opportunity for leisure, social and culture experience outside normal range of choices or beyond everyday experience', (Getz, 1991, 2005). By extension, family events incorporate opportunities for family leisure, social and cultural experiences within or outside their local communities. Fletcher (2022) notes that family events are either events 'experienced by' members of a family, events 'experienced as' family or events that 'impact' families. Family events extend towards community engagement events that promote inter-generational family interactions. This broad spectrum of family events brings out the diverse experiential and social nature of events that are experienced by families and by extension, children. The positive impacts of such events include the creation of safe environments for children to enjoy the diverse cultural, entertainment and leisure spaces. Family events are either expected or unexpected and have become an important part of every community, culture and society. They represent either gains or losses and are typically shared with the members of the family. Specifically, family events have been considered to be central towards engaging children with the society around them as well as building relationships around them that last within their lifetime (Gowresunkaar et al., 2022; Seraphin, Yallop, Seyfi, & Hall, 2022). Family events indicate how children perceive their position and roles within society and the environment around them, (Willet, 2015). Studies have shown that children's early experiences in life have an effect on their consumption and preferences (Birbili, 2013; Pretes, 2013). Despite the dearth in literature on the economic effects of family events, the family-based context of children involvement in tourism has been a growing tradition in the tourism sector accounting for a significant 30% of the leisure travel market (Shanzel & Yeoman, 2015). Family events are not just positive to children but also without proper management can present negative impacts and risks to children such as child-abusive behaviours, bullying, consumption of alcohol, bring accidental harm to the children and also affect the mental health and well-being of children (Patterson & Mccubbin, 1983; Simons, 2015).

Nostalgic Family Events, Childhood Memories and Sustainability Discourse: Conceptual Perspectives

According to Seraphin and Green (2019), children play a significant role in conceptualising future consumption. As an additional tourist cohort, children play a very important role in the events industry. It is a segment that is expected to grow and form the future of events industry in the developing world. The experiences of children in early life have a significant effect on 'memorable events experiences' in later years of life. The emotional link, family cultural environment and the events–memory nexus between the children and places/spaces play a significant role in influencing the children's events experiences (Farmaki, 2021; Guo & Liu, 2022; Xu et al., 2021). Consumers are hedonic beings, and they are constantly in search for emotional arousal as the dominant motivator for their consumption process. Therefore, affect has been considered as a consequence of the rational consideration of the product attributes (Hyde, 2008). Childhood memories have been considered as a strong factor in evoking nostalgic longing and an escape to the past. This longing for the past has developed either directly and indirectly through memorable tourism events and experiences (Tung, Lin, Zhang, & Zhao, 2017), positive feelings towards nature and culture (Lee & Ma, 2006) as well as travel motives (Waileong et al., 2015). Various social psychology and cultural anthropology studies have been trying to understand 'why' childhood memories were significant influencers (Levy, 1981; Rook, 2001). However, according to Foster, Zin, Keto, and Pulkki (2022), the childhood memories are always eco-socialized, i.e. socially and ecologically integrated with other forms of life. To the extent that these childhood memories form the basis for future choices. According to Lee and Ma (2006), direct childhood experiences with the environment has also contributed to positive feelings and attitude towards nature. Nostalgia has been perceived as the yearning of memories that is experienced by individuals in the context of a positive and/or negative feeling (Mandal, Gunasekar, Dixit, & Das, 2022). Children build their physical, social and cognitive dispositions and skills that influence their future actions. It is in their early years in life that children form connections and relationships with the environment, communities and the world around them. The nostalgic memories later on form their specific references and drives in life.

Family Events Management: Implications on Childhood Identity Development

In order to address the 16th Sustainable Development Goal (SDG 16), promoting inclusive societies is the bedrock of developing inclusive and integrated societies. To a particular extent, family events play an important role in embedding inclusivity and enhancing a cohesive, inclusive and integrated society (Maingi, 2018). At the heart of any society is the family and its cohesiveness. The health and welfare of the family institution is fundamental to the well-being of every society. Family events, when properly designed and managed, can have a positive impact on children's identity and individual psychosocial development. This involves understanding the unique psychological and social needs of children. The psychosocial needs of children were mapped by Erickson (1959) through his model for individual identity development that examined the different dilemmas that must be solved at the different stages of childhood and adulthood. The model maintained that personality develops at a certain pre-determined order which integrates the psychological needs of the individual as well as the societal needs. These are highlighted in Table 1. The model shows that infants need care that is consistent and reliable, therefore developing a sense of trust and security as they engage and develop other relationships. Family events need to provide consistent and reliable care to the infants therefore developing a sense of hope and support

Table 1. Childhood Psychosocial Development.

Stage (Years)	Psychosocial Dilemma (Main Process)	Virtue (Positive Self-Description)	Pathology (Negative Self-Description)
Infancy (0–2)	Trust versus mistrust (Mutuality with caregiver)	Hope and support	Detachment
Early childhood (2–4)	Autonomy versus shame and doubt (limitation)	Will	Compulsion
Middle childhood (4–6)	Initiative versus guilt (Identification)	Purpose	Inhibition
Late childhood (7–11)	Industry versus inferiority (Education)	Competence	Inertia
Early adolescence (12–18)	Group identity versus alienation)	Affiliation	Isolation
Adolescence (19–22)	Identity versus role confusion (Role experimentation)	Fidelity	Confusion
Young adulthood (23–34)	Intimacy versus isolation (Mutuality with peers)	Love	Exclusivity
Middle age (34–60)	Productivity versus stagnation (Person–environment fit and creativity)	Care	Rejectivity
Old age (60–75)	Integrity versus despair (Introspection)	Wisdom	Despair
Very old age (75–death)	Immortality versus extinction (Social support)	Confidence	Diffidence

Source: Adapted from Erickson (1959) and Newman and Newman (2003).

to the infants. Engaging the infants in day care play-based activities can be important in building the support that they need. At the second stage of early childhood, the child is developing some level of personal control and independence. Children at this stage are encouraged to be more confident and autonomous. At this stage, the children need to be encouraged to gain more self-esteem and achieve more personal control and independence. Family events in this stage need to provide children with physical activities that encourage them to be more active and independent as this helps the children develop psychosocially.

At the third and fourth stage of childhood, the children are in need for identity and education. At this stage, children are regularly interacting with other children and family events provide them with an opportunity to explore their interpersonal skills. The children can engage at their level and initiate activities with other children. At these stages of childhood, the teachers play a very important role as they engage them in learning activities. Their drive to learn new skills takes a significant role in their lives. Family events provide the best opportunity for the children at this stage to engage with their peers and develop unique virtues as a result.

Eco-Socialisation of Childhood (Adapting Bronfenbrenner's (1992) Ecological Systems Theory Perspective)

There has been a growing evidence suggesting that children were fundamental towards developing sustainable and responsible domains early in life (Kaefer, 2022; Maingi & Gowreesunkar, 2022; Seraphin et al., 2022). Children have their own refined ideas and thinking concerning things that affect them. However, more often than not, they end up being consumers and not producers of solutions to problems that surround them. In later life, most of the adults are influenced by the childhood memories. In this context, this study tries to understand the roles and impacts of childhood memories on sustainable events framework by adapting to the ecological systems theoretical perspective as explained in different studies, (Bronfenbrenner, 1992; Woodside, Caldwell, & Spurr, 2005). The ecological systems theory perspective explains childhood behaviour from both a micro- and macro-systems lens of the person's environment. Bronfenbrenner divided a person's ecological system into five major parts, i.e. the microsystem, the meso-system, the exosystem, the macrosystem and the chronosystem. The microsystem represents the first level of the ecological system, and it involves the childhood's immediate environment including the parents, siblings, religious institutions, the teachers and school peers. The children are influenced by the immediate environment to the extent that the immediate environment becomes the reference point. Reconstruction of personal memories can be based on this ecological level. Research on reconstructed childhood memories has shown that information sources such as family stories, photos and videos served as significant triggers of childhood memories (Wang & Gulgoz, 2019). In addition, the presence of family members and other adults provided significant reference cues for autobiographical childhood memories (Bauer, Bodner, Erdogan, Truxillo, Tucker, 2007). At the mesosystem level, this represents the interaction between the different microsystems. It includes the socio-cultural, regulatory and educational institutions surrounding the children. These institutions are very important in educating and facilitating the provision of important services to the children. Social interaction with people in different settings have an important influence on the development of the child. Mesosystems are social in nature, and they contribute towards positive behaviour. Experiences in different cultural contexts can give personalised and customised meanings of childhood. Childhood memories are subject to reconstruction with reference to the child's mesosystem across different contexts and time. Studies such as Foster et al. (2022) and Keto and Foster (2021) confirm that children are always eco-socialised, and this defines their ecological and social relations in the future. At the exosystems level, the other social structures which includes the children policy and mass media are the centre stage in developing the setting of childhood. Inside this policy-making exosystem, the child's rights and roles are defined. Indeed, social policy with regards to children and tourism is key towards developing the direction on children engagement in tourism. The macrosystem composes of the cultural values, customs and traditions that define childhood memories from an immediate societal point of view. Culture affects the adult's earliest recollection and autobiographical memory (Ross & Wang, 2010; Wang, 2001). The chronosystem represents the external environmental events and transitions that have significant influence on the life of the child. Each of the environments has an influence on childhood and by extension on childhood memories to the extent that these ecological systems serve either as facilitators or constraints.

Childhood experiences create sensory wonders where children view events as active proceedings in their web of life. The scope of this web revolves around ecological systems that do not operate within a vacuum. There are social, economic and environmental conditions that influence the childhood experiences and memories and define what they expect in future travel. Within the childhood's landscape, memories of family events become souvenirs of life that invoke nostalgia and a longing of the sensory wonders of memories. Such genealogical motives behind people searching for their family roots and revisiting their childhood has been well documented in research (McCain & Ray, 2003). The roles of memories in motivational research were earlier noted by Bird, Leighton, and McLean (2020) as a means of evoking the sensual remembrance of the past experiences. Family events in a way evoked the philoxenic and altruistic nature of childhood experiences, sending the visitors towards a memory lane of family tourism events and experiences. The deeper meanings of philoxenia according to Christou and Sharpley (2019) include physical, psychological and hedonic elements. However, the absence of children and childhood memories in event management studies tends to ignore the philoxenic nature of events and experiences. To the extent that sustainability needs are nostalgic ecological, social and economic expressions of the past. The 1987 United Nations Brundtland Commission report defines sustainability as

> Meeting the needs of the present without compromising the ability
> of future generations to meet their own needs.
>
> (UN, 2022)

Sustainability as a concept has been perceived as 'reflective' and 'restorative' in nature, indicative of the need for preservation and conservation of events and resources to a previous image of childhood memories. A notable reference on research on sustainable nostalgia shows that sustainability in a way is a nostalgic expression of the future (Bandyopadhyay, 2022; Chi & Chi, 2022; Davies, 2010; Hajra & Aggarwal, 2022). Nostalgia has been an imposing drive for wish fulfilment (Shin & Jeong, 2022; Yoon & Uysal, 2005) as well as a yearning desire for an attainable future, (Cheung, Sedikides, & Wildschut, 2016). Studies on the repeat-visit phenomena have shown that leisure vacationing has been to a significant extent influenced by memories, (Braun-LaTour, LaTour, & Zinkan, 2007; Rhoden, Hunter-Jones, & Miller, 2016). Sentimental feelings and nostalgia have been an important determinant of product attachment and explaining customer–product relationships (Page, 2014). Idealised family events have capitalised on nostalgic sentiments of the visitors, therefore enhancing social connectedness, identity and reconnection with the past and therefore developing strong pro-environmental behaviours (Wang, Jia, & Sun, 2018), pro-social behaviours (Gino & Desai, 2012) as well as pro-cultural behaviours, (Chang, Lin, & Wu, 2021). To the extent that this imagining to the sustainable future could create a different or better future for all. In the converse, the opposite may hold by noting that the longing for family events may be a product of nostalgia and childhood memories (Christou, 2018). The love and defence for nature and culture can be nurtured by engaging children in sustainable family events at a tender age. Children can learn more about nature and the threats that face wildlife to inculcate within them the passion for conservation, restoration and protection of the environment. Their exposure to different cultures and traditions also helps them to create a longer-lasting global culture for the children.

Family events can play a role in engaging children to be active change agents and proponents of change in the world through storytelling as well as through eco-conscious play. True to Benjamin franklin words; 'tell me and I forget, teach me and I may remember, involve me and I learn?', experiential learning as noted by Oloo (2022) is an important component associated with the children's cognitive, creative, emotional and social skills development. Active engagement of children through nature play events further promotes education for sustainability outcomes such as sustainability knowledge, skills and values on SDGs. However, there are exceptions of stressful life events that affect the participation of children in family events which include children being in broken homes, children living in poverty, orphaned children, as well as children living with chronic illnesses and disabilities leading to social isolation.

Conclusion

In conclusion, it is worth noting that family events create an eco-socialized childhood that idealises events and experiences. Family events provide the gestalt focus in adulthood and become the focal point of future event preferences. It is important that ecological systems theoretical approach as well as the theories on Childhood psychosocial development are adopted to develop sustainable events for children. There is need for events stakeholders to understand the unique ecological systems and psychosocial factors surrounding children and childhood and devise policies that are children sensitive in order to guarantee the children a safe and secure environment as well as memorable experiences for adulthood. It is important that the lifecycle approach towards events is adapted in devising the marketing policies and strategies such that the view of the children are integrated within the marketing plans and policies than a spatial analysis of the market. The integration of sustainability themes in children events products such as democracy, inclusivity, conservation, mutual respect, equality, life skills etc. is critical towards integrating sustainability. Children have an opportunity to build a new world from their perspective. In turn, these aspects influence their future lives and behaviours. There is need for further research towards memorable and sustainable events and experiences for children and young people, therefore guaranteeing conservation action and sustainable events and experiences for all. There is need towards promoting sustainability in children/family education, events and experiences therefore ensuring that the future generations are able to relive their nostalgic childhood experiences later in life.

References

Bandyopadhyay, R. (2022). Consuming colonial nostalgia in Kolkata, India. *Annals of Tourism Research, 95.* doi:10.1016/j.annals.2022.103427

Bartoletti, R. (2010). Memory tourism and the commodification of nostalgia. In P. Burns, C. Palmer, & J.-A. Lester (Eds.), *Tourism and visual culture* (Vol. 1, pp. 23–42). Wallingford: CABI.

Bauer, T. N., Bodner, T., Erdogan, B., Truxillo, D. M., Tucker, J. S. (2007, May). Newcomer adjustment during organizational socialization: A meta-analytic review of antecedents, outcomes, and methods. *Journal of Applied Psychology, 92*(3), 707–721. doi:10.1037/0021-9010.92.3.707. PMID: 17484552.

Birbili, M. (2013). Developing young children's thinking skills in Greek early childhood classrooms: Curriculum and practice. *Early Child Development and Care, 183*(8), 1101–1114.

Bird, G. R., Leighton, H., & McLean, A. K. (2020). A matter of life and death: Tourism as sensual remembrance. In C. Palmer & H. Andrews (Eds.), *Tourism and embodiment.* New York, NY: Routledge.

Braun-LaTour, K. A., LaTour, M. S., & Zinkan, G. M. (2007). Using childhood memories to gain insight into brand meaning. *Journal of Marketing, 71*(2), 45–60.

Bronfenbrenner, U. (1992). Ecological systems theory. In R. Vasta (Ed.), *Six theories of child development revised formulations and current ideas.* London: Jessica Kingsley.

Canosa, A., & Graham, A. (2022). Reimagining children's participation: A child rights informed approach to social justice in tourism. *Journal of Sustainable Tourism, 1–13.*

Chang, J., Lin, S. H. H., & Wu, L. S. (2021). Searching memories of pleasures in local cuisine: How nostalgia and hedonic values affect tourists' behavior at hot spring destinations? *British Food Journal.*

Cheung, W., Sedikides, C., & Wildschut, T. (2016). Induced nostalgia increases optimism (via social-connectedness and self-esteem) among individuals high, but not low, in trait nostalgia. *Personality and Individual Differences, 90,* 283–288.

Chi, O. H., & Chi, C. G. (2022). Reminiscing other people's memories: Conceptualizing and measuring vicarious nostalgia evoked by heritage tourism. *Journal of Travel Research, 61*(1), 33–49.

Christou, P. A. (2018). Tourism experiences as the remedy to nostalgia: Conceptualizing the nostalgia and tourism nexus. *Current Issues in Tourism, 23*(5), 612–625.

Christou, P., & Sharpley, R. (2019). Philoxenia offered to tourists? A rural tourism perspective. *Tourism Management, 72*, 39–51.

Dann, G. M. (1995). Tourism: The nostalgia industry of the future. In W. F. Theobald (Eds.), *Global tourism: The next decade* (pp. 55–67). Oxford: Butterworth-Heinemann.

Davies, J. (2010). Sustainable nostalgia. *Memory Studies, 3*(3), 262–268.

Erickson, E. (1959). *Identity and the life cycle.* New York, NY: International University Press.

Farmaki, A. (2021). Memory and forgetfulness in tourism crisis research. *Tourism Management, 83*(1). Retrieved from https://www.ncbi.nlm.nih.gov/pmc/articles/PMC7456263/pdf/main.pdf

Fletcher, T. (Ed.). (2022). *Family events: Practices, displays and intimacies.* Abingdon, Oxon: Routledge.

Foster, R., Zin, M., Keto, S., & Pulkki, J. (2022). Recorgnizing ecosocialization in childhood memories. *Educational Studies.* doi:10.1080/00131946.2022.2051031

Getz, D. (1991). *Festivals, special events, and tourism.* Van Nostrand Reinhold.

Getz, D. (2005). *Event management and event tourism* (2nd ed.). New York, NY: Cognizant Communications Corporation.

Gino, F., & Desai, S. D. (2012). Memory lane and morality: How childhood memories promote pro-social behaviors. *Journal of Personality and Social behaviors, 104*(2), 1–16.

Gowresunkaar, V. G. B., Mohanty, P. P., & Maingi, S. W. (2022). Children as ambassadors in sustainability initiatives of ANPRAS, mauritius. In H. Seraphin (Ed.), *Children in sustainable and responsible tourism.* Bingley: Emerald Publishing Limited.

Guo, X., & Liu, T. (2022). The psychological process and emotional cognition of children's tourism experiences in Chinese family culture. *Frontiers in Public Health, 11*(1), 1–13.

Hajra, V., & Aggarwal, A. (2022). Nostalgia: An antecedent of tourist motivations in senior citizens. *ECS Transactions, 107*(1). doi:10.1149/10701.6569ecst

Horowitz, M. J., Wilner, N., & Alvarez, W. (1979). Impact of event scale: A measure of subjective stress. *Psychosomatic Medicine, 41*, 209–218.

Huang, X., Zhang, L., & Ihnatoliova, L. (2020). Spatial memory bias in children tourists. *Journal of China Tourism Research, 16*(1), 78–95. doi:10.1080/19388160.2020.1718051

Hyde, K. F. (2008). Independent traveler decision-making. In A. G. Woodside (Ed.), *Advances in culture, tourism and hospitality research* (Vol. 2). Bingley: Emerald Publishing Limited.

Kaefer, F. (2022). Understanding sustainable tourism. In *Sustainability leadership in tourism* (pp. 7–25). Cham: Springer.

Keto, S., & Foster, R. (2021). Eco-socialization – An ecological turn in the process of socialization. *International Studies in Sociology of Education, 30*(1), 34–52.

Kim, J. H., Ritchie, J. B., & McCormick, B. (2012). Development of a scale of a memorable tourism experience scale (MTES). *Journal of Travel Research, 53*(3), 323–335.

Lee, J. C., & Ma, W. H. (2006). Early childhood environmental education: A Hong Kong example. *Applied Environmental Education and Communication, 5*(2), 83–94.

Levy, S. J. (1981, Summer). Interpreting consumer mythology: A structural approach to consumer behavior. *Journal of Marketing, 45*, 49–61.

Lin, C. (2009). *Developmental psychology*. Beijing: People's Education Press.

Liu, Y., & Draper, J. (2022). The influence of attending festivals with children of family quality of life, subjective well-being and event experience. *Event Management, 26*, 25–40.

Lohr, V. I., Pearson-Mims, C. H., Tarnai, J., & Dillman, D. (2000). *A multicultural survey of the influence of childhood environmental experiences on adult sensitivities to urban and community forests*. Department of Horticulture and Landscape Architecture, Washington State University. Retrieved from https://public.wsu.edu/~lohr/hih/nucfac/prop.htm

Lugosi, P., Robinson, R. N., Golubovskaya, M., & Foley, L. (2016). The hospitality consumption experiences of parents and carers with children: A qualitative study of foodservice settings. *International Journal of Hospitality Management, 54*, 84–94.

Maingi, S. W. (2018). Tourism and event management trends and policies: A regional approach. In H. Seraphin & M. Korstanje (Eds.), *International event management: Bridging the gap between theory and practice*. Newyork: Nova Science Publishers.

Maingi, S. W., & Gowreesunkar, V. G. (2022). Child rights and inclusive sustainable tourism development in east Africa: Case of Kenya. In H. Seraphin (Ed.), *Children in sustainable and responsible tourism*. Bingley: Emerald Publishing Limited.

Mandal, S., Gunasekar, S., Dixit, S. K., & Das, P. (2022). Gastro-nostalgia: Towards a higher order measurement scale based on two gastro festivals. *Tourism Recreation Research, 47*(3), 293–315.

Marschall, S. (2015). 'Homesick tourism': Memory, identity and belonging. *Current Issues in Tourism, 18*(9), 876–892.

Martin, D. (2010). Uncovering unconscious memories and myths for understanding international tourism behavior. *Journal of Business Research, 63*(4), 372–383.

McCain, G., & Ray, N. M. (2003). Legacy tourism: The search for personal meaning in heritage travel. *Tourism Management, 26*(6), 713–717.

Newman, B., & Newman, P. (2003). *Development through life* (8th ed.). Pacific Grove, CA: Brookes/Cole.

Oloo, L. A. (2022). A sustainable urban future: The role of early childhood education. Urbanet. Retrieved from https://www.urbanet.info/sustainable-future-role-of-early-childhood-education/

Page, T. (2014). Product attachment and replacement: Implications for sustainable design. *International Journal of Sustainable Design, 2*(3), 265–282.

Park, S. Y., Pan, B., & Ahn, J. B. (2020). Family trip and academic achievement in early childhood. *Annals of Tourism Research, 80*. doi:10.1016/j.annals.2019.102795

Patterson, J. M., & Mccubbin, H. I. (1983). The impact of family life events and changes on the health of a chronically III child. *Family Relations*, 255–264.

Pezdek, K., Finger, K., & Hodge, D. (1997). Planting false childhood memories: The role of event plausibility. *Psychological Science, 8*(6), 437–441. doi:10.1111/j.1467-9280.1997.tb00457.x

Pomfret, D. M. (2020). Battle for the peak: Childhood, the great war and cultural heritage tourism in Hong Kong. *Cultural and Social History, 17*(5), 677–696.

Pretes, M. (2013). Postmodern tourism: The Santa Claus industry. *Annals of Tourism Research, 22*(1), 1–15.

Radic, A. (2017). Toward an understanding of child's, cruise experience. *Current Issues in Tourism, 22*(2), 237–252.

Rhoden, S., Hunter-Jones, P., & Miller, A. (2016). Tourism experiences through the eyes of a child. *Annals of Leisure Research, 19*(4), 424–443.

Rook, D. W. (2001). Researching consumer fantasy. In E. Hirshman & J. N. Sheth (Eds.), *Research on consumer behaviour* (Vol. 3, pp. 247–270). Greenwhich, CT: JAI Press.

Ross, M., & Wang, Q. (2010). Why we remember and what we remember: Culture and autobiographical memory. *Perspectives on Psychological Science, 5*(4), 401–409.

Rydell, A. M. (2010). Family factors and children's disruptive behaviour: An investigation of links between demographic characteristics, negative life events and symptoms of ODD and ADHD. *Social Psychiatry and Psychiatric Epidemiology, 45*(2), 233–244.

Sebba, R. (1991). The landscapes of childhood: The reflection of childhood's environment in adult memories and in children's attitudes. *Environment and Behavior, 23*(4), 395–422.

Seraphin, H. (2020). Childhood experience and (de) diasporisation: Potential impacts on the tourism industry. *Journal of Tourism, Heritage & Services Marketing (JTHSM), 6*(3), 14–24.

Seraphin, H., & Green, S. (2019). The significance of the contribution of children to conceptualizing the destination of the future. *International Journal of Tourism Cities, 5*(4), 544–559. doi:10.1108/IJTC-12-2018-0097

Seraphin, H., Yallop, A. C., Seyfi, S., & Hall, C. M. (2022). Responsible tourism: The 'why' and 'how' of empowering children. *Tourism Recreation Research, 47*(1), 62–77.

Seyfi, S., Hall, C. M., & Rasoolimanesh, S. M. (2019). Exploring memorable cultural tourism experiences. *Journal of Heritage Tourism, 15*(3), 341–357.

Shanzel, H. A. (2013). The importance of 'social' in family tourism. *Asia-Pacific Journal of Innovation in Hospitality and Tourism, 2*(1), 1–15.

Shanzel, H. A., & Yeoman. (2015). Trends in family tourism. *Journal of Tourism Futures, 1*(2), 141–147.

Shi, Y., Bettache, K., Zhang, N., & Xue, L. (2021). Constructing nostalgia in tourism: A comparison analysis of genuine and artificial approaches. *Journal of Destination Marketing & Management, 19.* doi:10.1016/j.jdmm.2020.100488

Shin, H. H., & Jeong, M. (2022). Does a virtual trip evoke travelers' nostalgia and derive intentions to visit the destination, a similar destination, and share?: Nostalgia-motivated tourism. *Journal of Travel & Tourism Marketing, 39*(1), 1–17.

Simons, D. A. (2015). *Adult sex offender typologies.* SOMAPI Research Brief. Retrieved from https://smart.ojp.gov/sites/g/files/xyckuh231/files/media/document/adultsexoffendertypologies.pdf

Stadler, R., & Jepson, A. (2017). Understanding the value of events for families, and the impact upon their quality of life. In E. Lundberg, J. Armbrecht, T. D. Andersson, & D. Getz (Eds.), *The value of events* (1st ed. eBook). Routeldge. ISBN: 9781317193241.

Stone, P. R. (2022). Epilogue: 'Monsters and mediating mortality moments': Dark tourism and childhood encounters. In M. M. Kerr, P. R. Stone, & R. H. Price (Eds.), *Children, young people and dark tourism* (pp. 285–291). Routledge.

Swarbrooke, J. (2002). *The development and management of visitor attractions*. Oxford: Butterworth-Heinemann.

Trdina, A., & Pusnik. (2022). Travel beyond place: Touring memories and displaced homecoming. *Journal of Tourism and Cultural Change*. doi:10.1080/14766825.2022. 2046015

Tung, V. W., Lin, P., Zhang, H. Q., & Zhao, A. (2017). A framework of memory management and tourism experiences. *Journal of Travel & Tourism Marketing*, *34*(7), 853–866.

Tung, V. W., & Ritchie, J. R. (2011). Exploring the essence of memorable tourism experiences. *Annals of Tourism Research*, *38*(4), 1367–1386. doi:10.1016/j.annals. 2011.03.009

United Nations. (2022). *Sustainability*. United Nations. Retrieved from https://www. un.org/en/academic-impact/sustainability

Ursin, M., & Skålevik, M. L. (2018). Volunteer tourism in Cambodian residential care facilities—A child rights-based approach. *The International Journal of Children's Rights*, *26*(4), 808–836.

Vesey, C., & Dimanche, F. (2003). From Storyville to Bourbon street: Vice, nostalgia and tourism. *Journal of Tourism and Cultural Change*, *1*(1), 54–70.

Villalonga-Olives, E., Rojas-Farreras, S., Vilagut, G., Palacio-Vieira, J. A., Valderas, J. M., Herdman, M., ... Alonso, J. (2010). Impact of recent life events on the health related quality of life of adolescents and youths: The role of gender and life events typologies in a follow-up study. *Health and Quality of Life Outcomes*, *8*, 71. doi:10.1186/1477-7525-8-71

Wagner, D. A. (1978). Memories of Morocco: The influence of age, schooling, and environment on memory. *Cognitive Psychology*, *10*(1), 1–28.

Wai Leong, A. M., Yeh, S., Hsiao, Y. C., & Huan, T. C. (2015). Nostalgia as travel motivation and its impact on tourists' loyalty. *Journal of Business Research*, *68*(1), 81–86.

Wang, Q. (2001). Culture effects on adults earliest childhood recollection and self-description: Implications for the relation between memory and the self. *Journal of Personality and Social Psychology*, *81*(2), 220–233.

Wang, Q., & Gulgoz, S. (2019). New perspectives on childhood memory: Introduction to the special issue. *Memory*, *27*(1), 1–5.

Wang, L., Jia, J., & Sun, D. (2018). Nostalgia and pro-environmental behaviour: The mediation effect of place attachment. *World Applied Sciences Journal*, *36*(3), 408–412.

Weidenfield, A., Butler, R., & Williams, A. M. (2016). *Visitor attractions and events: Locations and linkages*. New York, NY: Routeledge Taylor and Francis.

Willet, R. (2015). Everyday game design on a school playground: Children are bri-coleurs. *International Journal of Play*, *4*(1), 32–44.

Woodside, A. G., Caldwell, M., & Spurr, R. (2005). Ecological systems in lifestyle, leisure and travel behaviour. In R. G. March & A. G. Woodside (Eds.), *Tourism behaviour: Travellers' decisions and actions*. Wallingford: CABI Publishing.

Xu, C., Zhong, S., Li, P., & Xiao, X. (2021). Tourist memory and childhood land-scape. *Journal of Tourism and Cultural Change*. doi:10.1080/14766825.2021. 2015358

Yoon, Y., & Uysal, M. (2005). An examination of the effects of motivation and satisfaction on destination loyalty: A structural model. *Tourism Management*, *26*(1), 45–56.

Chapter 3

Marketing Sustainable Events for Children

Marco Martins, Ricardo Jorge da Costa Guerra, Lara Santos and Luísa Lopes

Abstract

In today's world, events are used as a mean to achieve an array of objectives including changing behaviours. This chapter asserts the importance of marketing in encouraging sustainable behaviours by children through events. Thus, it examines the most effective way of marketing to contribute to shift behaviours in a young age having events as an ally. The question that poses is how marketing and more specifically social marketing can help to plan, create, design and promote sustainable events for children. Bearing that in mind, and based on a semi-systematic literature review, one developed a comprehensive conceptual framework intending to show how it is possible to encourage sustainable children's behaviour through events. Results suggest that social marketing can play a significant role in changing children's behaviour towards sustainability. It is argued that there is a creation of 'value' even that behaviour change is only temporary. Furthermore, it is suggested that social marketing represents a viable approach when seeking to educate children and change their behaviours towards the adoption of more sustainable practices. This chapter advances theoretical knowledge by offering a conceptual framework and by suggesting a way forward in marketing sustainable events for children.

Keywords: Marketing; social marketing; sustainable events; children; sustainable development; framework

Introduction

As Lean (2009, p. 191) puts it, 'to fully realise ideals like sustainability, the industry must work towards inspiring enduring changes of behaviour that ensure the wealth and wellbeing of the individual and their economic, sociocultural, and

Events Management for the Infant and Youth Market, 39–51
Copyright © 2023 Marco Martins, Ricardo Jorge da Costa Guerra, Lara Santos and Luísa Lopes
Published under exclusive licence by Emerald Publishing Limited
doi:10.1108/978-1-80455-690-020231007

ecological environments. These changes of action will help deliver individual and global wellness'.

Events can be a powerful tool to change people's thinking and behaviour. However, having success in combining events, sustainability and children is no easy task. Nevertheless, children could potentially play a role in sustainable development implementation if they are empowered to do so (Séraphin, 2020), and 'youth can be harnessed as a major agent of change in achieving sustainable development' (UNESCAP, 2017, p. 7).

In social marketing, the adoption of an alternative behaviour should result in value perceived by consumers. However, there are a variety of definitions of social marketing that represent different points of view and emphasise other elements of social marketing than the 'change individual behavior for social good' theme (Lefebvre, 2012). The literature suggests that exchanges for behaviour changes must be attractive for consumers to adopt a social marketing product (French & Russel-Bennet, 2015).

Although, marketing and events could be seen as the antithesis of sustainability, one demonstrates here that both can contribute if well planned to achieve a more sustainable product, process and contribute to change behaviours amongst the participants in an event. It was our intent to understand how marketing and more specifically social marketing can help to plan, create, design and promote sustainable events for children. The proposed framework in the current research shows how to make awareness, engagement and empowerment strategies central when developing events for children.

The structure of this chapter is as follows. After describing the research's methodology, one addressed the meaning of sustainable events. Afterwards, social marketing and the role played by social marketing in events were discussed. Then, one debated the thematic structure of this chapter, how can we market sustainable events for children, and it was here a possible framework was proposed. Finally, one narrates our findings and discusses them, presenting the various implications and contributions of our study.

Methodology

This research is based on a semi-systematic review. This kind of methodology allows researchers to overview a topic and/or to look how research within a selected field has evolved over time (Snyder, 2019). In general, this type of research pretends to identify and comprehend all potentially pertinent research traditions that have connotations with the topic under study with the objective of synthesizing these using meta-narratives (Wong, Greenhalgh, Westhorp, Buckingham, & Pawson, 2013). When well conducted a literature review as research method creates a firm foundation for the advancement of knowledge facilitating theoretical-conceptual development (Webster & Watson, 2002).

Theorisation and conceptualisation are processes that require abstract thinking that involves the mental representation of an idea; pure conceptual papers may include among other possibilities 'integrative models' and 'conceptual frameworks' (MacInnis, 2011). Conceptualisation of constructs is critical because they are the basis on which measures are derived from and on which theories are tested (Engel & Schutt, 2014). Therefore, a conceptual framework serves as a guide and support to research (Ravitch & Riggan, 2016), and so it can be considered as a huge step for a rigorous qualitative research.

Nevertheless, some limitations exist when one carries out an exploratory study; because being an interpretation of a completely new reality, it is only possible to make suppositions without having the possibility of verifying them.

What Is a Sustainable Event?

The World Commission on Environment and Development (WECD, 1987, p. 43) defined sustainable development as the 'development that meets the needs of the present without compromising the ability of future generations to meet their own needs'. In 2015, the United Nations (UN) adopted Sustainable Development Goals (SDGs) in a General Assembly (UN, 2020), these SDGs collectively help to guide actions for global sustainable development and shape visions for the future.

Research concerning sustainability of festivals and events is relatively advanced (Séraphin, Platania, Spencer, & Modica, 2018). Getz (2009, p. 70) regarding sustainable events says that 'sustainable events are not just those that can endure indefinitely, they are also events that fulfil important social, cultural, economic and environmental roles that people value. In this way, they can become institutions that are permanently supported in a community or nation'.

Meanwhile, for the Events Industry Council (EIC, 2022) a sustainable event is the event that acts towards preserving our natural environment, promoting at the same time a healthy and inclusive society, and supporting a thriving economy. To the events industry, however, would be advisable to have a broader vision of its sustainable development encompassing both the 'product' and 'process' aspects, that is, to organise events that meet sustainable standards when being enjoyed by its audience. It is imperative that a shift in thinking to occur so that one goes from pollution prevention to product stewardship (Hart, 1997; Musgrave & Henderson, 2011). More importantly even, the purpose of sustainable events, especially when marketed for children, should focus on a values-led trans-formation that goes far beyond the dynamics identified in literature concerning responsible events and sustainability in events (Higgins-Desbiolles & Monga, 2020).

Social Marketing

Within the marketing discipline, social marketing stands out for being a field that involves behaviour changing. Social marketing can intervene upstream or downstream. In the first it tries to influence individual behaviours and in the second it tries to influence the behaviours of those that shape the environment in which the individual is inserted. Coined by Kotler and Zaltman (1971, p. 5), it was defined by them as 'the design, implementation, and control of programs calculated to influence the acceptability of social ideas and involving considerations of product planning, pricing, communication, distribution, and marketing research. Thus, it is the explicit use of marketing skills to help translate present social action efforts into more effectively designed and communicated programs that elicit desired audience response'. According to Jutbring (2018, p. 238) 'in social marketing, the adoption of an alternative behaviour should result in value perceived by consumers'. Creating progress with meaning towards sustainability requires more far-reaching approaches than just the development of new products or altering the existing ones, including promoting and accepting concepts such as consumption reduction, responsible consumption and sustainable lifestyles (Peattie & Peattie, 2009). In an attempt to come to a consensus iSMA (International Social Marketing Association), ESMA (European Social Marketing Association) and AASM (Australian Association of Social Marketing) (2017) approved the definition that follows – 'Social marketing seeks to develop and integrate marketing concepts with other approaches to influence behaviour that benefit individuals and communities for the greater social good. Social marketing practice is guided by ethical principles. It seeks to integrate research, best practice, theory, audience and partnership insight, to inform the delivery of competition sensitive and segmented social change programmes that are effective, efficient, equitable and sustainable'.

The use of social marketing when it comes to the promotion of sustainability is well established. Since the first moment that social marketing campaigns have addressed environmental issues, for example, on promoting eco-literacy (Taylor & Muller, 1992), involvement in recycling (Zikmund & Stanton, 1971), sustainability (McKenzie & Smith, 2000), events (Andersson, Jutbring, & Lundberg, 2013) and/or education for sustainability (Arbuthnott, 2009).

According to French and Gordon (2015), social marketing has proven to be a powerful set of tools and principles that link the knowledge generated by behavioural sciences and other fields of human behaviour, with our comprehension of the design, implementation and management of effective action programmes drawn from the field of management and marketing.

Social Marketing and Events

Although a unified social marketing theoretical framework is still lacking (Cohen & Andrade, 2018), it is still possible to go back to literature for narrowing down the existent ones to the following benchmark criteria for social marketing interventions developed by Andreasen (2002) when seeking to apply social marketing in events looking to change children's behaviour:

(1) Behaviour change is the 'bottom line' and at the same time the superior objective to design sustainable management interventions;
(2) Analysis of the target audience;
(3) Identification of the desired behaviour, a careful segmentation of the target must be conducted;

(4) Implementation of the transformational programme; it is needed the creation of attractive and motivational exchanges with the children's.
(5) Combining all traditional marketing mix Ps for this target group;
(6) Careful attention must be given to the competition faced by the desired behaviour.

Planned events 'facilitate or constrain experiences for participants, guests spectators, and other stakeholders. Every event experience is personal and unique, arising from the interactions of setting, programme and people' (Getz, 2008, p. 21). However, one must refocus our marketing programmes as an exchange, and the centre piece of that exchange is co-creation. That means, that one should recognise that our focus should not just be our target audience, in this case children, but also all stakeholders, those that are critical to the behaviour change success through events and with whom one must actively engage in developing customised, competitively compelling value propositions (Lefebvre, 2012).

In August 2012, the privately owned music festival Way Out West 'went veggie' without emphasising the links between meat consumption, carbon emissions and their contribution to global warming (Anderson, Jutbring, & Lundberg, 2013). A follow-up study about the participants' behaviour after attending this event revealed that 47.4% of them reduced their meat consumption that indicates that the social proposition marketed by the festival had a clear effect amongst attendees (Jutbring, 2018). This leads us to the idea that if events manage to create awareness through social marketing, they will contribute to change behaviours and even maintain them in time because consumers will perceive that a value was created and exchanged (French & Russell-Bennett, 2015).

Marketing Sustainable Events for Children

The number of people (children are no exception) seeking to engage in experiences that supply emotional value, as well as a learning process to create long-lasting positive changes, personal growth, inner fulfilment and well-being is growing (Ateljevic, Sheldon, & Tomljenovic, 2016; Kirilova, Lehto, & Cai, 2017; Martins & Santos, 2022; Sheldon, 2020).

Children's sustainable behaviour can be defined as a set of actions taken by children that will result in a reduction in the damage caused to the environment and in a better use of natural resources (White, Habib, & Hardisty, 2019). When marketing sustainable events for children and aiming for sustainable development, event managers and marketers should bear in mind the important role that these events can play in accelerating SDGs (Table 1.). It is in our childhood and more specifically in the early years of adolescence that identity formation happens, and as such, can be more easily moulded; it is then crucial to expose at this stage youngsters to sustainable tourism development goals through examples (Martins & Guerra, 2022).

Events design for children can embody the idea expressed by Telzer, van Hoorn, Rogers, and Do (2018, p. 219) that 'the more one's patterns of

Table 1. The Role of Sustainable Events for Children and SDG's Acceleration.

Goal 1. End poverty in all forms.

Events role: Enrol in your event organisation local members of the community

Goal 2. End hunger, achieve food security and improved nutrition, and promote sustainable agriculture.

Events role: Offer meals to children in need and/or work to donate food post event to children in need; use only local products originated from sustainable agriculture; promote healthy food.

Goal 3. Ensure healthy lives and promote well-being for all at all ages.

Events role: Supply health exams to children and to their parents.

Goal 4. Ensure quality education and promote lifelong learning for all.

Events role: Provide tutorials and simulations for educating children for sustainable development

Goal 5. Achieve gender equality and empower all women and girls.

Events role: Ensure that in your event gender is not an issue – all must have equal opportunities; provide activities in which neither gender can excel because of their nature or genetic treats – this is paramount in such a young age.

Goal 6. Ensure availability and sustainable management of water and sanitation for all.

Events role: Partner with entities that can provide clean drinking water; sanitation must meet all the requirements in terms of sustainability.

Goal 7. Ensure access to affordable, reliable, sustainable and modern energy for all.

Events role: Choose venues that use renewable energy.

Goal 8. Promote sustained, inclusive and sustainable economic growth.

Events role: Make sure you prioritise local suppliers and especially those that possess some kind of 'green' certification.

Goal 9. Build resilient infrastructure, promote inclusive and sustainable industrialisation, and foster innovation.

Events role: Use certified buildings; make sure to incorporate virtual elements in your event and tech support to children that may have limited access to technology.

Goal 10. Reduce inequality within and among countries.

Events role: Make sure your event provides equal opportunities to children of all countries and to all populations

Goal 11. Make cities and human settlements inclusive, safe, resilient and sustainable.

Table 1. *(Continued)*

Events role: Events can be used to provide greater insights to children regarding smart cities, climate change and even about pandemics.

Goal 12. Ensure sustainable consumption and production patterns.

Events role: Explore events capabilities for production, inventory management and for supply chain improvements; place recycling and compost bins throughout the event; reduce paper via the use of technology tools.

Goal 13. Take urgent action to combat climate change and its impacts.

Events role: Measure your event's carbon footprint making at the same time this information available to the children attending it; create a way of measuring their footprint aiming to help them understand how they can reduce it in next events and day-to-day practices.

Goal 14. Conserve and sustainably use the oceans, seas and marine resources for sustainable development.

Events role: Eliminate all plastics use from your events; make children aware of the dangers for the oceans sustainability of the use of plastics, sunscreen lotion, among other harmful practices; Promote sustainable fishing and seafood consumable practices.

Goal 15. Protect, restore and promote sustainable use of terrestrial ecosystems, sustainably manage forests, combat desertification and halt and reverse land degradation, and halt biodiversity loss.

Events role: Make children aware of the important of trees and of planting them; use reusable items in your event making sure you communicate to children why doing so. Promote a healthy diet like the Mediterranean one.

Goal 16. Promote peaceful and inclusive societies for sustainable development, provide access to justice for all and build effective, accountable and inclusive institutions at all levels.

Events role: Make children aware of the importance in their present and future lives of contributing for the promotion of peaceful communities, having access to a fair and inclusive justice, and build effective, accountable and inclusive institutions at all levels. It is crucial in events to promote and incentivise freedom of expression, respect for human rights and reduction of inequalities.

Goal 17. Strengthen the means of implementation and revitalise the global partnership for sustainable development.

Events role: Make children's aware of the importance of 'Green' labels and certifications. Show how sustainable practices can improve their lives.

Source: The author (Developed by the authors based on UN's SDGs, UN, 2020).

differential association are balanced towards exposure to prosocial, positive behaviour and attitudes, the greater the probability that one will also engage in positive behaviours'.

In our proposed framework (Fig. 1), it is proposed that when creating and marketing sustainable events for children, social marketers must focus in designing and implementing strategies that first of all create awareness, that is the first step, without creating awareness it is our understanding that promoting the engagement of such young attendees will be harder, and the final step will be to achieve empowerment.

Awareness is a construct with many layers, and so Carden, Jones, and Passmore (2022) stated that such reality has led to the fact that the concept has been defined under several perspectives originating a somewhat diffuse picture. In this chapter, one understands awareness as a combination of two ideas. First, like Fisher (1998) says, it is 'thinking about thinking', what in a way is about the development of critical thinking (see Ennis, 1981; Hitchcock, 2017). Secondly, it is our understanding that it is one's perspective awareness in relation with the perception of the feelings of others that considers one's impact in others' lives (Beck, Baruch, Balter, Steer, & Warman, 2004; Lane, Quinlan, Schwartz, Walker, & Zeitlin, 1990; Trentacosta & Izard, 2007); that considers the impact of one's in others life.

Regarding engagement and its importance, it has been proved through time that engaged people display positive attitudes towards events they consider important; engagement has been established as an important construct for youngsters and adult's performance and well-being (Halbesleben, 2010). Engagement presupposes youngsters' participation in the life of their community and society, developing lifelong relationships in it. According to Hur (2013),

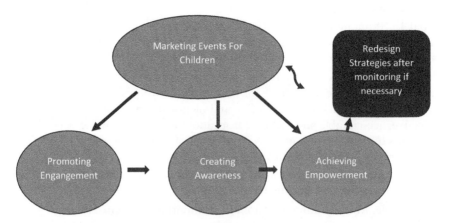

Fig. 1.   Marketing Sustainable Events for Children – A Framework.
Source: The authors.

empowerment finds its origins as a form of theory with Freire (1991), when suggesting a plan for liberating the oppressed through education. Empowerment is defined in different ways in literature. Shulman and Luechauer and Shulman (1992) define empowerment as the process of enabling people to take personal responsibility and ownership of the tasks they perform. Theories of empowerment include both processes and outcomes, suggesting that actions, activities or structures may be empowering, and that the outcome of such processes result in a level of being empowered (Swift & Levin, 1987). Empowerment, on the other hand, means an increase or reinforcement of 'power'. In it 'individuals take possession of their own lives through interaction with other individuals, generating critical thinking in relation to reality, favouring the construction of personal and social capacity' (Baquero, 2012, p. 181).

One good example of children feels engaged with it, because they feel part of a community, becoming aware of social problems, and afterwards empowered to critically think and intervene, is the Greta Thunberg's 'Fridays for Future Initiative' movement. On 15 March 2018, Youth for the Climate, the digital platform created to coordinate these students protests, called a strike and meetings that united more than a million young people in 2,083 cities in 125 countries. The objective is to raise awareness of climate change in society and demand that governments act to counteract the effects (UNICEF, 2021). These events should enable children to perceive, reflect and interpret their social reality (individually and/or collectively), and consequently producing changes that can result in the construction of a better human and fairer society through participating in a social engagement process (Jeyaraj & Gandolfi, 2022).

When designing a strategy to create and promote sustainable events, social marketers should intervene in three dimensions, they must promote engagement (dimension 1); create awareness (dimension 3) and achieve empowerment (dimension 3). Finally, they must create a monitoring tool, one that will allow to change their strategy during the sustainable event, but also one that will allow to make a follow-up – one that will permit them to make adaptations if necessary in the sustainable event design and strategy itself in the future.

Promoting Engagement – when sustainable events managers and social marketers propose an engaging content, one that appeals to children's strengths and involvement, that will result in children to go beyond just knowing and will enable them to push boundaries; they will become more attentive, will reduce the degree of uncertainty in terms of what they know and what they should do with that knowledge, and that will increase their degree of confidence.

Creating Awareness – Children's awareness about sustainability issues can be increased through attending events – the particular skills and knowledge gained will or at least would help changing behaviours towards the environment that surrounds them. The idea of social market campaigns is that after creating awareness what it follows is interest, desire and action.

Achieving Empowerment – Empowering children and making them aware in sustainable events is not an easy task, but is possible when there is a presenting stage where children share ideas and discuss them with their fellow companions and with adults; in this stage they become empowered because they will feel they own their thoughts, are getting skills to pursue their passions and they are following their own path not their parents or other adults' path.

Human beings are naturally curious, and that curiosity comes hand in hand with an increased engagement with the world including exploratory behaviour, active experimenting, meaning-making and learning (Panksepp, 2011). Then, ideally, events should be taking advantage of this human singularity through the application of engagement and empowerment strategies. This study comes forward with a new model, one that provides an integrated link between the constructs' engagement, empowerment and awareness (Fig. 1).

Conclusion

This exploratory study, because such is the nature of exploratory studies, contains theoretical-conceptual and methodological limitations that could be target in future empirical studies. It would be of interest to study perceived consumer value, amongst broader audiences, and how these form negative and/or positive values having the same event as background. Furthermore, one could say that more important than just the adoption of behaviours would be to understand if they maintain as time passes through, for example, from childhood to adulthood or from infants to teenagers it is crucial to make pot follow-up studies such as the one of Jutbring (2018).

This study also shows that events, if well planned and implemented by social marketers and managers, can play an important role in influencing children to change behaviours and embrace sustainable practices more easily.

Therefore, awareness engagement and empowerment must be strategic in enhancing children's ability to be resilient and proactive, so that they can therefore be considered essential to succeed in our ever-changing society and contribute to change it also.

However, one must not forget that Kemp (2020) expresses that serious limitations and ethical pitfalls exist in transformative experiences. In particular, he argues that transformative experiences can lead us away from our own personal flourishing path.

References

Andersson, T. D., Jutbring, H., & Lundberg, E. (2013). When a music festival goes veggie. *International Journal of Event and Festival Management, 4*(3), 224–235. doi: 10.1108/IJEFM-06-2013-0015

Andreasen, A. R. (2002). Marketing social marketing in the social change marketplace. *Journal of Public Policy and Marketing, 21*(1), 3–13. doi:10.1509/jppm.21.1. 3.17602

Arbuthnott, K. D. (2009). Education for sustainable development beyond attitude change. *International Journal of Sustainability in Higher Education, 10*(2), 152–163. doi:10.1108/14676370910945954

Ateljevic, I., Sheldon, P., & Tomljenovic, R. (2016). *Global report on the transformative power of tourism.* Madrid: UNWTO.

Baquero, R. (2012). Empoderamento: instrumento de emancipação social? Uma discussão conceitual. *Revista Debates, 6*(1), 173–187. doi:10.22456/1982-5269.26722

Beck, A. T., Baruch, E., Balter, J. M., Steer, R. A., & Warman, D. M. (2004). A new instrument for measuring insight: The Beck cognitive insight scale. *Schizophrenia Research, 68*(2–3), 319–329. doi:10.1016/S0920-9964(03)00189-0

Carden, J., Jones, R. J., & Passmore, J. (2022). Defining self-awareness in the context of adult development: A systematic literature review. *Journal of Management Education, 46*(1), 140–177. doi:10.1177/1052562921990065

Cohen, J. B., & Andrade, E. B. (2018). The ADF framework: A parsimonious model for developing successful behavior change interventions. *Journal of Marketing Behavior, 3*(2). doi:10.1561/107.00000046

EIC. (2022). Principles for sustainable events. Retrieved from https://www.eventscouncil.org/Portals/0/EIC%20Documents/Sustainability/Principles%20for%20sustainable%20events.pdf?ver=2019-01-18-123244-787

Engel, R. J., & Schutt, R. K. (2014). *Fundamentals of social work research* (2nd ed.). Thousand Oaks, CA: Sage Publishing, Inc.

Ennis, R. H. (1981). Rational thinking and educational practice. In J. Soltis (Ed.), *Philosophy of education. Eightieth Yearbook of the National Society for the Study of Education, Part I* (pp. 143–183). Chicago: The National Society for the Study of Education.

Fisher, R. (1998). Thinking about thinking: Developing metacognition in children. *Early Child Development and Care, 141*, 1–13. doi:10.1080/0300443981410101

Freire, P. (1991). *A Educação na Cidade*. São Paulo: Cortez.

French, J., & Gordon, R. (2015). *Strategic social marketing*. London: SAGE.

French, J., & Russell-Bennett, R. (2015). A hierarchical model of social marketing. *Journal of Social Marketing, 5*(2), 139–159. doi:10.1108/JSOCM-06-2014-0042

Getz, D. (2008). Event tourism: Definition, evolution, and research. *Tourism Management, 29*(3), 403–428. doi:10.1016/j.tourman.2007.07.017

Getz, D. (2009). Policy for sustainable and responsible festivals and events: Institutionalization of a new paradigm. *Journal of Policy Research in Tourism, Leisure and Events, 1*(1), 61–78. doi:10.1080/19407960802703524

Halbesleben, J. R. B. (2010). A meta-analysis of work engagement: Relationship with burnout, demands, resources and consequences. In A. B. Bakker & M. P. Leiter (Eds.), *Work engagement: A handbook of essential theory and research* (pp. 10–24). Hove: Psychology Press.

Hart, S. L. (1997). Beyond greening – Strategies for a sustainable world. *Harvard Business Review, 75*, 66–76.

Higgins-Desbiolles, F., & Monga, M. (2020). Transformative change through events business: A feminist ethic of care analysis of building the purpose economy. *Journal of Sustainable Tourism, 29*(11–12), 1989–2007. doi:10.1080/09669582.2020.1856857

Hitchcock, D. (2017). Critical thinking as an educational ideal. In D. Hitchcock (Ed.), *On reasoning and argument: Essays in informal logic and on critical thinking* (pp. 477–497). Dordrecht: Springer. doi:10.1007/978-3-319-53562-3_30

Hur, M. H. (2013). Empowerment. In M. D. Gellman & J. R. Turner (Eds.), *Encyclopedia of behavioral medicine*. New York, NY: Springer. doi:10.1007/978-1-4419-1005-9

iSMA, AASM, & ESMA. (2017, July). *Global consensus on social marketing principles, concepts and techniques*. Retrieved from http://smana.org/wp-content/uploads/

2017/04/ESMA-AASM-SMANA-endorsed-Consensus-Principles-and-concepts-paper.pdf

Jeyaraj, J. J., & Gandolfi, F. (2022). Empowering students for social justice through a critical pedagogy inspired framework of servant leadership. *Pedagogy, Culture & Society, 30*(2), 169–184. doi:10.1080/14681366.2020.1793216

Jutbring, H. (2018). Social marketing through a music festival: Value perceived by festival visitors who reduced meat consumption. *Journal of Social Marketing, 8*(2), 237–256. doi:10.1108/JSOCM-03-2017-0017

Kemp, R. S. (2020). Lessons in self-betrayal: On the pitfalls of transformative education. *Educational Theory, 70,* 603–616. doi:10.1111/edth.12446

Kirilova, K., Lehto, X., & Cai, L. (2017). What triggers transformative tourism experiences? *Tourism Recreation Research, 42*(4), 498–511. doi:10.1080/02508281.2017.1342349

Kotler, P., & Zaltman, G. (1971). Social marketing: An approach to planned social change. *Journal of Marketing, 35*(3), 3–12. doi:10.1177/002224297103500302

Lane, R. D., Quinlan, D. M., Schwartz, G. E., Walker, P. A., & Zeitlin, S. B. (1990). The levels of emotional awareness scale: A cognitive-developmental measure of emotion. *Journal of Personality Assessment, 55,* 124–134. doi:10.1080/00223891.1990.9674052

Lean, G. L. (2009). Transformative travel: Inspiring sustainability. In R. Bushell & P. J. Sheldon (Eds.), *Wellness and tourism: Mind, body, spirit, place* (pp. 191–205). Elmsford: Cognizant Communication.

Lefebvre, C. R. (2012). Transformative social marketing: Co-creating the social marketing discipline and brand. *Journal of Social Marketing, 2*(2), 118–129. doi:10.1108/20426761211243955

Luechauer, D. L., & Shulman, G. M. (1992, April). Moving from bureaucracy to empowerment: Shifting paradigms to practice what we preach in class. Paper presented at the *Annual Midwest Academy of Management*. Retrieved from https://files.eric.ed.gov/fulltext/ED360666.pdf

MacInnis, D. J. (2011). A framework for conceptual contributions in marketing. *Journal of Marketing, 75*(4), 136–154. doi:10.1509/jmkg.75.4.136

Martins, M., & Guerra, R. (2022). Transformational education for sustainable tourism in middle schools. In H. Séraphin (Ed.), *Children in responsible and sustainable tourism* (pp. 129–142). Bingley: Emerald Publishing Limited. doi:10.1108/978-1-80117-656-920221010

Martins, M., & Santos, L. (2022). Transformational marketing and transformational travel. *Journal of Tourism Futures, 8*(3), 397–401. doi:10.1108/JTF-01-2022-0025

McKenzie-Mohr, D., & Smith, W. (2000). *Fostering sustainable behavior: An introduction to community-based social marketing.* Garbiola Island, BC: New Society Publishers.

Musgrave, J., & Henderson, S. (2011). The development of competitive advantage through sustainable event management. *Worldwide Hospitality and Tourism Themes, 3*(3), 245–257. doi:10.1108/17554211111142202

Panksepp, J. (2011). The primary process affects in human development, happiness, and thriving. In M. Kennon, T. B. Kashdan, & M. F. Steger (Eds.), *Designing positive psychology: Taking stock and moving forward* (pp. 51–85). New York, NY: Oxford University Press.

Peattie, K., & Peattie, S. (2009). Social marketing: A pathway to consumption reduction? *Journal of Business Research, 62*(2), 260–268. doi:10.1016/j.jbusres.2008. 01.033

Ravitch, S. M., & Riggan, M. (2016). *Reason and Rigor. How conceptual framework guide research* (2nd ed.). Thousand Oaks, CA: Sage.

Séraphin, H. (2020). Responsible tourism education of younger consumers: The role of mini-clubs in mountain resorts. *Worldwide Hospitality and Tourism Themes, 12*(4), 409–419. doi:10.1108/WHATT-05-2020-0022

Séraphin, H., Platania, M., Spencer, P., & Modica, G. (2018). Events and tourism development within a Local community: The case of Winchester (UK). *Sustainability, 10*(10). doi:10.3390/su10103728

Sheldon, P. (2020). Designing tourism experiences for inner transformation. *Annals of Tourism Research, 83*. doi:10.1016/j.annals.2020.102935

Snyder, H. (2019). Literature review as a research methodology: An overview and guidelines. *Journal of Business Research, 104*, 333–339. doi:10.1016/j.jbusres.2019. 07.039

Swift, C., & Levin, G. (1987). Empowerment: An emerging mental health technology. *Journal of Primary Prevention, 8*, 71–94. doi:10.1007/BF01695019

Taylor, D. W., & Muller, T. E. (1992). Eco-literacy and environmental citizenship: A social marketing challenge for public sector management. *Optimum, 23*(3), 6–16.

Telzer, E. H., van Hoorn, J., Rogers, C. R., & Do, K. T. (2018). Social influence on positive youth development: A developmental neuroscience perspective. *Advances in Child Development and Behavior, 54*, 215–258. doi:10.1016/bs.acdb.2017.10.003

Trentacosta, C. J., & Izard, C. E. (2007). Kindergarten children's emotion competence as a predictor of their academic competence in first grade. *Emotion, 7*, 77–88. doi: 10.1037/1528-3542.7.1.77

UN. (2020). *Global indicator framework for the sustainable development goals and targets of the 2030 agenda for sustainable development.* UNSD. Retrieved from: https://unstats.un.org/sdgs/indicators/Global%20Indicator%20Framework% 20after%202020%20review_Eng.pdf

UNESCAP. (2017). *UN and SDGs. A handbook for youth.* Retrieved from: https:// www.unescap.org/sites/default/files/UN%20and%20SDGs_A%20Handbook% 20for%20Youth.pdf

UNICEF. (2021). Youth for climate action. Retrieved from https://www.unicef.org/ environment-and-climate-change/youth-action

Webster, J., & Watson, R. T. (2002). Analyzing the past to prepare for the future: Writing a literature review. *MIS Quarterly, 26*(2), xiii–xxiii. Retrieved from http:// www.jstor.org/stable/4132319

WECD. (1987). *Our common future.* Oxford: Oxford University Press.

White, K., Habib, R., & Hardisty, D. J. (2019). How to SHIFT consumer behaviors to be more sustainable: A literature review and guiding framework. *Journal of Marketing, 83*(3), 22–49. doi:10.1177/0022242919825649

Wong, G., Greenhalgh, T., Westhorp, G., Buckingham, J., & Pawson, R. (2013). RAMESES publication standards: Meta-narrative reviews. *BMC Medicine, 11*, 20. doi:10.1186/1741-7015-11-20

Zikmund, W. G., & Stanton, W. J. (1971). Recycling of solid wastes: A channel-of-distribution problem. *Journal of Marketing, 35*(3), 34–39. doi:10.1177/0022242971 035003

Section 2
A Youth and Childism Perspective of Events

Chapter 4

University Sustainability Career Information Events for Future Leaders

Karen Cripps

Abstract

Education for Sustainable Development and graduate employability are key agendas within Higher Education, and career-related events provide a context that caters to both simultaneously. There is a need for greater integration of academic department and career service teams in developing event management that systematically considers the potential to raise awareness of sustainability-related careers. This can maximise student personal and professional growth through sustainability-related career events, which simultaneously benefit the student through shaping personal and professional 'purpose', society through impact on the United Nations Sustainable Development Goals and university impact-related measures. By approaching events as a source of empowering students to become aware of, and actively seek out careers in which they can have a positive impact on people and planet, universities can provide a pipeline of sustainability 'actioners and transformers'. This chapter illuminates the potential actions between career service teams and academic departments in developing information-related events about sustainability-related careers. It extends a popular employability framework to sustainability, presented with an illustrative case in a UK study context aligned with the sustainability 'Thinker, Actioner and Transformer' typology. An analysis of career service information enables clear recommendations to be provided on how academic teams, career and other operational services might coordinate approaches. It is proposed that the ultimate commitment of growth in transformation might well be to nurture students as activists for change, presented through the topical analysis of 'fossil-free' career events. This is very much a starting point, and it is hoped that the chapter provides an opening for further discussion.

Keywords: Education for Sustainable Development; Sustainable Development Goals; employability; career event planning; universities; students

Events Management for the Infant and Youth Market, 55–65
Copyright © 2023 Karen Cripps
Published under exclusive licence by Emerald Publishing Limited
doi:10.1108/978-1-80455-690-020231009

Introduction

This chapter explores the nexus of sustainability and employability, within the context of Higher Education career events. It provides insights into how sustainability-related career information events can be managed to most effectively support the personal and professional development of graduates. The management of such University events for young adults (primarily aged between 18 and 24) sets the context for twenty-first-century leadership that addresses the United Nations 'Sustainable Development Goals' (SDGs).

Surprisingly little literature can be found on the Education for Sustainable Development (UNESCO, 2017) agenda as it relates to graduate employability, and there is a marked dearth of insight as it relates to career events. There is, however, evidence of a movement towards such alignment, with Norton and Penaluna (2022) for Advance HE (the UK Higher Education professional body) capturing current educational policy and practice initiatives as the '3Es for Wicked Problems: Employability, Enterprise and Entrepreneurship' (Norton & Penaluna, 2022).

Séraphin, Yallop, Seyfi, and Hall (2020) typology of 'Sustainability Thinker, Actioner and Transformer' aligns with Bloom's (1968) taxonomy of learning which classifies learning objectives as a hierarchical model of complexity beginning with a basic comprehension of knowledge (i.e. Thinker) through to the advanced evaluation and creation of knowledge (i.e. Transformer). If education is to be effective in developing the sustainability skills required for graduates to become 'change agents' (Cook, 2020) (i.e. Transformers), and students are to be prepared for the burgeoning 'green' skills job market (LinkedIn, 2022), then it follows that education should provide an integrated approach to sustainability and employability.

Progress towards the SDGs depends upon a systematic and integrated approach to embedding them in educational processes. In the United Kingdom, educators may be aware of the importance of employability outcomes in measurements such as the UK Teaching Excellence Framework (TEF), or UK Quality and Assurance Agency for Higher Education's guidance on 'Education for Sustainable Development' (QAA and Advance HE, 2021). Several global accreditation bodies (such as AACSB and EQUIS within a Business School context) require evidence of societal impact in strategic, curriculum and scholarly activities. This provides the 'formal curriculum' (Blasco, 2011) context for nurturing the progression of sustainability 'thinkers'.

It is proposed here that more insight is needed into how Education for Sustainable Development and employability can be more aligned, and that university events are a mechanism to develop this. This chapter therefore responds to the call for universities to embed sustainability more into the curriculum and linking it to employability to help prepare students for careers (Gamlath, 2022), and to continued interest by students to learn about sustainability (SOS-UK, 2022). The broader 'informal curriculum' (Blasco, 2011) can be a powerful influence on developing students as sustainability 'actioners and transformers' in operational areas such as sustainable and ethical catering, transportation and building design.

International University sustainability ratings such as the *Times* 'Higher Education Impact Ratings' and the student network 'People and Planet' ratings illustrate the importance of Universities 'walking the talk'. Yet curiously such rankings tend not to extend to University services that are linked to the student learning and employability experience, such as Career Services.

If universities are viewed as complex multi-internal stakeholders comprising differing academic faculties, student service and administrative teams, then a lens of SDG17 'Partnership' is a guiding imperative. This also extends to career event management which depends on outreach and connection to organisations and alumni. Career Services teams are a central component of student empowerment, working alongside academic teams to inspire, inform and shape student employability. Academics may be time challenged to integrate job market information and opportunities alongside other module learning outcomes, and therefore rely on Careers Services. Yet academics hold subject expertise that can support and develop information provided by Career teams. Equally, by keeping abreast of job market openings and skill requirements, academics are better placed to support students' development in formal curriculum delivery. It is therefore important for academic departments, careers teams and operational services to work together and support students' employability trajectories through combining expertise in initiatives such as careers-related events.

This chapter maps the type of events UK university careers teams promote that can engage students in sustainability 'actioners and transformers'. It provides insights gleaned from mapping University career web site pages to identify what type of information is provided related to sustainability careers, leading to recommendations for greater integration across University structures in event planning to support student employability for sustainability-related careers. To begin, the 'SOAR' employability framework (Kumar, 2015) is presented in the next section to illustrate connections between sustainability related events as part of employability. Finally, a case example of the 'Fossil Free Careers Campaign' (People and Planet, 2022a) mapped against Séraphin et al.'s (2020) 'sustainability transformers' typology exemplifies the power of event management design to inform and shape students as future leaders and activists.

SOAR Employability Framework to Inform Sustainability Career Information Events

SOAR stands for Self, Opportunity, Aspirations and Results and has been used and evaluated globally and in the United Kingdom as a learning and development tool which leads to transferable Higher Education graduate-level skills and attributes (Kumar, 2015). It is a reformulation of the DOTS model which traditionally underpins many careers education programmes. DOTS stands for Decision-learning, Opportunity-awareness, Transition skills and Self-awareness. SOAR reformulates DOTS so that learners start with 'Self-awareness', and addresses evaluation and impact of learning behaviours and attributes through the final stage of 'Results', which is vital to understanding self and collective impact of learning.

The SOAR employability framework (Kumar, 2007, 2022) sets out a process map of how student learning *for* and *about* the SDGs can be facilitated alongside academic, personal and professional development. It is based on the principles of appreciative enquiry (Cooperider & Fry, 2012) which is key, since such holistic, whole-person pedagogy is said to be central to the development of 'global competence' (OECD, 2022). Applied to the design and implementation of career-related information events by Universities, the SOAR framework provides an integrated structure to formal academic interests with careers services, for the mutual benefit of both student development and supportive progress to the SDGs.

SOAR's first step of 'Self-awareness' engages students' mindset and heart set in contributing to the SDGs, which might, for example, be achieved through career events which feature guest speakers working in sustainability and passionate about what they do. 'Opportunity' aligns students' knowledge and skillsets to collaborate on projects and activities both on campus and beyond. Events based on volunteering opportunities and feature local through to international projects can be instrumental here. The third step of 'Aspirations' might feature alumni events, who showcase their career journeys and what is possible post-degree. The final stage of 'Results' encourages reflection on meaningful and mindful engagement in career planning and might be facilitated through internal events both with career services professionals and the academic team.

Consideration of the SOAR framework in event planning facilitates consideration of the employability-sustainability connections applied to all projects which can trigger further collaboration. Discussions can be further extended through consideration of Séraphin and Yallop (2019) typology as seen in Table 1 which presents an example of a sustainability-related event at Oxford Brookes University in 2023 (Oxford Brookes University, 2022). The event in this case is an Instagram cooking competition (@lovestudentleftovers) based on creative leftover food recipes rolled out over some months, followed by a closing and panel discussion event and on-campus celebration activities. The event was initiated as part of the United Nations supported 'Principles of Responsible Management Education' 10th anniversary celebrations of the UK network, on the theme of good sustainability. The event was designed to raise awareness of food waste problems and solutions among the student population. Supported by academic members of staff, the competition and on-campus events are organised by students.

Analysis of University Career Pages

Research Method

An exploratory, scoping analysis was carried out of UK University Career external facing website pages for explicit mention of employability for green/sustainable/corporate responsible/environmental careers. Qualitative information

Table 1. Applying the SOAR Employability Framework and Sustainability Typology to an Event.

SOAR Employability Framework (Kumar, 2015)	@Lovestudentleftovers Competition (Oxford Brookes University, 2022)	Sustainability Typology (Séraphin & Yallop, 2019)
Self	Students learn about the project and step forward to engage. They design website and social media materials to capture interest in food waste and promote engagement in the competition and get to know students from other programmes and faculties working on the event.	Thinker
Opportunity	Students network with local community partners and seek promotional opportunities with partners both online and on campus.	Actioner
Aspirations	Student participation as organiser, competition entrant or on campus attendee enables engagement with business and community partners, and knowledge building to inspire career aspirations. The Careers Service follows the on-campus event up with an alumni 'food' careers event.	Actioner
Results	Students are supported by academic teams and career services to capture and develop learning reflections that result from engagement in the event, to inform career planning for further SDG impact.	Transformer

Source: The Author.

was captured to identify the types of information and events featured that support student awareness of sustainability-related careers such as:

- Information on job sites/recruitment agencies
- Supporting resources – professional associations, trade/public/media/governmental organisations
- Internships/placements/work experience (internal/external)
- Current sustainability jobs advertised
- Employer insights/events/fairs with sustainability focus
- University opportunities – (awards, challenge projects, volunteering)
- Graduate/alumni connections and insights
- Connection to University Sustainability Team (role profiles, project opportunities such as auditing, teams and committees, Green Impact)

The People and Planet (2022b) University League rankings for 2021–2022 were followed in identifying and collating information, but the results were not compared against these rankings since it was found that relevant information might only be available on internal University pages. Initially, the plan was to analyse pages specifically part of the Careers/Employability sections of University websites. However, it soon became apparent that information relevant to careers such as volunteering opportunities, or opportunities and insights might also be located within faculty course pages, sustainability management team pages or as part of blogs/event entries were identified through a web search but did not necessarily feature on career pages, or volunteering information was often not featured on career pages.

Therefore, the search process became one of entering into the web search 'sustainability and careers' alongside the University name. This identified potential separate pages, alongside direct examination of the pages offered within the Careers/employability sections of websites. Although the particular interest of this study was sustainability careers information for business and management, it frequently needed to be considered alongside broader information provided for faculty areas such as environmental science studies as there is clear integration between the two and they were often not distinguished between.

Due to the limitations of accessing all areas of University careers pages, the results provide only an indicative exploration of differing University approaches across the range of criteria. The qualitative insights gained in terms of the type of content provided, how it is presented, accessibility in terms of where it features on web pages, and the degree to which careers information is integrated with academic study related information, revealed the most interesting insights.

Findings

With increasing imperative for Universities to be demonstrating engagement in the SDGs, it is common practice for Universities to feature how sustainability projects and events are addressed at operational, teaching and research level.

Where this is not reflected in careers information either reflects a lack of integration, a minimum and arguably surface level of engagement or at worst, greenwashing if bold claims are made on the website that are only loosely substantiated. Worse are cases where the University pages make a strong commitment to sustainability, but Business and Management career pages make no reference to sustainability at all. There is significant disconnect here and presents significant opportunity for Universities to engage in events that develop cross-university collaboration.

Key findings below indicate how various types of University events can be more explicitly aligned with employability strategy:

- Sustainability strategy
  Information on sustainability management is frequently presented under operational/campus, teaching, research and sustainability engagement. Other campus services such as 'catering' initiatives are detailed, but the links to careers as a University service are lacking. In some limited cases, the features of the sustainability management team were fully explored and applied to careers through, for example, career profiles and advice of employees working within these teams, and the opportunities for students to engage in operational/ campus related sustainability projects with explicit reference to how this can build skills and experiences for employability. It was extremely rare, however, for such explicit links on sustainability pages to be linked from the careers websites. It is recommended that operational/campus opportunities are presented in the same way as volunteering opportunities (i.e. directly linked from career pages).
- Volunteering
  Almost all University websites analysed offered volunteering opportunities, but these were not systematically linked to careers pages. By doing so, it would help to reinforce the connections to students and potentially increase engagement (and thereby personal and collective impact).
- Internal operational opportunities
  The website review identified best practice examples as offering opportunities for students to gain skills and experiences through working on campus-related events. This might include setting up competitions, projects and funding opportunities, supporting with campus audits as part of Green Impact and Responsible Futures accreditations, and Internship opportunities with the operational team.
- Faculty and career service collaboration
  In many cases, careers specialists are located within academic departments. Best practice cases identified in this research in terms of the richness of career information on sustainability, mirrored broader academic expertise within the context of sustainable business management. This might reflect collaboration between academics and professional careers advisors. Such collaboration would seem beneficial in relation to identifying and keeping up to date with job market reports and insights, and career development opportunities such as

Internships. Blog pages written by academics with careers professionals are beneficial, and can be extended to students and alumni. There is also great opportunity here to align training events such as the popular 'Carbon Literacy Project' as career development alongside enriching academic learning.

- Communication capture on the sustainability-employability nexus

  There is significant opportunity to develop a more consistent and integrated approach to the sustainability-employability nexus. The research found that careers information might be located under careers/employability team pages, within Student Union pages or within academic department/programme pages. Added to this, relevant events and opportunities might be offered through student engagement pages and/or sustainability management team pages. Some very useful insights might be captured within blog pages that might not be linked to key pages. It is therefore recommended that an employability perspective is considered in relation to all services and academic departments. Developing a system of hashtags or consistent guidelines in approach to shared information links across pages can be helpful.

- Presentation appeal for engagement

  If sustainability-related information and events are to reach out and inspire interest and engagement, they need to be appealing. The research identified that career information pages related to sustainability vary from very basic design approaches based on basic text-based information which might include links to PDF documents, through to more visually appealing pages with images and supported by media such as videos and podcasts. Information needs to be accessible and engaging, down to even the most basic detail of adding contextual information to job roles rather than just a list of role titles. The development of engaging communicative approaches can in turn generate interest and engagement in broader campus events.

- External website career event information

  Universities strategically design career information for prospective and current students. Some secure career pages are only comprised of career tools, others encompass all information on career training and events. It is suggested from this study that even where information is securely held, clear indication on the nature of the information also needs to be presented on the public facing site. For example, if there is rich and detailed information on career sectors, or events relating to sustainable careers, to describe this on public sites.

  The introductory section to this chapter set out the potential alignment in university sustainability career information events with SDG17 on 'Partnership'. Career opportunities for graduates span public, private and civil society, and an open approach enables shared learning and collaboration. Interestingly, only one university was found to include the direct links to other Universities with detailed sustainability for career resources. This seems a time efficient approach, and one which recognises and celebrates leaders in the field.

'Fossil Free Careers' Fairs Campaign

'People and Planet' (2022) (a UK student network that campaigns for social and environmental justice) is running a campaign which calls on University careers services to stop 'end recruitment pipelines into the oil, gas, and mining industries'. This requires Universities to stop advertising vacancies of any extractive industry businesses and to stop inviting them to attend careers events. Birbeck University (2022) was an early signatory, providing a policy statement that:

> Birkbeck Careers will not hold relationships with any companies that have not demonstrated a commitment to positive environmental and ethical business models. This is part of our commitment to increased sustainability and addressing the climate crisis. This includes, but is not limited to, attendance at careers events and other recruitment opportunities, posting role vacancies, sponsorships and advertising.

It is not the purpose here to discuss the operational considerations for Universities in whether or not to become a signatory to this campaign, but rather to illustrate how student engagement in the campaign generates engagement in becoming a 'sustainability transformer'. At the time of writing, the campaign website details that four Universities have made a 'Fossil Free Career' statement/ policy. While this might appear limited, the impact is more significant in the presentation of 58, 640 students at these Universities. Furthermore, the campaign site states the support of 10 UK Students Unions which collectively represent 238, 395 students in committing to boycott any oil, gas and mining recruitment events. The reach of the campaign is therefore clearly aligned to triggering awareness and 'sustainability thinkers'.

A 'Fossil Free Career Guide' (People and Planet, 2022a) encourages student 'action' under such appeals as 'students have the power to win'. Rich resources and advice are provided for students on how to initiate and build a campaign at their respective Universities including representation at events such as (Re) Freshers Fairs. Campaign training is offered to build student skills, and broader engagement is encouraged in raising money for this 'radical, student-led organisation'. It is a very clear example of developing 'sustainability transformers' through the employability-sustainability nexus. Séraphin (2022) points to the importance of 'Becoming' (i.e. learning a new way of doing things) as part of the 'life course framework', which links to the role of education in empowering students to become 'sustainability activists'.

Conclusion

This chapter has illustrated how events related to sustainability and employability in a University context can be formulated and managed in order to generate greater individual and collective impact. Careers-related information and events for sustainability can be effectively approached through the lens of sustainability thinker, action and transformer in order to generate greater cross-University collaboration. This was illustrated through the case example of a student online and on-campus event. The latter case example based on the 'Fossil Free Careers' campaign further underlines the sustainability-employability nexus, and the rise of the student 'activist'. This can be considered powerful in developing future leaders that speak up and speak out on behalf of people and planet, as part of the movement of employee 'activism' (Reitz & Higgins, 2022).

Séraphin et al.'s (2020) analysis of empowerment draws on Boley, McGehee, Perdue, and Long (2014) forms of empowerment as psychological, social and political forms. Applied to the context of activism experiences in Higher Education, students can be identified as empowered psychologically through a purpose-driven cause, 'social' empowerment through spending time with friends away from developing a collective identify with peers and a broader network and 'political' empowerment through taking action to speak out and mitigate climate risk. It can be seen as instrumental in the development of 'significant life experiences' (Chawla, 2007) that influence lifelong pro-environmental and sustainable behaviours in a professional and personal context.

It is therefore proposed that sustainability-related careers events offer significant potential to contribute transformative, whole-person teaching pedagogy (Mezirow, 2016). Insights based on the review of University career website pages provide several recommendations concerning alignment and integration across University functions. By generating more awareness through sustainability-related careers projects and events, Universities can simultaneously enrich students career development and organisational impact for collective benefit in progressing positively towards the SDGs.

References

Birbeck University. (2022). Birbeck futures ethical careers policy. Retrieved from https://www.bbk.ac.uk/student-services/careers-service/ethical-careers-policy

Blasco, M. (2011). Aligning the hidden curriculum of management education with PRME. *Journal of Management Education*, *36*(3), 364–388. doi:10.1177/1052562911420213

Bloom, B. S. (1968). *Taxonomy of educational objectives: The classification of educational goals*. New York, NY: Longman: Greens.

Boley, B. B., McGehee, N. G., Perdue, R. R., & Long, P. (2014). Empowerment and resident attitudes toward tourism: Strengthening the theoretical foundation through a Weberian lens. *Annals of Tourism Research*, *49*, 33–50. doi:10.1016/j.annals.2014.08.005

Chawla, L. (2007). Childhood experiences associated with care for the natural world: A theoretical framework for empirical results. *Children, Youth, and Environments*, *17*(4), 144–170.

Cook, I. (2020). Future graduate skills: A scoping study. Change agents UK and EAUC. Retrieved from https://www.sustainabilityexchange.ac.uk/files/future_graduate_skills_report_change_agents_uk_eauc_october_2020.pdf

Cooperider, D., & Fry, R. (2012). Mirror flourishing and the positive psychology of sustainability+. *The Journal of Corporate Citizenship*, (46), 1–12.

Gamlath, S. L. (2022). Sustainability based careers and graduate prospects. *New Vistas*, *8*, 3–7.

Kumar, A. (2007). *Personal, academic and career development in higher education: SOARing to success.* London and New York, NY: Routledge.

Kumar, A. (2015). Enabling all learners to SOAR for employability: An inclusive integrative pedagogy. Retrieved from https://www.advance-he.ac.uk/knowledge-hub/enabling-all-learners-soar-employability-inclusive-integrative-pedagogy

Kumar, A. (2022). *Personal, social, academic and career development: SOARing to success* (2 ed.). London and New York, NY: Routledge Taylor and Francis.

LinkedIn (2022). *Global green skills report.* Retrieved from https://economicgraph.linkedin.com/content/dam/me/economicgraph/en-us/global-green-skills-report/global-green-skills-report-pdf/li-green-economy-report-2022-annex.pdf

Mezirow, J. (2016). Transformative learning as discourse. *Journal of Transformative Education, 1*(1), 58–63. doi:10.1177/1541344603252172

Norton, S., & Penaluna, A. (2022). 3 Es for wicked problems: Employability, enterprise, and entrepreneurship: Solving wicked problems. In *Advance HE.* Retrieved from https://www.advance-he.ac.uk/knowledge-hub/3-es-wicked-problems-employability-enterprise-and-entrepreneurship-solving-wicked

OECD. (2022). Big picture thinking: How to educate the whole person for an interconnected world. Retrieved from https://issuu.com/oecd.publishing/docs/big-picture-thinking-educating-global-competence

Oxford Brookes University. (2022). Student Engagement – @lovestudentleftovers digital cooking competition. Retrieved from https://www.brookes.ac.uk/sustainability/student-engagement/

People and Planet. (2022a). Fossil free careers. Retrieved from https://peopleandplanet.org/fossil-free-careers

People and Planet. (2022b). University League 2021–2022. Retrieved from https://peopleandplanet.org/university-league

QAA and Advance HE. (2021). Education for sustainable development guidance. Retrieved from https://www.qaa.ac.uk/quality-code/education-for-sustainable-development

Reitz, M., & Higgins, J. (2022). Leading in an age of employee activism. *MIT Sloan Management Review, 63*, 61–67.

Séraphin, H. (2022). Understanding the traits of tourism sustainability activists through a life course framework. *Journal of Policy Research in Tourism, Leisure and Events.* doi:10.1080/19407963.2022.2029873

Séraphin, H., & Yallop, A. (2019). An analysis of children's play in resort mini-clubs: potential strategic implications for the hospitality and tourism industry. *World Leisure Journal, 62*(2), 114–131.

Séraphin, H., Yallop, A. C., Seyfi, S., & Hall, C. M. (2020). Responsible tourism: The 'why' and 'how' of empowering children. *Tourism Recreation Research*, 1–16. doi: 10.1080/02508281.2020.1819109

SOS-UK. (2022). Students organising for sustainability – Sustainability skills survey. Retrieved from https://www.sos-uk.org/research/sustainability-skills-survey

UNESCO. (2017). Education for Sustainable Development Goals: Learning objectives. Retrieved from https://www.unesco.de/sites/default/files/2018-08/unesco_education_for_sustainable_development_goals.pdf

Chapter 5

How Children Experience Major Sports Events: Narratives of the Mediterranean Games, Oran, Algeria 2022

Yasmine Ait-Challal, Souad Djedi-Birady, Faouzi Ghidouche and Kamila Ait-Yahia Ghidouche

Abstract

This research work explores the perception of children's experiences as spectators of a sporting event. The study focusses on the 19th Mediterranean Games hosted by Oran in the summer of 2022 and aims to analyse the trace of emotions and memories that the event left in their minds. A qualitative survey was conducted with 22 resident children who attended the event as spectators. The results show that a child's experience at a sporting event is holistic, appearing in several dimensions: a cognitive dimension, referring to what the child learnt from the event, and an affective dimension, which is important for creating strong and meaningful experiences for children at sporting events.

Keywords: Mediterranean Games; Oran; children; experience; emotion; memories

Introduction

Research in the context of sports events has long focussed on their economic impacts, which is an indisputable fact when one considers the number of capital destinations that invest in hosting a sporting event (Murugan & Tuck Sai, 2018). Nevertheless, it should be noted (Preuss & Arne Solberg, 2006) that economic analyses do not reflect the initial value of sports events, which is a carrier of social values for residents, offering them the opportunity to attend high-quality sports competitions and enjoy a festive atmosphere in their city. Moreover, residents play a crucial role in the success of a sporting event not only through their

Events Management for the Infant and Youth Market, 67–83
Copyright © 2023 Yasmine Ait-Challal, Souad Djedi-Birady, Faouzi Ghidouche and Kamila Ait-Yahia Ghidouche
Published under exclusive licence by Emerald Publishing Limited
doi:10.1108/978-1-80455-690-020231011

commitment and support for the event (Gursoy & Kendall, 2006; Zhou & Ap, 2009) but also through the positive atmosphere they create at the sporting event (Chen, 2011). The findings attest that residents are spectators of the event to the same 'degree' as tourists, and it is essential to understand their perceptions as spectators.

Children represent an under-explored segment in the sports event context literature review, yet researchers acknowledge their influence on family purchasing decisions (Cullingford, 1995; Séraphin & Yallop, 2019). Séraphin and Gowreesunkar (2020) work highlighted the importance of children in the tourism and hospitality sector. This importance is reflected in children's influence in choosing a tourist destination (Séraphin & Yallop, 2019) or even the type of vacation (Li, Wang, Xu, & Mao, 2017). This interest is further justified by the fact that children represent both the future actors and consumers of the tourism and hospitality sector. In this sense, children should represent an essential component of any tourism destination initiative (Séraphin & Gowreesunkar, 2020).

Séraphin and Yallop (2019) proposed an ambidextrous management approach to improve the experience of children by giving particular importance to the 'fun' dimension, which is an essential factor in the satisfaction of children (and parents). This importance is also found in event industries. However, Séraphin and Gowreesunkar (2020) noted that in the scientific journals specialising in event management, few researchers have been interested in children and even less in children's experience in large events. Dallari and Mariotti (2016) and Canosa and Graham (2020) proposed postmodernist approaches and argued for focussing on individual experiences. Children are also seen as 'disseminators' of sociocultural values that they derive from the event, as they have proximity to their family and peers (Schulenkorf & Edwards, 2012). Their predispositions (freshness of mind and lack of prejudice) make it easier for them to take advantage of the psychological income generated by the event that Howard and Crompton (2003) summed up as the pride of belonging to the host city and the sense of national unity that this brings.

To this end, building on the researchers' idea of the need to understand spectator experiences and their influence on post-event behaviour (Hallmann, Zehrer, & Rietz, 2021), we believe it is crucial to understand how residents in the broadest sense and child residents in particular experience the sporting event. This study fills a gap in the literature by exploring children's experiences of major sporting events. This research proposes to explore both (1) the perception (subjective and material) of children's experiences as spectators of an event, (2) the trace of emotions and memories left in the mind of the events, and finally, (3) the implications of children's experiences on future sports practice.

This chapter is organised as follows: the section on 'literature review' presents events and children. The section on 'context of the study' discusses the Mediterranean Games (MG) organised by the city of Oran in 2022 and then describes the methodological approach used. Next results of the research are provided after which finally a discussion of the research results and the conclusion and implications of our research are presented.

Literature Review

Sports Event Experience

The concept of experience is defined from a marketing point of view as an internal and subjective response of the consumer to the direct or indirect encounter with a product, a company or the components of the associated organisation (Meyer & Schwager, 2007). Brakus, Schmitt, and Zarantonello (2009) proposed a practical definition in the context of our study, that of sports events (Sorrentino, Fu, Romano, Quintano, & Risitano, 2020). These authors conceive the experience as a model composed of four latent sub-dimensions: a 'sense' dimension that refers to the impact of marketing on the five senses (eyesight, hearing, taste, touch and smell); a dimension of affective and emotional 'sensation', and a third one, cognitive, concerning the 'thoughts' on a lived experience. The last and most important dimension is 'action'. It is a question of seeing if the experience produced translates into action, such as a purchase or a recommendation. In our case, this translates into the intention to revisit the destination or to attend the event again.

This holistic conception of experience is appropriate for sporting events because being a spectator is like listening to a functional orchestra where several musical instruments contribute to the overall performance (Pearce, 2011). In this sense, sporting events elicit in the spectator a mixture of sensations and emotions that merge to create a holistic experience (Ayob, Wahid, & Omar, 2013; Song, Ahn, & Lee, 2015; Sorrentino et al., 2020). The notion of experience has been introduced into sports tourism research recently (Kim, Ritchie, & McCormick, 2012; Song, Kim, & Choe, 2019; Sorrentino et al., 2020) and matches the development of the sports event industry.

Destinations invest large amounts of money in hosting sporting events. Therefore, there is a need to ensure that the event provides a satisfying experience for spectators because, as the literature points out, a satisfying experience influences behavioural intentions towards the event and/or the host destination, which will translate into future behaviour (Duan & Dai, 2018). In the era of the 'experience economy' (Hung, Lee, & Huang, 2016), researchers have increasingly given importance to the topic of experience in tourism in recent years (Moon & Han, 2019). Nevertheless, only a few studies have been conducted in the sports industry (Wu & Ai, 2016; Wu & Cheng, 2018).

Children's Experience of a Sporting Event

The experience of an event takes the person on a journey from the ordinary daily routine to a space where extraordinary joy and fun are created and shared (Kuykendall, Tay, & Ng, 2015; Morgan, 2008). Regarding travel, fun and games lead us to think of children seeking exciting and fun vacation activities that offer immersive sensory experiences (Gram, 2005). However, if there is interest in conducting more research on the experience of a sporting event, the focus should not be limited to adults only. However, it should be broadened to include children who, for a long time, have been neglected because the child does not meet the main criterion of a good respondent to scientific research, which is 'the abstract thinking that characterizes the maturity of adolescence and later adulthood' (Scott, 2000).

There has been an increase in awareness over the past 20 years where tourism researchers have shown particular interest in the target audience of children because they influenced family decision-making (Aït-Yahia Ghidouche & Ghidouche, 2020; Carr, 2006; Khoo-Lattimore, Prayag, & Cheah, 2015) and the fact that children have distinct needs and interests that need to be taken into account (Djedi & Aït-Yahia, 2022; Schänzel & Yeoman, 2015). Indeed, the literature on a child's tourism experience reveals that children remember fun experiences. They enjoy being active and learning through play; vacations allow them to meet new friends and spend time with family (Rhoden, Hunter-Jones, & Miller, 2016).

When children are happy by having a fun tourism experience, they positively influence parental happiness (Khoo-Lattimore, delChiappa, & Yang, 2018). This opportunity to share family experiences and memories is why more research is being conducted on the family tourism experience. Poria and Timothy (2014) argue that even within this lens of children's vacation experiences and the concept of family tourism, the child's voice continues to be absent as research focusses on parental perspectives rather than children's. Rhoden et al. (2016) and Radic (2019) share this view and call on researchers to put children more at the centre of studies, especially by telling their perceptions and experiences.

If children are not frequent subjects of research on the tourism experience, they remain absent from the experience of sports events. Nevertheless, since Pierre de Coubertin, we know that sports events are bearers of educational values. Futada (2007) highlighted that Olympism promoted the integral education of the human being and that the connection between sporting events and the heroic and agonistic imaginary would help the sport to develop as a pedagogical tool. Extending this idea, Carton and Winnykamen (1999) stated that games and sports constitute a compensatory space that 'exerts of this fact a cathartic function by allowing the realization of desires and the liquidation of conflicts'.

Weed (2010) referred to the 'demonstration effect' as 'a process by which people are inspired by elite sport, sports people, or sports events to participate themselves'. Potwarka and Leatherdale (2016) stated that this effect is most effective among the younger population and in communities where events are held. Potwarka, Snelgrove, Wood, Teare, and Wigfield (2020) confirmed this effect by arguing that watching an elite sporting event can contribute to increasing youths' intention to participate in a new sport and explains these inspirational moments experienced through the cognitive-affective-behavioural mechanism which suggests that how people think about and process particular cognitive stimuli can influence the emotional (affective) states experienced by a person which, in turn, can influence particular responses to stimuli such as the formation of a behavioural intention (Holbrook & Hirschman, 1982). From this observation, we believe that hosting sports events can be seen as an opportunity to inspire children to be more active, play a sport, and participate in sports events. Aware of the lack of research on children in sports events, we rely on the theoretical foundations of the tourist experience in children. We will try through this research to understand how children live the experience of the sports events of the MG.

Methodology

Study Background

The MG are a major sporting event organised every four years in the countries of the Mediterranean Basin. In the summer of 2022, Algeria organised the 19th edition of the MG in Oran. It was a dozen days of competition, sport and celebration with the participation of 3,390 athletes from 26 countries in 24 sports (athletics, swimming, horseback riding, Judo, football etc.).

Methodological Approach

This study on the perception of resident children's experiences as spectators of a sporting event was conducted based on an exploratory qualitative study with children aged 11–15. Smith (2008) justified using qualitative research because of its ability to bring out individuals' experiences. Our research was conducted in accordance with the main guidelines for conducting such research with children (Brée, 2012). Also, we scrupulously respected the principles of respect, confidentiality and consent.

Therefore, the research explores how the children experienced the MG competition. We tried to understand what they thought of this event and to identify the image they had of it. Then, we asked the children to tell us about their experience during the MG period, i.e. what they did or wished to do, what they learnt and what they remembered about the event to bring out their cognitive experience. We questioned their feelings to bring out their affective experience and evaluate this experience (event satisfaction) and finally to see their behavioural intentions towards sports events in general and sports practice in particular.

The recruitment of children participating in the survey was done conveniently because of the difficulty of obtaining parental consent and the necessary authorisations from schools for this study. Also, we used canvassing on social networks (publication by a group of volunteers of the MG on Facebook) and by recommendation. The survey took place over three days in Oran between September 29 and 1 October 2022. Twenty-two children living in Oran participated in this study, 14 Males and 8 Females (Table 1). All of them were enrolled in public schools. We chose to conduct individual face-to-face interviews. The duration of the interviews varied between 20 and 35 minutes.

Data Analysis and Results

The results represent the outcomes of content analysis, carried out in two phases on a corpus consisting of 22 transcripts faithful to the audio recordings made with the participants in the study. The software MAXQDA22 was used to carry out

Table 1. Interviewees Profile.

First Names	Age	Gender	Educational Level	Participant
Adam	11	Male	Secondary education	Spectator
Ahlem	11	Female	Secondary education	Spectator
Aissa	15	Male	Secondary education	Spectator + volunteer
Hana	11	Female	Secondary education	Spectator
Houssem	13	Male	Secondary education	Spectator
Malak	14	Female	Secondary education	Spectator
Mehdi	13	Male	Secondary education	Spectator
Ryad	11	Male	Secondary education	Spectator
Sohaib	12	Male	Secondary education	Spectator
Yacine	15	Male	Secondary education	Spectator + volunteer
Lylia	13	Female	Secondary education	Spectator
Ghozlane	11	Female	Secondary education	Spectator
Ayoub	13	Male	Secondary education	Spectator
Sara	12	Female	Secondary education	Spectator
Mouad	13	Male	Secondary education	Spectator
Aymen	12	Male	Secondary education	Spectator
Aissa	11	Male	Secondary education	Spectator + volunteer
Abdelkrim	14	Male	Secondary education	Spectator

Table 1. *(Continued)*

First Names	Age	Gender	Educational Level	Participant
Bilal	15	Male	Secondary education	Spectator
Yassine	11	Male	Secondary education	TV spectator (indirect experience)
Habiba	13	Female	Secondary education	Spectator + volunteer
Zakaria	15	Male	Secondary education	Spectator + volunteer

Source: The Authors.

the first and second stages of analysis. For some, the following categories correspond to the themes mentioned in the in-depth interview guide, while others emerged during the two analysis phases. Verbatims will be used to illustrate the categories presented.

Mediterranean Games: Catalyst of Emotions and Sensations

The event of the MG seems to stimulate many emotions in the different categories of people who live in the city where the event was held. Mainly, joy and happiness to host a sporting event of such magnitude as the MG. The enthusiasm of the local population especially induced this joy. The dimension 'popular enthusiasm' was found in the speech of the majority of the interviewed teenagers. 'R: I remember the special atmosphere that prevailed and the popular fervour around the event. People around me always talked about it, especially the sports competitions, and all wished the Algerian athletes to win (Mehdi_13)'. The enthusiasm of the people around this event was reinforced by the online and offline communications. 'R: outside everyone was talking about MG, with my friends, on TV everyone was talking about it, all Algeria (Bilel_14)'. This enthusiastic attitude was perceptible by the children, and helped to create a positive general atmosphere, whether it be for the sports events, 'R: what I liked is the general atmosphere during the sports events and the encouragement of the supporters towards the athletes and the participants (Yacine_15)' or outside the sports structures, through festivities in several locations in the city of Oran, 'R: Yes, in "place d'armes" site, there was music, competitions, clowning... that made the children happy, as well as drawing contests (Abdelkrim_14)'. The cultural activities that accompanied the sports event appeared to have been appreciated by the local population and positively associated with the MG.

The second most cited dimension by participants is 'enjoyment and happiness'. Indeed, the uniqueness and unprecedented nature of the event seem to arouse curiosity combined with enjoyment to witness the organisation of this event for the first time in Algeria and the city of Oran. 'R: I was happy because it was new for me, and not only me, all the children were happy (Adam_11)'. 'R: Yes, it is the first time that we organised such a thing in Oran... I was proud, and I felt the joy...it was a lot of emotions... (Aymen_12)'.

The teenagers seem to have experienced the MG under the sign of 'pride' as well. Pride is the most commonly quoted emotion by children. The majority of participants, whether they attended the MG in person or through the media platforms, expressed great pride that the country was able to organise an event of such stature. 'R: I was proud, I said to myself, at least we participated in a world event because it included several countries (Yassine_11)'. The feeling of pride is more present in Oran. 'R: Proud that the city is hosting the games. I consider that the games were a total success for the city of Oran (Ahlem_11)'.

The pride concerning the performance of the country's athletes (Algerian athletes) comes back very often in the participants' speeches. 'R: Especially on the occasion of the atmosphere in the stadium when the Algerian athletes entered. I felt a pride that the city of Oran is in the spotlight in several countries such as France (Mehdi_13)'. Some children expressed their 'relief' at the smooth running of the MG, particularly the fact that there were no major incidents that could damage the country's reputation. 'R: I feel many positive emotions because I attended this event. The fact that there were no incidents is also a relief (Yacine_15)'.

Positive Impacts: Bringing People and Visibility to the City

According to the children's perspective, the organisation of an international sports event has given the city of Oran international *visibility and reputation*. Most respondents spontaneously mentioned this dimension, considering it a positive and substantial impact of the MG. 'R: so that all the people can discover it...Oran has become more known than before (Mouad_13). Several respondents thus grasped the intercultural dimension of this sporting event, referring to the tangible heritage (tourist sites of the city) and intangible heritage (all the traditions, values and gastronomy of Algeria and the city of Oran in particular). For teenagers, such a sports event has improved awareness about the city and the country internationally, which may be considered a trigger for international tourism. 'R: Almost half of the countries that came did not know Algeria. During the MG, they took knowledge of our traditions, our dishes, and that is something good! (Lylia_13)'. The tourist activity emanating from this event was also linked to the economic development of the city of Oran, considering these large-scale sports events as a creator of wealth for the cities that host them. 'R: There will be more tourists for the city of Oran. There will be a positive effect on the economic situation of the city of Oran (Yacine_15)'.

Another dimension that the teenagers massively reported is the one that concerns all the *urban improvements* made on the occasion of the MG. Children reported a better organisation in the city, like property, reinforced security, and the opening of new places and infrastructures, in addition to ephemeral/transitory arts places. 'R: Yes, the city of Oran has changed. The new stadium was opened for the MG. The schools were refurbished. The tourist spots like "La place d'armes" were decorated with flowers and flags (Houssam_13)'.

Mediterranean Games: Motivating and Inspiring

MG appear to *motivate and inspire* children and youth on many levels. Indeed, many children express their will to become professional and high-level athletes. 'R: I would like to improve my judo skills and be among the athletes chosen to represent and honour my country (Aissa_15)'. The MG have opened the field of possibilities for children, who probably never considered that they could make such achievements. 'R: when I was in the stadium, I imagined myself as an athlete and that I could win in a judo competition (Houssam_13)'. Some children are said to witness a greater craze in terms of practicing sports since the MG, whether from the children themselves or from their parents, who seem to recognise the importance of high-performance sports. 'R: When we attended the gymnastics events, I told my mother to enrol me to practice this sport and participate in the events of the MG in other countries and that I would get gold medals and become famous (Hana_11)'.

Another significant fact is the development of *positive behaviours and attitudes* among teenagers on many levels. 'R: I learned a lot about the right way to behave and to be at my best (Ahlem_11), whether it is in terms of commitment to the country, in terms of good sportsmanship, or respect during competitions. 'R: I learnt that it is necessary to have a sporting spirit and to remain motivated and to persevere to become a champion like them (Habiba_13)'. In this regard, several children pointed to the negative attitude of some Algerian supporters, who whistled at the opposing team. 'R: I also did not like the behaviour of some Algerians towards foreigners like those from Mali, saying bad words, throwing bottles. It influences the image of our country badly (Aymen_12)'.

Mediterranean Games: Triggering new Knowledge

Attending the MG seems to have allowed the children to *acquire knowledge and develop organisational skills*. 'R: I also developed skills in the hospitality of tourists during the games (Yacine_15)'. They also seem to link the sports dimension to that of tourists. For them, the two aspects are closely connected. 'R: I learnt to be disciplined, respect the tourists, and convey a good image to the tourists (Malak Radja_14)'. Though children acquired new knowledge about new sports and the event itself (MG), they say they learnt less about the city of Oran. It seems like the MG were not a trigger for the city of Oran regarding knowledge development (in history, arts and culture, among others). 'R: On the other hand, concerning the city of Oran, the event did not provide me with any new information (Sohaib_12).'

Discussion

The consumer experience, as described by Brakus et al. (2009), provided an adequate basis for discussing the obtained results. Other lines of inquiry related to major sports events clarify and complement the results presented here. Brakus et al. (2009) defined experiences as a combination of 'sensations, feelings, cognitions, and behavioral responses evoked by brand-related stimuli'. In fact, in this definition alone, we encounter most of our insights, namely the emotions and sensations produced by the MG, different types of knowledge (cognition) and a behavioural response represented in our case by the participants' willingness to revisit and take part in this event in the future.

The most salient result of this research is that this event seems to produce a confluence of feelings and emotions in visitors, ranging from joy and admiration to a sense of identity (the sense of pride among the inhabitants of the host city). Our findings are in line with those of many other researchers who have confirmed the importance of feelings and emotions in creating strong and significant experiences in sports events (Sorrentino et al., 2020). Brakus et al. (2009) confirm that experiences can give rise to general evaluations and attitudes, particularly evaluations of the experience itself. This dimension was also found in children expressing their feelings about the overall experience in the MG.

It is suggested that experience with a brand (in this case study, an event) occurs as a subjective response to experiential attributes associated with the brand in a particular context (Brakus et al., 2009). Among the attributes that were most reported is 'popular enthusiasm', combining different emotions/feelings triggered by the event, such as the local populations' fervour and the host city's atmosphere.

Our findings highlight that pride is the most recurrent emotion among children. This pattern of results is consistent with the previous literature that considers sport to be a tremendous lever for increasing national pride (Elling, Hilvoorde, & van den Dool, 2014) and a means of creating a kind of national identity (Haut, Prohl, & Emrich, 2016). This pride was manifested in two ways, as synthesised by Storm and Jakobsen (2020): in one way, pride in belonging to the host city of the event, and pride that the event was successful and, in another way, pride in the achievement of national athletes at the event.

These results also confirm that there is no longer a need to focus solely on economic arguments to justify the hosting of sports events, as it is increasingly clear that the event provides intangible effects such as pride (Gibson, Kaplanidou, & Kang, 2012). Still, in this idea of intangible effects, it emerges from our results that children perceive social benefits of MG that are manifested as 'bringing visibility, notoriety and a good reputation to their city' and 'relief' at the smooth running of MG. This finding is in line with the results of Kim and Petrick (2005), who found that image improvement, the opportunity to increase international recognition and community pride are the main social benefits perceived by residents.

This finding is consistent with previous research that announces that resident support, considered a key to the success of major sporting events, is closely related to perceptions of event impact (Al-Emadi et al., 2017). Social exchange theory provides a theoretical framework for understanding this relationship; it states that one person's action is dependent on another person's actions (Inoue & Havard, 2014), which suggests that children's support is related to their perceptions of the impacts generated by MG.

The results of this research provide supporting evidence that the children, as a result of their experience of the MG, were strongly influenced by the sports performance and expressed a desire to play the sport in question, and many acted on it. These results are consistent with the claim that affective states of inspiration are more goal-oriented because there is often an object towards which the resulting motivation is directed (Potwarka et al., 2020). In this sense, the work of Veal, Toohey, and Frawley (2012) revealed a likely relationship between mega sport events and sport participation among children.

Whang (2006) confirmed that the organisation of sports events like the Football World Cup had created a generation of young Koreans who are committed to the community and have had their label changed from 'irresponsible generation' to 'generation W' about the positive changes brought about by the World Cup sports event. This idea is further supported by the finding of our qualitative study that the MG event has produced a set of positive and engaging attitudes among young resident people in terms of commitment to the country, good sportsmanship and respect.

The study findings indicate that teenagers acquired different types of knowledge, especially about new sports and the event itself. Concerning the practice of sports, the lack of knowledge proved to be an obstacle to developing a behavioural intention concerning the practice of a sport among the children surveyed. It is the case, particularly for certain sports, such as gymnastics for females. Moreover, the children surveyed who participated in the MG as volunteers (immersive experience) declared having acquired new skills and knowledge. These results are consistent with the claim that volunteering promotes the development of transferable skills (Fairley, Gardiner, & Filo, 2016).

Conclusion

Key Findings

The objective of this research was to explore the experience of a sporting event as lived by the child resident of the host city. The results confirm that the conception of the experience of a child in the context of a sporting event is holistic and manifests itself in several dimensions: a cognitive dimension that refers to what the child has developed as knowledge, thanks to the event, and an affective dimension, the most telling in our research with children. The mixture of emotions, such as joy and pride, provoked by their strength and impact on the children is a transformational dynamic that influences their future behavioural intentions by serving as an inspiring lever on their practices (sport), lifestyle and way of thinking (surpassing oneself). It appears that feelings and emotions, in accordance with the findings of Sorrentino et al. (2020), are important in creating strong and meaningful experiences for children in sports events. Their positive evaluation of the experience and the satisfaction they derive from it is a predictable indicator of their future actions.

Theoretical Contributions

This research focussed on the notion of children's experience of a sporting event as host city residents. To our knowledge, no research has been conducted on children in this context (child residents). This theoretical choice responds, on the one hand, to the recommendations of researchers (Hallmaan et al., 2021) to give more importance to the concept of experience of sporting events, given that this variable would influence future behaviours, and on the other hand to be interested in children as a research subject to fill the theoretical void linked to the problem of underestimation and the little interest given to the child (Thornton, Shaw, & Williams, 1997).

Managerial Contributions

The results suggest several practical implications for event stakeholders, especially in the case of Algeria, where few studies have investigated the organisation of events in this country (Ait-Yahia Ghidouche & Ghidouche, 2018). First, organisers should focus their marketing campaign on the event's intangible aspects, such as sharing information and stories related to the event and the host city to benefit potential residents and tourists. The goal is to create a permanent link with the event – before, during and after – and to generate interest among residents and visitors. In addition, event organisers need to integrate and combine entertainment with the event. This means offering additional spectator-oriented activities that will increase the overall value of the event and develop a positive experience of visiting the event.

In this sense, and to reinforce children's immersive experience, organisers should, for example, organise children's days in the image of what is proposed in the mega sports events in the world. However, it also promotes contact between children and participating athletes, increasing and strengthening the event experience. Finally, as far as the public authorities of the host city are concerned, they must direct their actions towards the resident children to promote social cohesion and pride in belonging. This can be done by setting up concerted actions with all the civil society stakeholders to reinforce the children's knowledge of the city's history and the event.

Limitations and Avenues of Research

There are at least three potential limitations concerning the results of this study. The first refers to the lack of previous research on children's experiences in tourism in general and the events industry. The second potential limitation refers to the age of the children who participated that we selected in our study, which is not representative of all age groups of children. In this sense, future research could analyse the differences in children's perception of events according to age groups, gender or the parents' socio-professional categories. In addition, the study focussed only on resident children; in future research frameworks, it would be interesting to broaden the reflection on the experience of 'tourist' children during a sports event. Finally, this research focussed on a regional sports event, which limits its scope for generalising its results. We, therefore, recommend that, in the context of Algeria, we look at the exploratory analysis of children's experiences in the case of other types of events (cultural festivities).

References

Ait-Yahia Ghidouche, K., & Ghidouche, F. (2018). Cultural events and their effect on city image: The case of Constantine capital of Arab culture 2015. In H. Séraphin & M. Korstanje (Eds.), *International event management: Bridging the gap between theory and practice* (pp. 101–114). New York, NY: Nova Science Publishers.

Aït-Yahia Ghidouche, K., & Ghidouche, F. (2020). 6 Good holidays in children's voices and drawings. In H. Séraphin & V. Gowreesunkar (Eds.), *Children in hospitality and tourism: Marketing and managing experiences* (pp. 91–106). Berlin: De Gruyter.

Al-Emadi, A., Kaplanidou, K., Diop, A., Sagas, M., Le, K. T., & Al-Ali Mustafa, S. (2017). 2022 Qatar World Cup: Impact perceptions among Qatar residents. *Journal of Travel Research, 56*(5), 678–694. doi:10.1177/0047287516652502

Ayob, N., Wahid, N. A., & Omar, A. (2013). Mediating effect of visitors' event experiences in relation to event features and post-consumption behaviors. *Journal of Convention & Event Tourism, 14*(3), 177–192. doi:10.1080/15470148.2013.814037

Brakus, J. J., Schmitt, B. H., & Zarantonello, L. (2009). Brand experience: What is it? How is it measured? Does it Affect loyalty? *Journal of Marketing, 73*(3), 52–68. doi: 10.1509/jmkg.73.3.052

Brée, J. (2012). *Kids marketing.* Paris: EMS.

Canosa, A., & Graham, A. (2020). Tracing the contribution of childhood studies: Maintaining momentum while navigating tensions. *Childhood, 27*(1), 25–47. doi: 10.1177/0907568219886619

Carr, N. (2006). A comparison of Adolescents' and parents' holiday motivations and desires. *Tourism and Hospitality Research, 6*(2), 129–142. doi:10.1057/palgrave.thr. 6040051

Carton, A., & Winnykamen, F. (1999). *Les relations chez l'enfant: Génèse, développement, fonctions.* Paris: Armand Colin.

Chen, S. C. (2011). Residents' perceptions of the impact of major Annual tourism events in Macao: Cluster analysis. *Journal of Convention & Event Tourism, 12*(2), 106–128. doi:10.1080/15470148.2011.569877

Cullingford, C. (1995). Children's attitudes to holidays overseas. *Tourism Management*, *16*(2), 121–127. doi:10.1016/0261-5177(94)00022-3

Dallari, F., & Mariotti, A. (2016). Les pratiques touristiques ciblées sur l'enfance: Vers une nouvelle perspective? Retrieved from https://journals.openedition.org/viatourism/1525

Djedi, S., & Aït-Yahia, G., K. (2022). Empowering children: A path toward sustainable tourism in emerging countries. In H. Séraphin (Ed.), *Children in sustainable and responsible tourism* (pp. 115–128). Bingley: Emerald Publishing Limited. doi:10.1108/978-1-80117-656-920221008

Duan, X., & Dai, L. (2018). Study on the relationship between experience quality, Co-created value and users' behavioral intention of making continuous contributions on internet UGC platforms. *Journal of Service Science and Management*, *11*(2), 267–277. doi:10.4236/jssm.2018.112019

Elling, A., Hilvoorde, I., & van den Dool, R. (2014). Creating or awakening national pride through sporting success? A longitudinal study on macro effects in The Netherlands. *International Review for the Sociology of Sport*, *49*(2), 129–151. doi:10.1177/1012690212455961

Fairley, S., Gardiner, S., & Filo, K. (2016). The spirit lives on: The legacy of volunteering at the Sydney 2000 Olympic Games. *Event Management*, *20*(2), 201–215.

Futada, F. M. (2007). Olympic education: Concept and models. In K. Rubio (Ed.), *Olympic education and social responsibility*. São Paulo: Casa do Psicólogo.

Gibson, H. J., Kaplanidou, K., & Kang, S. J. (2012). Small-scale event sport tourism: A case study in sustainable tourism. *Sport Management Review*, *15*(2), 160–170. doi:10.1016/j.smr.2011.08.013

Gram, M. (2005). Family holidays. A qualitative analysis of family holiday experiences. *Scandinavian Journal of Hospitality and Tourism*, *5*(1), 2–22. doi:10.1080/15022250510014255

Gursoy, D., & Kendall, K. W. (2006). Hosting mega events. *Annals of Tourism Research*, *33*(3), 603–623. doi:10.1016/j.annals.2006.01.005

Hallmann, K., Zehrer, A., & Rietz, J. (2021). Sport events as experience scapes: The spectator's perspective. *International Journal of Sports Marketing & Sponsorship*, *22*(4), 764–779. doi:10.1108/IJSMS-04-2020-0056

Haut, J., Prohl, R., & Emrich, E. (2016). Nothing but medals? Attitudes towards the importance of Olympic success. *International Review for the Sociology of Sport*, *51*(3), 332–348. doi:10.1177/1012690214526400

Holbrook, M. B., & Hirschman, E. C. (1982). The experiential aspects of consumption: Consumer fantasies, feelings, and fun. *Journal of Consumer Research*, *9*(2), 132–140.

Howard, D. R., & Crompton, J. L. (2003). *Financing sport* (2nd ed.). Morgantown, WV: Fitness Information Technology.

Hung, W.-L., Lee, Y.-J., & Huang, P.-H. (2016). Creative experiences, memorability and revisit intention in creative tourism. *Current Issues in Tourism*, *19*(8), 763–770. doi:10.1080/13683500.2013.877422

Inoue, Y., & Havard, C. T. (2014). Determinants and consequences of the perceived social impact of a sport event. *Journal of Sport Management*, *28*(3), 295–310. doi:10.1123/jsm.2013-0136

Khoo-Lattimore, C., delChiappa, G., & Yang, M. J. (2018). A family for the holidays: Delineating the hospitality needs of European parents with young children. *Young Consumers, 19*(2), 159–171. doi:10.1108/YC-08-2017-00730

Khoo-Lattimore, C., Prayag, G., & Cheah, B. L. (2015). Kids on Board: Exploring the choice process and vacation needs of Asian parents with young children in resort hotels. *Journal of Hospitality Marketing & Management, 24*(5), 511–531. doi:10.1080/19368623.2014.914862

Kim, S. S., & Petrick, J. F. (2005). Residents' perceptions on impacts of the FIFA 2002 World Cup: The case of Seoul as a host city. *Tourism Management, 26*(1), 25–38. doi:10.1016/j.tourman.2003.09.013

Kim, J.-H., Ritchie, J. R. B., & McCormick, B. (2012). Development of a scale to measure memorable tourism experiences. *Journal of Travel Research, 51*(1), 12–25. doi:10.1177/0047287510385467

Kuykendall, L., Tay, L., & Ng, V. (2015). Leisure engagement and subjective well-being: A meta-analysis. *Psychological Bulletin, 141*(2), 364–403. doi:10.1037/a0038508

Li, M., Wang, D., Xu, W., & Mao, Z. (Eddie). (2017). Motivation for family vacations with young children: Anecdotes from the Internet. *Journal of Travel & Tourism Marketing,* 1–11. doi:10.1080/10548408.2016.1276007

Meyer, C., & Schwager, A. (2007). Understanding customer experience. *Harvard Business Review, 85*, 116–126.

Moon, H., & Han, H. (2019). Tourist experience quality and loyalty to an island destination: The moderating impact of destination image. *Journal of Travel & Tourism Marketing, 36*(1), 43–59. doi:10.1080/10548408.2018.1494083

Morgan, M. (2008). What makes a good festival? Understanding the event experience. *Event Management, 12*(2), 81–93. doi:10.3727/152599509787992562

Murugan, N., & Sai, B. T. (2018). Residents' perceptions on social impacts of hosting the 29th SEA games. *Asia-Pacific Journal of Innovation in Hospitality and Tourism, 7*, 11–33.

Pearce, P. L. (2011). *Tourist behaviour and the contemporary world.* Bristol: Channel View Publications.

Poria, Y., & Timothy, D. J. (2014). Where are the children in tourism research? *Annals of Tourism Research, 47*, 93–95. doi:10.1016/j.annals.2014.03.002

Potwarka, L. R., & Leatherdale, S. T. (2016). The Vancouver 2010 Olympics and leisure-time physical activity rates among youth in Canada: Any evidence of a trickle-down effect? *Leisure Studies, 35*(2), 241–257. doi:10.1080/02614367.2015.1040826

Potwarka, L. R., Snelgrove, R., Wood, L., Teare, G., & Wigfield, D. (2020). Understanding demonstration effects among youth sport spectators: Cognitive and affective explanations. *Sport, Business and Management: International Journal, 10*(2), 187–206. doi:10.1108/SBM-11-2019-0106

Preuss, H., & Arne Solberg, H. (2006). Attracting major sporting events: The role of local residents. *European Sport Management Quarterly, 6*(4), 391–411. doi:10.1080/16184740601154524

Radic, A. (2019). Towards an understanding of a child's cruise experience. *Current Issues in Tourism, 22*(2), 237–252. doi:10.1080/13683500.2017.1368463

Rhoden, S., Hunter-Jones, P., & Miller, A. (2016). Tourism experiences through the eyes of a child. *Annals of Leisure Research, 19*(4), 424–443. doi:10.1080/11745398. 2015.1134337

Schänzel, H. A., & Yeoman, I. (2015). Trends in family tourism. *Journal of Tourism Futures, 1*(2), 141–147. doi:10.1108/JTF-12-2014-0006

Schulenkorf, N., & Edwards, D. (2012). Maximizing positive social impacts: Strategies for sustaining and leveraging the benefits of intercommunity sport events in divided societies. *Journal of Sport Management, 26*(5), 379–390. doi:10.1123/jsm.26.5.379

Scott, J. (2000). Children as respondents: The challenges for qualitative researchers. In P. Christensen & A. James (Eds.), *Research with children: Perspectives and practices* (pp. 98–119). London: Falmer Press.

Séraphin, H., & Gowreesunkar, V. (Eds.). (2020). *Children in hospitality and tourism: Marketing and managing experiences.* Berlin: De Gruyter.

Séraphin, H., & Yallop, A. (2019). Proposed framework for the management of resorts Mini Clubs: An ambidextrous approach. *Leisure Studies, 38*(4), 535–547. doi:10.1080/02614367.2019.1581249

Smith, J. A. (2008). *Qualitative psychology: A practical guide to research methods.* London: Sage.

Song, H.-J., Ahn, Y., & Lee, C.-K. (2015). Structural relationships among strategic experiential modules, emotion and satisfaction at the Expo 2012 Yeosu Korea: Experiential modules, emotion and satisfaction. *International Journal of Tourism Research, 17*(3), 239–248. doi:10.1002/jtr.1981

Song, H., Kim, M., & Choe, Y. (2019). Structural relationships among mega-event experiences, emotional responses, and satisfaction: Focused on the 2014 Incheon Asian Games. *Current Issues in Tourism, 22*(5), 575–581. doi:10.1080/13683500. 2018.1462310

Sorrentino, A., Fu, X., Romano, R., Quintano, M., & Risitano, M. (2020). Measuring event experience and its behavioral consequences in the context of a sports mega-event. *Journal of Hospitality and Tourism Insights, 3*(5), 589–605. doi:10.1108/JHTI-03-2020-0026

Storm, R. K., & Jakobsen, T. G. (2020). National pride, sporting success and event hosting: An analysis of intangible effects related to major athletic tournaments. *International Journal of Sport Policy and Politics, 12*(1), 163–178. doi:10.1080/19406940.2019.1646303

Thornton, P. R., Shaw, G., & Williams, A. M. (1997). Tourist group holiday decision-making and behaviour: The influence of children. *Tourism Management, 18*(5), 287–298. doi:10.1177/0047287598036004137

Veal, A. J., Toohey, K., & Frawley, S. (2012). The sport participation legacy of the Sydney 2000 Olympic Games and other international sporting events hosted in Australia. *Journal of Policy Research in Tourism, Leisure and Events, 4*(2), 155–184. doi:10.1080/19407963.2012.662619

Weed, M. (2010). The potential of the demonstration effect from Olympic Games and major sport events to grow and sustain participation in sport. Paper presented at *North American Society of Sport Management Conference*, Florida, US.

Whang, S.-H. (2006). Korea and Japan 2002: Public space and popular celebration. In A. Tomlinson & C. Young (Eds.), *National identity and global sports events* (pp. 215–231). Albany, NY: State University of New York Press.

Wu, H.-C., & Ai, C.-H. (2016). Synthesizing the effects of experiential quality, excitement, equity, experiential satisfaction on experiential loyalty for the golf industry: The case of Hainan Island. *Journal of Hospitality and Tourism Management, 29,* 41–59. doi:10.1016/j.jhtm.2016.05.005

Wu, H.-C., & Cheng, C.-C. (2018). What drives spectators' experiential loyalty? A case study of the Olympic Football Tournament Rio 2016. *Asia Pacific Journal of Marketing & Logistics, 30*(4), 837–866. doi:10.1108/APJML-08-2017-0174

Zhou, Y., & Ap, J. (2009). Residents' perceptions towards the impacts of the Beijing 2008 Olympic Games. *Journal of Travel Research, 48*(1), 78–91. doi:10.1177/0047287508328792

Chapter 6

The Agency of Children and Young People in Sustainability Transitions: Eco-Spiritual Events on Hare Krishna Eco-Farms in Europe

Tamas Lestar and Giuseppe Pellegrini-Masini

Abstract

The role of children and young people is not outlined in the sustainability transitions literature. The aim of this work is to illustrate the significance of young people's agency by showcasing Hare Krishna eco-farms organising cultural/eco-spiritual events. This work forms part of a wider sustainability study focussing on food in spiritual communities in Europe. Data were collected through observation and interviews on three Hare Krishna farms. The agency of children and youths and the significance of their presence at eco-events emerged as an unexpected theme. Findings show that Hare Krishna events in Europe are visited by a relatively high number of children and young people who learn about more sustainable practices through extracurricular activities. By describing the cognitive and experiential encounters, the authors draw attention to the significance of children's involvement in ecologically geared events in the context of sustainability transitions.

Keywords: Sustainability; eco-spiritual events; agency; children; Hare Krishna; religion

Introduction

Getz and Page (2016) position festivals and cultural programmes as one of the four main types of events in event tourism, often taking place in (religious) communities. Hare Krishna eco-farms in Europe offer a clear example of this category as they hold a wide range of cultural and eco-spiritual events to

Events Management for the Infant and Youth Market, 85–99
Copyright © 2023 Tamas Lestar and Giuseppe Pellegrini-Masini
Published under exclusive licence by Emerald Publishing Limited
doi:10.1108/978-1-80455-690-020231012

community members and outsiders alike. The role of eco-spiritual communities is highlighted in the broad sustainability literature, suggesting that they are more successful in maintaining more sustainable practices than their secular counterparts (Lestar, 2020). More specifically for our purposes, the sustainability transitions literature has recently highlighted the agency of spirituality and religion in and for system-wide change (Köhrsen, 2018; Lestar & Böhm, 2020).

In contrast, the agency of children provides a theme which has largely been missed in several areas of social scientific enquiries. The lack of investigations and conceptualisations concerning children was foregrounded only recently in tourism research, for example (Seraphin, Yallop, Seyfi, & Hall, 2022). In sustainability transitions, on the other hand, the focus of which often remains on technological innovations and regime-wide interventions, the agency of children has not been incorporated into the theoretical framework.

In short, sustainability transition frameworks are interested in system-wide change through the dislocation of the current socio-technical regime(s) and systems of provision (e.g. energy) (Geels & Schot, 2010). Emphasised in their vocabulary, one often finds words like innovation, technology, transport, food systems, systems of provision, business and policymaking, to name a few. While the importance of regime-level (mezzo) change is stressed, the micro players on the community level (termed as niches), and interconnections between all levels and players, are also recognised. This is evident, for example, in research investigating the energy transition, where the importance of community energy schemes is highlighted (Pellegrini-Masini, 2020; Pellegrini-Masini, Pirni, Maran, & Klöckner, 2020). These niches are perceived as experimental spaces where more sustainable practices can be 'tested' before their wider dissemination (Geels, 2004, 2005; Geels & Schot, 2010). Due to the wide range of exemplary practices in the community, the Hare Krishna movement offers a unique case for analysis in the context of sustainability transitions. A traditional transitions analysis would consider specific frameworks of the niche and its transitional role for systemic change (e.g. Pellegrini-Masini et al., 2021). However, the purpose of this current chapter is primarily to highlight some areas concerning children and pro-environmental events. This could later be developed further into a conceptualisation of children's agency for sustainability transitions.

In what follows, we first provide a contextual section about two Hare Krishna eco-farms and their eco-spiritual events experienced by children. In particular, we will focus on school trips and the attendance of an annual fair that take place in two different Hare Krishna communities. While fairs are classified as event tourism opportunities (Getz & Page, 2016), school trips (or field trip) have a deliberate educational purpose that goes beyond the aim of entertaining and providing pleasurable experiences to participants, 'in which students interact with the setting, displays, and exhibits to gain an experiential connection to the ideas, concepts, and subject matter' (Behrendt & Franklin, 2014, p. 236).

The description of the cases is followed by a discussion in which key elements are presented in the context of sustainability transitions. Finally, a brief summary highlights the key insights while a call is made to consider and conceptualise children's agency for sustainability transitions.

Hare Krishna Eco-Tourism

The Hare Krishna community was the target of social and academic criticism in and around the 1980s (Rochford, 2007, pp. 115–138). Critics questioned the organisation's recruitment process and turned their works to theories of brain-washing, pathologising or new religious movements. The organisation's commitment to Indian cultures (cuisine, clothes, dress, music etc.) and perceived gender inequality have also prompted critical investigation (Rochford, 2007). Today, the community engages in philosophical debates and runs research institutions (such as the Oxford Centre for Hindu Studies) and publishes interfaith statements to promote dialogue. With an increasing focus on charitable and eco-farm projects, the movement appears to have overcome the crises posed by internal and external conflicts and criticism. This chapter approaches International Society for Krishna Consciousness (ISKCON) as a social innovation rather than a religious movement. The controversial issues mentioned above are beyond the scope of this article.

The following account forms part of a wider research looking into Hare Krishna practices with a focus on food and diet. The broad research was conducted in three European farm communities where the researcher spent altogether 10 weeks participating in daily activities and events while observing and interviewing believers and farm visitors. Findings were reported in several papers focussing on specific aspects of Hare Krishna ecology and spirituality (Lestar, 2017, 2018, 2020). The theme of children's agency emerged during the later stages of data collection. To repeat, this current account primarily focusses on children's involvement in ecological events. Several other aspects of the farms' achievements, however significant, are not considered here.

Bhaktivedenta Manor, Watford (London)

The Manor, as it is frequently called, was established near the town of Watford (16 miles northwest of London) in 1973. The property was donated to the ISKCON by George Harrison of the Beatles. Since its establishment, the Manor has become the UK centre of the ISKCON movement, listing some 250,000 visits a year.

Currently, there are about 50 employees, some 300 regular volunteers and about 1,800 Sunday congregation attendees. Two major ecological achievements in the community are the total eradication of fuel-based technology from food production (machinery or fertilisers) and an extensive daily food distribution programme that has been running for several decades. Environmental sustainability occupies a central place in the teachings and practices of the farm. The establishment attracts hundreds of visitors, tourists and friends weekly from London and across the country. Sundays are special occasions when followers of Krishna and other Hindu faiths meet to share in devotional and recreational activities. On these days, religious services may be attended, and time spent with family and community gatherings in the nearby fields that also offer dining facilities and a playground.

To help visitors, neat signposts give directions and information about expected behaviour regarding dress code, smoking and meat consumption. Next to the arrival area there is a contemplative garden dedicated to the theme of spirituality and vegetarianism. At the entrance, a poster advocates meat-free Mondays with Paul McCartney, a dedicated supporter of the community's food projects. Rock bands, soloists and actors are portrayed as either vegetarians or sympathisers in promoting equality in the world. On a separate poster, famous people such as Tolstoy, Einstein and Leonardo da Vinci are portrayed, together with their photographs, in support of the vegetarian ethos. Children can also take a lesson home by studying pictures displayed on the garden wall to explain non-violent practices on their level.

The spacious parks, ornamental gardens, ponds, footpaths and educational trails provide an elevating atmosphere for community members and visitors alike.

Children and the Bhaktivedenta Manor

Eco-tourism, which is under the educational department, is the main attraction for outsiders. Coaches carrying school children, elderly and disabled people visit the farm to learn about Krishna spirituality connected with sustainable farming and lifestyle practices, and to taste the special vegetarian food. Most visitors are secondary school students who visit as in compliance with the national curriculum for religious studies. In 2019, the farm was visited by 8,000 school children, accompanied by about 400 adults: teachers, helpers and parents. About 90% of school visits were made by primary children, 10% were sixth-form students. In addition to the primary and secondary school students, there are university students, researchers, disabled groups and diverse groups of adult and elderly people who also visit the farm for its ecological and spiritual attractions.

Apart from the school trips, an estimated 20,000–30,000 pupils visit the centre every year.

A close spiritual connection to land and nature, including animals, is demonstrated by visiting the stops on the eco-tour. An entire bundle of practices is thus introduced from the growing of plants and specific herbs through ploughing and milking to food preparation and sharing Krishna prasadam: food offered to the deities before consumption. Ox-cart tours are offered two–four days a week to demonstrate the various aspects of eco-farming such as ploughing, rearing, milking, milling and organic gardening.

Children can also find messages of compassion specifically addressed to them in pictures displayed on the garden wall. While the nature of these encounters is ephemeral as school trips only last for a few hours, it is likely that these rare experiences will remain with the children and youths for the rest of their lives (DeWitt & Storksdieck, 2008).

After visiting the centre, schoolteachers and students express their gratitude and appreciation on the community's website, where they can also post questions. At times children post their drawings to illustrate what they learnt. Below are some reflective comments made by a teacher:

- It was a wonderful day, the children learnt so much about diversity and religious education, so much more than from a book!

Other teachers wrote:

- It was a pleasure to hear the children of Bhaktivedanta Manor School singing and playing music at the end. It was a powerful experience for our children who don't often experience that kind of communal joy.
- The students and staff thoroughly enjoyed this.
- The students have all been very positive and thrilled in respect of the welcome that was extended to them. Thank you so very much.
- Students really appreciated the opportunity to purchase a reminder of their visit.
- Everyone was very warm, friendly and polite. We have never had such a super school trip. We were treated like special guests. Wonderful little gifts to take home.

One of the authors observed a few student groups around the goshala (cowshed), which is the first stop of the bullock tour. They enjoyed feeding the cows, seeing them milked and listening to the guide's words about Hindu cow protection. Cow protection in the Manor has five basic requirements. (1) No cow or bull is ever slaughtered. (2) Calves suckle from their mothers. (3) Oxen are engaged in work. (4) Cows are hand-milked. (5) Cows and bulls are fed appropriate, natural food. Cows in the stable are called by their first name. They have their name, photo and description displayed as follows: 'Cintamini 27/11/2014 Breed: Dairy Shorthorn. One of her horns is much shorter than the other, and her stomach fur is an unusual red-white colour'.

The ox-cart tour has several other stops where visitors learn about ploughing, farming and organic gardening. At the end of the tour, guides in the temple offer a spiritual journey into the faith, after which visitors taste Krishna food and dress in Krishna clothing.

Krishna Valley, Hungary

Started in 1993 by a handful of devotees, the Krishna Valley has become a sizeable eco-village with 700 acres of land. The valley is a member of both international Global Ecovillage Network (GEN) and national Hungarian Network of Living Villages (MEH) eco-village networks. The valley forms part of the mediaeval village of Somogyvamos which has a population of about 600 people, 120 of whom are gypsies who are mostly unemployed, and 220 Krishna believers. Arriving on the farm the researcher was impressed by its spacious yet orderly landscape, a bicycle rental scheme, the neat parking lots, the many trees and ornamental plants, and an appealing natural setting. The spatial arrangement is most inviting and favourable for gardening, appreciating nature, outdoor exercise, eating together, cultivating friendships, reading and communal activities. It was ISKCON founder's legacy to create farming communities to cultivate 'simple living and high thinking', and to demonstrate this philosophy in practice to the outside world. As such, to 'live off the land' and 'off the cows', and in harmony with nature – on the basis of serving rather than exploitation – is of paramount value for the believer.

Regarding sustainability, selective waste collection, alternative energy (e.g. wind turbines and heating system), water management, food, land use, eco-tours, ecological reading groups and cow protection are all spatially set to stabilise pro-environmental attitudes and practices. Demand-side resource reduction is key in domestic practices, especially in the Krishna Valley where external electricity is ruled out of the space. Devotees juxtapose simplicity to materialist greed or associate it with health (e.g. simple food, cold water shower), contentment or a less carbon-intensive lifestyle. In Krishna Valley, personal boreholes and compost toilets are being introduced at the expense of the more comfortable but complicated use of centralised water supply and sewage management system. Labour, domestic or not, is purposefully made manual where machinery is avoidable. Drawing water from the well, doing the laundry or milking the cow are all done by hand.

During the 24 years of its existence, community members have planted 350,000 trees on the farm, roughly an average of 200 trees per person each year. More trees are left in place then felled, resulting in a designed regeneration of biodiversity on the land. Shifting from previous monocultural cultivations and reforestation resulted in the re-introduction of several species in the area, a project that has been highly successful. The established monoculture was completely changed into woodlands and small-scale and organic production. Biodiversity has greatly improved through polycultural methods and arrangements.

All people who were asked in the village knew about the valley and the Hare Krishna farm. In about a twenty-mile radius, the valley is signposted on the roadsides, and most people are aware of its existence (Table 1).

Children and the Krishna Valley

During the annual village fair – or rather, Valley Fair (each July) – all accommodation in the region is booked up in advance to host some 7,000 visitors. The farm's attractions include a guided tour of six stops where visitors learn about natural grey water filtering and reuse, wind and solar systems, Hare Krishna schooling, organic production, Krishna food and cow protection. Some forty-thousand people book the tour annually.

Guides are available in Hungarian and German languages. By observing and talking to visitors, the researcher found them to be thrilled about tasting prasadam (food offered to the deities before consumption) and having a ride on the ox-pulled cart. The two-hour trip may not lead to a direct life-changing experience for many, but ecological knowledge and experience may contribute to incremental changes in lifestyle practices (Gifford & Nilsson, 2014; Stern, 2000). The income raised through the eco-programme contributes towards the valley's maintenance.

Table 1. Visitors in Hungarian Krishna Valley.

Year	Individual Visitors			Other	Total
	Children	**Elderly/Retired**	**Adult**	**Groups, Festivals**	**Total**
2002	1,600	1,040	8,650	8,497	19,787
2003	2,286	3,120	8,790	15,359	29,555
2004	2,082	1,313	5,399	13,254	22,048
2005	1,612	1,038	8,657	8,616	19,923
2006	1,957	1,313	5,313	10,327	18,910
2007	1,967	1,438	5,584	13,923	22,912
2008	1,921	1,702	5,552	12,531	21,706
2009	1,813	1,757	5,471	10,889	19,930
2010	1,666	1,724	5,310	13,186	21,886
2011	1,471	1,771	5,240	9,275	17,757
2012	792	2,147	4,543	9,456	16,938
2013	777	1,757	4,273	10,701	17,508
2014	1,559	1,593	4,699	9,842	17,693
2015	1,565	1,382	4,526	10,560	18,033
2016	1,475	1,640	5,465	11,310	19,890
2017	2,163	1,997	6,205	10,703	21,068
2018	2,315	2,173	6,986	13,679	25,153
2019	2,164	2,116	8,010	11,842	24,132
2020	1,657	1,435	6,371	6,652	16,115

Source: The Authors.

Visitors to the valley arrive by cars, bicycles or coaches carrying groups of school children, company workers or holiday makers. Due to the close vicinity of the Lake Balaton, there are a considerable number of foreign visitors, especially from Germany. On passing through the main gate, visitors have the option to rent a bike or walk through the ecological trail across the farm. They can also opt for a bullock ride, a scheme resembling that of the Watford community. The trail has several stops where visitors can observe the activities described in the previous section. The work of the organisational units, such as gardens, primary school, temple, preservation cellar, is introduced by the tour guide. Alongside the path, billboards displaying photos and texts explain the ecological achievements and endeavours of the community. One of the eco-tour stops displays an air-shot photograph of what the flat monocrop-surrounding landscape looks like and how the patchwork valley is nested in it, showing an altogether different picture. There is a radical difference between the valley and the outside world.

To secure crop variety, members grow several types of cereal grains (spelt, millet, buckwheat, legumes and amaranth) and produce 10 times more than what the community consumes. As a general principle in food production, the focus is on prevention of disease rather than treatment. One of the main attractions to children, not unlike in Watford, is the goshala, the cowshed. A well-kept dirt road, on which workers walk or cycle back and forth, leads directly into the impressive and inviting building. Visitors are encouraged to cross through the large wooden gate and step into what feels like an Eastern palace rather than a cowshed. The site is memorable. As in Watford, ethical treatment of animals is emphasised. Training oxen and putting them under yoke is not against Krishna philosophy, as serving and exercise is deemed beneficial for humans and animals alike. Apart from the bullock rides, Krishna eco-farms use oxen for ploughing, grinding grains and other farm-related activities.

An accredited primary school in the Krishna Valley may also offer memorable experiences. As we pass by the building, we notice the small bicycles lining up in the front yard. Cycling and walking are the two main sources of travel here as car ownership is not allowed. Simple living appears to be a dominant project in the community.

Discussion

Studying Hare Krishna eco-farms is interesting for sustainable transitions because they offer pro-environmental alternatives to mainstream lifestyle practices. The aim of this chapter, however, is to explore children's agency for change through an understanding of their participation in eco-activities and learning offered by community events and more specifically 'sustainability focussed events', defined as 'community events...encouraging pro-environmental behaviour of attendees' (Mair & Laing, 2013, p. 1114). While sustainability transitions frameworks offer specific tools to analyse, among others, the effectiveness and feasibility of more sustainable niches from the aspect of its community members and in its entirety, this time the authors are interested in how children as visitors relate to potential change. What is important from this aspect is (1) what children learn/gain through these eco-events, (2) how many persons are impacted through this and (3) what event managers and policy intervention could do to bolster involvement. In what follows, we draw on concepts highlighted in the sustainability transitions literature as well as supporting literature(s) to showcase the significance of children's presence at eco-tourism events and their potential (and proposed) agency for future transitions.

Cognitive and Experiential Learning

From a transitions perspective, the existence and spread of second-order learning is a key indicator for successful niche management because this type of learning fosters potentials to maintain practices which are – in the initial phase of transitions – less conventional and more sustainable (Pellicer-Sifres, Belda-Miquel,

Cuesta-Fernandez, & Boni, 2018). Second-order learning, also second-order change, double-loop learning etc. is conceptualised by Sterling (2011) who used it in pedagogic literature to address theoretical and pragmatic issues in sustainability education. Following Bateson (1972), Sterling (2011) builds a model of transformative learning (also transformative change, epistemic learning) by ranking and differentiating several levels of learning. According to this model, first-order learning or change

> ...refers to doing 'more of the same', that is, change within particular boundaries and without examining or changing the assumptions or values that inform what you are doing or thinking. In this sort of learning, meaning is assumed or given and relates primarily to the external objective world. [...] Second-order learning is more challenging and involves the learner (or learning organisation) critically examining, and if necessary, changing, his/her/its beliefs, values and assumptions. Therefore, this learning experience can be said to be deeper. It is more difficult and often uncomfortable for the learner because it is challenging and, because it involves reflecting critically on learning and change that takes place at the first-order level, it generates an awareness and understanding that goes beyond that level.
> (Sterling, 2011, p. 23)

Sterling then goes on to say that first-order change is often characterised by *doing things better* (efficiency) while second-order change is *doing better things* (efficiency in what areas?). Several scholars (e.g. Thomas, 2009) use the term transformative learning which equates with second-order learning in this model (Lestar, 2020). By application, children visiting Hare Krishna eco-farms encounter a wide range of practices that can be linked to second-order learning. According to the reference quoted above, a wide range of practices represented at Krishna eco-events can be perceived as transformative or 'deeper'. Taking vegetarianism as an example, children learn about this dietary option through cognitive (examples of famous vegetarians) as well as experiential lessons (tasting the food). In addition, gardening, farming, waste management, alternative energy and even dairy production in the community offer sustainable alternatives to the baseline practices of the outside world. The tours are arranged to educate children about the whole cycle of food production from ploughing without the use of fossil fuels through the use of conservation techniques to cooking, eating and sharing.

Another key point to consider in education is the importance of novel experiences (Ballarini, Martínez, Díaz Perez, Moncada, & Viola, 2013) and learning outside the classroom (Dillon et al., 2016). We believe that vacation and being outside (evident characteristics of school trips) are among the most memorable experiences adults reminisce from early childhood, and previous research appear to confirm that childhood outdoor experience is a predictor of environmental concern (Gifford & Nilsson, 2014). Further, Ernst and Burcak (2019) establish correlations between nature play, creative thinking and resilience. While Chawla (1992, p. 76) argues that memories are more intense when children have freedom to 'explore and manipulate' the environment.

By implication, Krishna communities show that the activities and events children participate in are based on involvement and enjoyment, aspects that may support future retrieval and pro-environmental behaviour, as research on pro-environmental behaviours has shown (Lindenberg & Steg, 2007). Not only are these activities novel in that they are arranged outside the classroom and in a natural environment, but they offer practical alternatives unique to mainstream societal practices.

Social Network(ing)

Another key indicator for the scalability of niche practices is the extent and type of social network maintained by practitioners. For sustainability transitions, close social ties with key role players such as business owners and government representatives prove useful (Fischer & Newig, 2016). Besides liaising with these key players, the number of persons impacted by a pro-environmental community and its organised events is also crucial, as Mair and Laing (103, p. 1117) put it '. . .a sustainable event can provide a platform to raise awareness about environmental issues and provide information on which individual behaviour changes can be made, which is a form of consciousness raising'. Apart from becoming the innovators and policymakers of the next generation, we, among other scholars (Walker, 2017), believe that children's future behaviour plays a crucial role in enabling or disabling sustainability transitions.

As presented in the previous sections, the visited eco-farms host a substantial number of school children (8,000 in 2019 in the Watford centre alone) who arrive as family members or school trip participants. A unique scheme in the United Kingdom invites primary and secondary students to visit the farms as part of the curriculum. Interestingly, the original rationale does not target pro-environmental activities but focusses on religious and cultural visits. Yet, religiosity is combined with an exemplary lifestyle manifested in more sustainable behaviours and practices supported by religious beliefs (Narayanan, 2001). Something that has been recently discussed by scholars (Ives & Kidwell, 2019; Johnston, 2014).

Crucially, following their visit, children may disseminate their learning by sharing their experience with their peers, in the classroom, and in the family circle, as in other sustainability education contexts, even young children appear doing (Stuhmcke, 2012). Barbieri, Stevenson, and Knollenberg (2019) point out the potential gains induced by intergenerational knowledge transfer. Applying this to Krishna eco-tourism, what is acquired through school trips and experiential encounters may, after sharing with parents, result in higher agricultural literacy for children and adults alike. After participating in the pro-environmental events, parents or schoolteachers may remind children of their learning experience, which helps to bolster more sustainable behaviours (Leichtman et al., 2017).

Bolstering Children's Participation in Pro-Environmental Events

Against the backdrop presented in the previous two sections, it appears to be beneficial to provide opportunities to an increasing number of children and youths to take part in events designed for ecological learning. Children appear suitable to benefit of environmental education through eco-tourism, as Seraphin et al. (2022) point out, children can be socially empowered through responsible tourism whose practice might contribute to the development of children's consciousness of sustainability and stimulate their pro-environmental actions. This appears confirmed by research on education for sustainable development (ESD), which (Percy-Smith & Burns, 2013; Walker, 2017) shows that children involved in educational programmes focussing on sustainable lifestyle could empower themselves to become active carriers of messages of change within their same families and communities.

In this context, the eco-tourism scheme developed in the Hare Krishna community might be a valuable contribution to ESD which promotes children's sustainable education and ultimately 'intergenerational co-learning' (Percy-Smith & Burns, 2013, p. 332) in children's families and communities. Therefore, sustainability transitions management could work on replicating similar practices in other sustainable communities as well as strengthening ties with the Hare Krishna farms themselves. Education policymaking and the public agencies could be informed, which in turn could potentially lead to an extension of the national curricula to include school trips to ecologically designed events.

Drawing on supporting literature and findings presented in Section 'Hare Krishna Eco-Tourism', practitioners could be made aware of the following extras to further improve the learning experience of children at pro-environmental events.

(1) Provide souvenirs to remind children of their participation in eco-events. (Menzel Baker, Schultz Kleine, & Bowen, 2006)
(2) Provide textual and visual aids to parents and teachers. (DeWitt & Storksdieck, 2008)
(3) Encourage adults to capture children's experiences and activities on camera. (Kisiel, 2006)
(4) Dedicate social media sites to children in eco-tourism. (For the importance of collective memory formation through social media, see: Groes, 2016)

Conclusion

In recent years the role of children in the general sustainability discourse has been increasingly highlighted (Walker, 2017), but it has not been conceptualised in the sustainability transitions literature. Apart from being the future innovators, the role of children's future behaviour in enabling or disabling sustainability transitions is crucial. Some research (Percy-Smith & Burns, 2013; Walker, 2017) is pointing at the potential of children to play a significant role in their immediate family and social circles, nevertheless the extent that this contribution might influence the ecological transition is unclear, even though it is sensible to hypothesise that the contribution is significant, given their possibility as agents to effect the present and future development of their communities unequivocally longer than adults. Given that transitions appear to occur, thanks to bi-directional, i.e. top-down and bottom-up actions, and that the importance of niches of change in the latter dynamics (bottom-up) has been highlighted (Geels & Schot, 2010), it is worth stressing that at this micro level, actions targeting young generations not only have a place but appear to have the potential to bear the greatest effects. Hence, eco-events could contribute, among other bottom-up initiatives,[1] to support the ecological transition as an impactful element of current ESD of young citizens.

By turning to eco-spiritual events organised in Hare Krishna communities, the authors presented the nature of the experiences children and youths gain by partaking in these events. Children receive cognitive and experiential lessons about more sustainable practices that radically differ from ordinary practices. The extracurricular activities and learning offered by the eco-spiritual events are particularly conducive to confirming and instigating pro-environmental behaviour because they take place in nature and away from the children's everyday environment. The type of learning (second order) taking place and the number of children reached at these events (and other persons through them) suggest that the alternative set of practices disseminated by the community provides an interesting case for the study of children's agency for sustainability transitions.

Apart from studying niches in relation to children visiting sustainability events, the public sector could further enhance their effectiveness by implementing changes in the curricula or providing incentives and support for these school trips or family visits. Through strengthening the organisational ties between the various stakeholders (transitions scholars, public sector and practitioners), eco-event organisers could be made aware of the significance of children and young people visitors at their events, and exchange insights on how to further improve their learning experience. These activities could well be included within the range of educational practices that form an effective educational agenda for sustainable development educators. It has to be pointed out that ESD is recognised as a key element of Sustainable Development Goal 4 (SDG 4) towards the transition to sustainability by the United Nations (UN General Assembly, 2015).

This chapter presented Hare Krishna eco-events in the context of children's involvement and sustainability transitions. Besides doing this, the aim of the authors was to invite transitions scholars to conceptualise children's agency in the theory and practice of sustainability transitions.

Note

1. Currently researched for the potential to accelerate the ecological transition in Europe, see e.g. the H2020 project ACCTING (https://accting.eu/).

References

Ballarini, F., Martínez, M. C., Díaz Perez, M., Moncada, D., & Viola, H. (2013). Memory in elementary school children is improved by an unrelated novel experience. *PloS one*, *8*(6), e66875.

Barbieri, C., Stevenson, K. T., & Knollenberg, W. (2019). Broadening the utilitarian epistemology of agritourism research through children and families. *Current Issues in Tourism*, *22*(19), 2333–2336.

Bateson, G. (1972). *Steps to an ecology of mind*. San Francisco: Chandler.

Behrendt, M., & Franklin, T. (2014). A review of research on school field trips and their value in education. *International Journal of Environmental & Science Education*, *9*(3), 235–245. doi:10.12973/ijese.2014.213a

DeWitt, J., & Storksdieck, M. (2008). A short review of school field trips: Key findings from the past and implications for the future. *Visitor Studies*, *11*(2), 181–197. doi: 10.1080/10645570802355562

Dillon, J., Rickinson, M., Teamey, K., Morris, M., Choi, M. Y., Sanders, D., & Benefield, P. (2016). The value of outdoor learning: Evidence from research in the UK and elsewhere. In *Towards a convergence between science and environmental education* (pp. 193–200). Abingdon: Routledge.

Ernst, J., & Burcak, F. (2019). Young children's contributions to sustainability: The influence of nature play on curiosity, executive function skills, creative thinking, and resilience. *Sustainability*, [online] *11*(15), 4212. doi:10.3390/su11154212

Fischer, L. B., & Newig, J. (2016). Importance of actors and agency in sustainability transitions: A systematic exploration of the literature. *Sustainability*, *8*(5). doi:10. 3390/su8050476

Geels, F. W. (2004). From sectoral systems of innovation to socio-technical systems: Insights about dynamics and change from sociology and institutional theory. *Research Policy*, *33*, 897–920.

Geels, F. W. (2005). Processes and patterns in transitions and system innovations: Refining the coevolutionary multi-level perspective. *Technological Forecasting and Social Change*, *72*, 681–696.

Geels, F. W., & Schot, J. (2010). The dynamics of transitions: A socio-technical perspective. In J. Grin, J. Rotmans, & J. Schot (Eds.), *Transitions to sustainable development*. New York, NY; London: Routledge.

Getz, D., & Page, S. J. (2016). Progress and prospects for event tourism research. *Tourism Management*, *52*(C), 593–631.

Gifford, R., & Nilsson, A. (2014). Personal and social factors that influence pro-environmental concern and behaviour: A review. *International Journal of Psychology*, *49*(3), 141–157. doi:10.1002/ijop.12034

Groes, S. (Ed.). (2016). *Memory in the twenty-first century: New critical perspectives from the arts, humanities, and sciences*. London: Palgrave Macmillan.

Ives, C. D., & Kidwell, J. (2019). Religion and social values for sustainability. *Sustainability Science*, *14*(5), 1355–1362.

Johnston, L. F. (2014). *Religion and sustainability: Social movements and the politics of the environment*. Abingdon: Routledge.

Kisiel, J. (2006). An examination of fieldtrip strategies and their implementation within a natural history museum. *Science Education*, *90*, 434–452.

Köhrsen, J. (2018). Religious agency in sustainability transitions: Between experimentation, upscaling, and regime support. *Environmental Innovation and Societal Transitions, 27*, 4–15.

Leichtman, M. D., Camilleri, K. A., Pillemer, D. B., Amato-Wierda, C. C., Hogan, J. E., & Dongo, M. D. (2017). Talking after school: Parents' conversational styles and children's memory for a science lesson. *Journal of Experimental Child Psychology, 156*, 1–15.

Lestar, T. (2017). Spiritual conversion and dietary change: Empirical investigations in two eco-spiritual communities. *Food Studies: An Interdisciplinary Journal, 7*(3), 23–34. doi:10.18848/2160-1933/CGP/v07i03/23-34

Lestar, T. (2018). Conviviality?: Eating together with Hare Krishna believers. *Food Studies: An Interdisciplinary Journal, 8*(3), 15–26. doi:10.18848/2160-1933/CGP/v08i03/15-26

Lestar, T. (2020, July 4). Religions going nuts? Faith-based veganism and transformative learning in the context of sustainability transitions (case 1: The Hare Krishna movement). *Journal of Organizational Change Management, 33*(5), 805–819.

Lestar, T., & Böhm, S. (2020). Ecospirituality and sustainability transitions: Agency towards degrowth. *Religion, State and Society, 48*(1), 56–73. doi:10.1080/09637494.2019.1702410

Lindenberg, S., & Steg, L. (2007). Normative, gain and hedonic goal frames guiding environmental behavior. *63*(1), 117–137. doi:10.1111/j.1540-4560.2007.00499.x

Mair, J., & Laing, J. H. (2013). Encouraging pro-environmental behaviour: The role of sustainability-focused events. *Journal of Sustainable Tourism, 21*(8), 1113–1128. doi:10.1080/09669582.2012.756494

Menzel Baker, S., Schultz Kleine, S., & Bowen, H. E. (2006). On the symbolic meanings of souvenirs for children. In R. W. Belk (Ed.), *Research in consumer behavior* (Vol. 10, pp. 209–248). Bingley: Emerald Publishing Limited. doi:10.1016/S0885-2111(06)10009-5

Narayanan, V. (2001). Water, wood, and wisdom: Ecological perspectives from the Hindu traditions. *Daedalus, 130*(4), 179–206.

Pellegrini-Masini, G. (2020). *Wind power and public engagement: Co-operatives and community ownership.* Abingdon: Routledge.

Pellegrini-Masini, G., Albulescu, P., Jager, W., Löfström, E., Macsinga, I., Alonso-Betanzos, A., … Sánchez-Maroño, N. (2021). *D6.2 report on the updated theoretical framework for social innovation diffusion.* Retrieved from https://local-social-innovation.eu/fileadmin/user_upload/Deliverables/SMARTEES-D6.2_theoretical_development_R1.pdf. Accessed on October 24, 2022.

Pellegrini-Masini, G., Pirni, A., Maran, S., & Klöckner, C. A. (2020). Delivering a timely and just energy transition: Which policy research priorities? *Environmental Policy and Governance, 30*(6), 293–305.

Pellicer-Sifres, V., Belda-Miquel, S., Cuesta-Fernandez, I., & Boni, A. (2018). Learning, transformative action, and grassroots innovation: Insights from the Spanish energy cooperative Som Energia. *Energy Research & Social Science, 42*, 100–111. doi:10.1016/J.ERSS.2018.03.001

Percy-Smith, B., & Burns, D. (2013). Exploring the role of children and young people as agents of change in sustainable community development. *Local Environment, 18*(3), 323–339. doi:10.1080/13549839.2012.72956

Rochford, E. B. (2007). *Hare Krishna transformed.* New York: New York University Press.

Seraphin, H., Yallop, A. C., Seyfi, S., & Hall, C. M. (2022). Responsible tourism: The 'why' and 'how' of empowering children. *Tourism Recreation Research, 47*(1), 62–77. doi:10.1080/02508281.2020.1819109

Sterling, S. (2011). Transformative learning and sustainability: Sketching the conceptual ground. *Learning and Teaching in Higher Education, 5*(11), 17–33.

Stern, P. C. (2000). Toward a coherent theory of environmentally significant behavior. *Journal of Social Issues, 56*(3), 407–424. doi:10.1111/0022-4537.00175

Stuhmcke, S. M. (2012). *Children as change agents for sustainability: An action research case study in a kindergarten.* Doctoral dissertation, Queensland University of Technology.

Thomas, I. (2009). Critical thinking, transformative learning, sustainable education, and problem-based learning in universities. *Journal of Transformative Education, 7*(3), 245–264. doi:10.1177/1541344610385753

UN General Assembly. (2015). *Transforming our world: The 2030 agenda for sustainable development.* New York: United Nations.

Walker, C. (2017). Tomorrow's leaders and today's agents of change? Children, sustainability education and environmental governance. *Children & Society, 31*(1), 72–83.

Chapter 7

Turning Winchester (UK) Into an Eventful Children City: Investigating the Creation of a Webtoon Festival

Charlie Mansfield and Hugues Seraphin

Abstract

The issues surrounding the scholarship on children-inclusive events man-agement are explored in depth to provide a context for this chapter. Focus then turns to the city of Winchester in the United Kingdom as a case study for potential events aimed at this age group. Through a synthesis of the findings from a thorough new research study along with emerging theories in narrative and storytelling as experience co-creation, a proposed design for a new event is put forward. It is hoped that this approach in the academic literature will encourage other researchers to include innovative proposals in their synthesis and conclusions. Finally, additional considerations of inte-grating city branding with a wider regional branding are explored through ethnobotany. Lessons are drawn from an example of brand management based on a city event for children in Scotland.

Keywords: Festival; Winchester; children; webtoon; destination; eventful city

Introduction

Events are playing an increasingly significant role in the life of individuals, alongside contributing to community cohesion (Andrews & Leopold, 2013; Fox, Gouthro, Morakabati, & Brackstone, 2014; Mallen & Adams, 2013; Yeoman, Robertson, Ali-Knight, Drummond, & McMahon-Beattie, 2012). The impor-tance of events for individuals and communities is evidenced by the fact that a significant number of events, particularly festivals and cultural events, are long existing ones, with their roots in either pre-modern or modern society (Fox et al., 2014). Beyond the social role that events play (Andrews & Leopold, 2013), they

Events Management for the Infant and Youth Market, 101–118
Copyright © 2023 Charlie Mansfield and Hugues Seraphin
Published under exclusive licence by Emerald Publishing Limited
doi:10.1108/978-1-80455-690-020231014

also bring considerable economic impact for communities, stakeholders and individuals (Yeoman et al., 2012).

Despite the wealth of literature on events (Getz & Page, 2020), practically no publication has focussed on the role and importance of children for the industry. This situation in events management literature could well be worse than the situation in academic literature in the wider field of tourism. Indeed, in tourism literature, all academics agree there is a paucity of research on the importance of children (Canosa & Graham, 2016; Cullingford, 1995; Hertzman, Anderson, & Rowley, 2008; Poria & Timothy, 2014; Séraphin & Vo-Than, 2020; Wall, 2019). However, these authors do not detect a total absence of research, which is the case in events management studies.

The purpose of this chapter is to address this gap in the academic literature, by investigating how important events are for children amongst other types of events organised in the specific location of Winchester, UK. This qualitative empirical study addresses the following research questions:

(1)   What types of events are organised in Winchester?
(2)   What types of events are organised specifically for children?
(3)   How important are events for children with regard to other types of events?

To address the above research questions, this empirical study is going to analyse the type of events organised by *WinchesterBid* and *Winchester City Council* over the period 2016–2020.

This chapter is of importance because (1) it provides a methodological approach to assess the importance of children events within a local community, (2) it addresses a major gap in the literature and (3) from a practical point of view, it could highlight to organisers of events in Winchester gaps that need to be addressed. However, considering the fact this chapter is based on a specific community, the results cannot be generalised.

Finally, this study (similar to the Lego, 2022 Report) defines children as any individual under the age of 18.

Literature Review

As it has already been established in the introduction, children as stakeholders of the event industry and related industries are poorly researched from an academic point of view. Indeed, when it comes to research methods to collect data from them, information is very limited and mainly focusses on the difficulties and hurdles (permission from parents; approach to collect the data; their level of understanding) in eliciting information from them (Brunt, Horner, & Semley, 2017). To avoid these difficulties, parents are often surveyed instead of the children (Fox et al., 2014; Poria & Timothy, 2014). However, there are a growing number of academics who have indeed developed research techniques specific to children and have surveyed them directly about their holiday experience, by asking them to draw and through interviews and questionnaires (Hixson, 2014;

Poria & Timothy, 2014; Radic, 2017). These academics are part of a growing number of researchers in tourism and related topics such as events, who believe that appropriate contexts should be put in place to enable meaningful participation of children in matters that could directly impact on them (Séraphin, 2021).

For many businesses, children are key customers; as a result, they put children at the centre of their strategies, particularly when it comes to digital marketing campaigns (Lego, 2022). More importantly, businesses endeavour to engage children for four principle reasons which include: (1) the fact that participation by children is a right which organisations strive to accommodate (2) developing strong links with the children market in order to create a sense of community and belonging between the children and the organisation (3) to ensure the products and services delivered actually meet the needs of the children market and (4) developing the creativity of employees (Lego, 2022). This collaboration also benefits children because when engaging children, it contributes to their empowerment, as they self-present themselves through the products and services delivered to them. This empowerment also happens through development of skills such as creativity, alongside the development of their social network as engaging with other children or adults.

Any approach from any business or organisation which aims at supporting the view that children engagement is as important as engagement of adults is referred as 'childism' (Wall, 2008, 2010). This concept also implies meeting or addressing the needs of children (Sundhall, 2017; Wall, 2008, 2010), as they are not passive stakeholders (James & Prout, 2003). It is also worth mentioning that 'children' is not a homogeneous group; therefore, when investigating this group, it is important to take into consideration the context (Katz, 2004).

Businesses have fully understood the importance of children, when the need to not only engage with them but also involve them in products and services development is pursued (Lego, 2022). However, academic literature on festivals and cultural events has not fully embraced children as stakeholders of local communities' events. Indeed, *Journal of Policy Research in Tourism, Leisure and Events* has a few articles published on community events, but none of them discusses it from a children perspective. *Journal of Policy Research in Tourism, Leisure and Events* only has one article related to children, but is related to sport events (Brackenridge, Rhind, & Palmer-Felgate, 2015). *International Journal of Event and Festival Management* is the same. Indeed, this journal does not have any publication specific to children. The closest one is about family events (Booth & Cameron, 2020). In *Journal of Convention & Event Tourism*, there is nothing on children.

Contextual Framework

An empirical study carried out by Séraphin, Platania, Spencer, and Modica (2018), revealed the following:

Winchester is a city in the South of the United Kingdom (Fig. 1), surrounded by some of the main tourist destinations of the country, namely London, Oxford and Cambridge.

As a city, Winchester is one of the wealthiest one in the country, with a growing and a rather healthy population in comparison with other parts of the country.

From an events point of view, Winchester is to be considered as an eventful city due to the variety of events offered which are happening all year round. Winchester is also to be considered as Special Interest Tourism Event (SITE) destination, due to the high proportion of cultural events held in the city.

These events are very popular with the locals, amongst these are the Christmas market, history, food and drink and art related events. The less popular ones are the fashion, film and literature related ones. Overall, these events are considered to contribute positively to the level of happiness and quality of life of locals.

Methodology

As suggested by Kamble (2022), the methodology section of this chapter is articulated around seven sections, namely: Methodological approach, the philosophical approach, research design, data collection methods, data analysis, research steps and trustworthiness.

Methodological approach – This study is based on a qualitative approach, which is an approach that not only enables the researcher to anchor the study within a context but also facilitates a thorough investigation of a topic. This study could also be said to have adopted a deductive approach which is about 'hypothesis testing and top-down application of theory' (Hammond & Wellington, 2013, p. 165).

Research design – Data for this study were collected through the analysis of festivals listed in the flyers 'Festivals in Winchester' over a period of five years (2016–2020). The unit of analysis for this study was mainly the type of festivals held in Winchester using the categories that are listed under in the brochure.

Data collection methods – The data from the flyers were recorded under three categories, i.e. the name of the event, the category and finally, the year the event was held.

Data analysis – The data collected from the flyers were reported into excel documents (Appendix 1 and 2), then a manual count of each type of events held in Winchester in 2020 was used to generate graphs using excel (Figs. 1 and 2). Content analysis is widely spread as a research method in the field of tourism and related topics as it is considered as very effective (Cakar, 2022).

Trustworthiness – The data used for this study are based on official documents (flyers) published by the main bodies (*WinchesterBid* and *Winchester City Council*) in charge of coordinating festivals in Winchester. These festivals are important for the local community due to their impacts on revitalisation, the

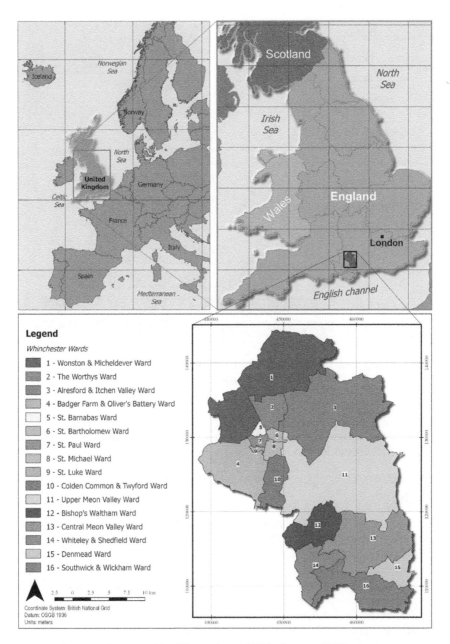

Fig. 1.   Geographical Location of Winchester (UK). *Source:* Séraphin, Platania, Spencer, & Modica (2018).

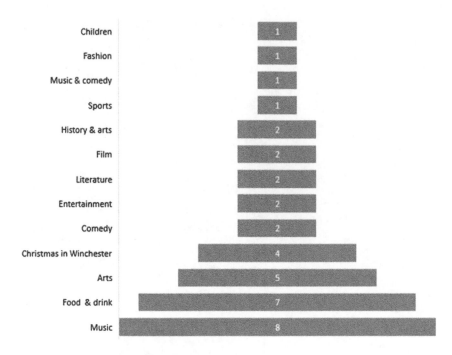

Fig. 2.   Types of Events Held in Séraphin et al. (2018). *Source:* The Author.

economy, the image of the destination and on the quality of life of locals in general (Richards & Palmer, 2010).

Results

The study (Fig. 2) reveals that most events held in Winchester fall under the category of (1) music festivals (2) food and drink festivals (3) art festivals and (4) festivals connected to Christmas. But overall, most of the events are adult-orientated. The family events such as the *Christmas market* or the *Hat Fair* (Appendix 1) are perfectly suitable for children, even designed specifically for them. There is only one event targeting them specifically, namely 'Children of Winchester Festival' (Appendix 1). The other event designed specifically for children 'Eastern Bunny Hop' only took place in 2017 (Appendix 2).

There is a good spread of events in Winchester throughout the year, knowing that most of them happen towards the end of the year between October and December (Fig. 3).

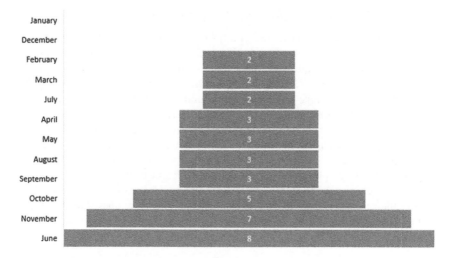

Fig. 3. When Events are Held in Séraphin et al. (2018). *Source:* The Author.

Discussion

The case study based on Winchester provides evidence that events dedicated exclusively to children are marginal. The objective of this study from this point onward is to provide a realistic and feasible strategy to the bodies in charge of events in Winchester on how to develop an eventful children city. To do so, a variety of frameworks are going to be used. First, a children consultation framework based on the Lego (2022) framework. Second, developing a suitable product or service (the *KidZania* framework). Third and final framework is based on storytelling, travel writing and destination branding.

Before developing an eventful children city strategy for Winchester, it is worth mentioning the fact that a previous study by Séraphin and Green (2019) which consulted children on their perception of what Winchester of the future should be like revealed that children have first and foremost a metaphorical perception of what the destination should be in the future, as opposed to an objective perception, meaning that their ideas are to be taken cautiously. Additionally, a study from Séraphin (2021) revealed that during COVID-19, Winchester engaged children in a trail across the city (creative and empowering fun activities) to educate them about COVID-19 (what it is, the impacts and how to keep safe). As a city, Winchester is not reluctant to engage with children (Séraphin, 2021). As for children and their parents, they are keen to be involved in consultation-related activities (Séraphin & Green, 2019).

Winchester as an Eventful City: Step 1 (Consultation)

Children consultation is considered as a form of engagement and empowerment, which implies: (1) providing them with a safe and suitable environment where they can be told about the issue under investigation (2) providing them with a suitable platform where they can share their view (3) conveying their message to the people who can make changes happen and (4) finally, feasible ideas from children should be implemented when possible (Lego, 2022). By consulting children, organisations are therefore complying (amongst other things) with some of the *Design for Children Rights* principles (2018), which includes Principle 1 ('Right to non-discrimination'); Principle 3 ('Right to participate'); Principle 4 ('Right to be protected'); Principle 10 ('Right to be heard' 'Right to participate').

Events such as the 'Easter Bunny Hop' or the 'Hat Fair' could be used to survey children using a variety of tools (interviews, drawing, questionnaire, focus groups, observations during games and activities) depending on their age.

Winchester as an Eventful City: Step 2 (Providing a Suitable Product or Service)

Developed products or services must cover some or all of the types of fun identified by Poris (2006), as playing is an important part of the development of children (Lego, 2022; Poris, 2006):

Friend-orientated fun (Interaction with others)
Empowering fun (Learning and achieving through fun activities)
Creative fun (Arts and music-related activities)
Silly fun (playful fun)
Sports-orientated fun (Physical activities)
Competitive fun (fun activity with something to win at the end for the best performer)
Family-orientated fun (displaying bonding within a family through games)
Surprising or adventurous fun (New experiences)
Relaxing fun (Relaxing activities)
Rebellious fun (Breaking rules)

The *KidZania* concept, also referred as the city of children, is basically the reproduction of a city, at a smaller scale within an indoor venue, with the overall objective to give children opportunities to have an experience which is close to that which would occur in the real life, while also offering real businesses (Shell, British Airways and H&M, among others) that have shops in high streets or online, an opportunity to promote their products and services to children and their families (Di Pietro et al., 2018; Tagg & Wang, 2016). The *KidZania* concept, built on the edutainment (education and entertainment) and advertainment (advertisement and entertainment) principles (Di Pietro et al., 2018; Tagg & Wang, 2016), is therefore to be related with all the types of fun developed by the Poris (2006) framework, making it a suitable concept for the empowerment of children.

As a city, Winchester could dedicate a day when the city would turn into a city for children, which means that on that day, all the partnered businesses would enable children not only to see the backstage of their activities but also get them involved whenever possible as a member of staff, and as customers (instead of or alongside their parents).

Winchester as an Eventful City: Step 3 (Storytelling, Travel Writing and Branding Around Children)

Destination branding is an important part of the role of Destination Marketing Organisations (DMOs) who are keen to stand out by constantly renewing their branding approach. This study, alongside existing research such as research in the field of travel writing and city branding (Mansfield & Potočnik Topler, 2023), presents storytelling and, more broadly speaking, travel writing as playing a significant role in the experience of visitors as closely related to the concept of affect (Mansfield & Potočnik Topler, 2023). This study is the first one to investigate how travel writing developed around events for children could contribute to the branding of a destination and the potential impacts on event tourism.

Save the Day, Place-Branding From Literary Travel Writing

Since 2000 the city of Clermont Ferrand has established a very specialised annual festival with young people in mind. Clermont is a French city in the volcano park of the old Auvergne region. Clermont's festival is based around making and sharing travel journals. In France, the travel journal in French, the *carnet de voyage*, is not just a written record of the day but includes stopping to sketch images of the city being explored and also, collecting printed mementos to keep in the travel journal. With a population of 147,000, Clermont is larger than Winchester with just 116,000, but the theme of journaling provides a useful model for the design of a new festival for children and teenagers in Winchester. The travel journal lends itself to mobility and identity growth for the individual festival participant, while for the host city it provides opportunities for attendees to explore in-depth particular points of architecture and urban space. This combination of participatory experience creates personalised place-branding. In research in the city of Cardiff in Wales, Coghlan and Filo (2013) worked with teenage boys to unlock their own routes through the city, and this work was built upon in tourism studies (Mansfield, 2018) to investigate the use of diaries or travel journals kept by participants in a case study of Concarneau, a seaside town in Brittany, France.

From the travel journals written throughout the day in Concarneau, the research findings uncovered a new concept for tourism and place-branding, 'the toureme' (Mansfield, 2018, p. 11), a way of recording experience which would transpose easily onto a day in the city of Winchester. The toureme arises during the journaling of a moment during the visit, often at a historical site or a site from a literary text when other sensory experiences are also taking place. The example from the French seaside study occurred at the historical site of the ruin of the fort at Cabellou Point; after a long walk, the participants stopped at the ruin to explore the rough granite stones with their hands when they hear live flute music being played in the trees nearby. The combination of experiences leads them to record this moment in their travel journals. After work by Ateljevic (2000), it is clear that this is cultural production taking place which will in future be associated with this spot in the urban landscape. Through the sharing of travel journals, for example, at festivals and online publishing, these toureme moments and their corresponding places can be enjoyed by a larger community.

Within the same study (Mansfield, 2018), it was found that journaling allowed deeper insight into the identities of those taking part in the walking and note-making; indeed, participants experienced positive changes in identity through well-being. A revelation towards the end of a section in one of the travel journals conveys this sense of identity growth and satisfaction:

> Actually, one thing I have realised is that I have enjoyed the last thirty minutes writing and reflecting. Perhaps I should do this more? From the field diary of Pete 2014, 32.
> (Mansfield, 2018, pp. 8–9)

In the proposed festival for Winchester, these research findings can be applied to create opportunities for young people and children to save the day for themselves in the form of travel journals. The travel journals will be in A5-format, hardback notebooks with spiral binding to allow them to lie-flat and provide a hard surface for the festival participants to write their journal of the day. Each of the children registered for the event via their guardian will be provided with their own travel journal to keep. Stopping points or plateaus on a circuit around the town (Mansfield & Potočnik Topler, 2021) can be created by the destination management team and stakeholders with commercial and social interests; these can include local colleges offering courses in drawing, illustration and sketching, stationery and arts material retailers demonstrating their products, paper and journal manufacturers offering specialist drawing and writing papers. In addition, professional creatives who make and publish *carnets de voyage* could be invited to the festival to hold workshops. As the participants make their journey around the mapped route, they will be given a branded sticker at each plateau by the stakeholder to put in their travel journal. Spaces to write will be available at each plateau and the participants will write about their experience and the place in their travel journal. This process will save the day's experiences and places for them.

Clermont Ferrand has successfully integrated their festival of carnets de voyage into their city's higher and secondary education institutions, and simultaneously into the professional and commercial life of the city. So much so, that within France, Clermont is known as a centre for the travel journal industry attracting creatives, university applicants and inward investment. Specialisation, though, is a well-developed model for French cities to build their brand from an annual festival to becoming a recognised commercial and creative centre, for example, consider Cannes, with its specialisation in the film industry.

The making and sharing of travel journals is popular, with 24,000 hashtag posts on Instagram at the time of writing (Instagram, 2022). This popularity though is hidden with the social media accessed by young people. This means that any new festival of travel journals for young people needs to incorporate cultural media used by that age group, a prime example is the vertical-scrolling webtoon format for smart phones which has gained a hold in South Korea. The webtoon industry was worth £330 million by 2020 (Jobst, 2022). In France, the home of printed comics, French TV financed a start-up called Delitoon in 2016, and at the time of writing, Delitoon has 400,000 subscribers to their webtoon releases (Croquet, 2022). In the United Kingdom, emerging channels are beginning to distribute webtoon strips, for example, the Google Play Books Store offered two webtoon comics through its eBook channel in mid-2022 for UK customers.

In summer 2022, a project was completed to create webtoon-formatted travel journals for destination development in Exeter (Mansfield, 2022). Workshops on creating this format can be part of the festival to give young attendees the digital skills to express their own designs and creativity in a format that is popular and accessible to this age group. The festival could be named Save the Day; this explains in a simple phrase what travel journaling can do. It lets children document and save the day's experiences to tell their own story for later reading. The phrase can easily become a hashtag, and it reminds parents and stakeholders to save that day in their diary. The programme contents are outlined above but to this must be added preparatory training and familiarisation with making travel journals. Because travel journals are so well established on Instagram, then this could be the preferred platform for raising awareness of the skills and enjoyment of the activity.

Shared Story Spaces to Build a Regional Brand

The role of the storyteller has been established in the United Kingdom since the early 1990s, as evidenced by the increased professionalisation of storytellers and the establishment of a society to represent and promote their activities (SFS, 2022). The Society for Storytelling, using guidelines from the National Association of Writers in Education, published a fee rate in 2022 of £250 per day for practitioners (SFS, 2022). As an exemplar in the creation of an event around storytellers, Aberdeen City Council offers a useful point of reference for cities such as Winchester, which may be considering storytelling as the basis for a new annual festival. In 1998 Aberdeen City Council launched its festival, which by its fourth year had become 'a six-week long celebration of storytelling and theatre, designed to engage Aberdeen nurseries, schools, community and family groups in the magical experience of storytelling' (McKay, 2002, p. 1). It is valuable to see that Aberdeen programmed their festival for the colder months, February and March, with the events indoors. As a model then, Winchester could use this winter season programming to provide a connection with children without clashing with summer outdoor events. Aberdeen council and arts organisations did not pursue a regional branding for its festival of storytellers, and so by the early 2020s their innovation was subsumed into the branding of Scottish National Storytelling, which shifted public focus away from Aberdeen to Scotland's capital, Edinburgh.

Winchester's Save the Day webtoon festival will need to prepare children, their guardians and teachers in both storytelling skills and in the technologies for developing their handwritten travel journals into digital media in suitable webtoon format. The impact of this type of training and further education will be to make Winchester a centre for new media creatives, in the way that Clermont in France has become a travel journaling centre. This will encourage start-ups and inward investment. The festival dates themselves will attract locals, holiday-makers and, importantly, suppliers and shoppers from the travel-to-work area to increase footfall in the town's heritage areas. For individuals, with their story-telling, journaling and webtoon creativity, they will be able to find new outlets to publish their work. One such enterprise for emerging creatives in digital story-telling is Panodyssey. Panodyssey is an EU-funded digital platform with online creative rooms to publish directly into Europe's cultural ecosystem and pay sto-rytellers directly for their work (Panodyssey, 2022).

Conclusion

To maintain recognition for its investment, then, Winchester would need a regional branding strategy for any new festival of storytellers, which created a dependence for the brand on local stories and local stakeholders (Mansfield & Potočnik Topler, 2023). Winchester has a ready-made regional identity which could be researched by storytellers and children. It was a central city in the Kingdom of Wessex, which existed from 519 to 927, and as such was the heart of the Old English language in its West Saxon dialect. This way of speaking Old English is preserved in the poem of Beowulf and we can still hear the accent spoken across the West Country of England today. The stories from this period were transmitted orally. They were written to be memorised by storytellers who could then travel from hamlet to town, storing the history without written copies (Foley, 1985). The long poem, *Memorial* (2011), by Alice Oswald, is a contem-porary example of this type of reciting from memory. The storyteller's festival for Winchester, called Save the Day, could bring this authenticity to life, with the theme of plants and foods brought from the branded region to the capital city as stories from the villages. An ethnobotany checklist is available for regional branding, which provides six key themes for local producers to contribute to destination brand development, see Table 1 developed from Mansfield and Potočnik Topler (2021, p. 201). In the lead-up to the event, the food suppliers and clothing manufacturers in the region supplying Winchester would have to pay particular attention in creating products suitable for children. It is envisaged that the local chamber of commerce and city council food hygiene officers would offer workshops and advice for suppliers to improve their offering for children, whilst

Table 1. The Ethnobotany Checklist, Developed Mansfield and Potočnik Topler (2021, p. 201).

The Ethnobotany Checklist
Eat and drink. Usually a main carbohydrate foodstuff, which can be prepared for both fine dining and as a tourist snack takeaway. Well-being must be incorporated in the meal preparation, for example, avoiding added refined sugar and other allergens. Seek to appeal to emerging food-consumption choices in new publics, for example, vegetarian, vegan, non-alcohol options.
Food for pollinators to maintain the plant and botanic life forms. These plants will require education panels, and links to local symbolic cultural capital for visitors to discover and appreciate.
Recyclable plant products. Raised social awareness of whose labour and whose knowledge is used and is valued in the collection, processing and re-use of the plant by-products.
Food taste or scent – a local herb, dating from ancient times, perhaps held in a local placename or the name of a river. Symbolic – positive symbolism with local connection to culture and literature will maintain authentic experiences for local identities and visitors.
Apparel. Wearable botanics, created and made with local craft skills. Institutions for this knowledge to be preserved enhanced and transmitted as part of local culture in colleges, workshops and through courses offered by regional universities.
Shelter – building with botanics and using local production knowledge and labour. Visitor attraction, equipment or building made of wood. For example, old wine press, bench, a tree park or arboretum. Wooden buildings using local timber rather than imported timber. Sponsorship and promotion of local timber and forestry businesses brought into the tourism space to support local carpentry industry and craft-workers.

remaining within the standards. These public organisations supporting local businesses can adapt the ethnobotany checklist to help their local economy.

The results of this single case study, alongside the discussions related to it, cannot be generalised to other destinations, unless they have a profile similar to

Winchester. Additionally, the recommendations formulated in this study are purely theoretical, meaning they have not been tested, which subsequently implies that empirical research is needed to confirm the validity and reliability of the research.

References

Andrews, H., & Leopold, T. (2013). *Events and the social sciences*. Abingdon: Routledge.

Ateljevic, I. (2000). Circuits of tourism: Stepping beyond the production consumption dichotomy. *Tourism Geographies: An International Journal of Tourism Space, Place and Environment, 24*, 369–388. doi:10.1080/146166800750035495

Booth, A. S., & Cameron, F. M. (2020). Family event participation: Building flourishing communities. *International Journal of Event and Festival Management, 11*(2), 223–238.

Brackenridge, C. H., Rhind, D., & Palmer-Felgate, S. (2015). Locating and mitigating risks to children associated with major sporting events. *Journal of Policy Research in Tourism, Leisure and Events, 7*(3), 237–250.

Brunt, P., Horner, S., & Semley, N. (2017). *Research methods in tourism, hospitality & events management*. London: Sage.

Cakar, K. (2022). The use of qualitative content analysis in hospitality and tourism. In Okumus, F., Rasoolimanesh, S. M., & Jahani, S. (Eds.), *Contemporary research methods in hospitality and tourism*. Emerald Publishing Limited: London.

Canosa, A., & Graham, A. (2016). Ethical tourism research involving children. *Annals of Tourism Research, 61*(15), 1–6. doi:10.1016/j.annals.2016.07.006

Coghlan, A., & Filo, K. (2013). 'Using constant comparison method and qualitative data to understand participants' experiences at the nexus of tourism, sport and charity events. *Tourism Management, 35*, 122–131. doi:10.1016/j.tourman.2012.06.007

Croquet, P. (2022). *Pourquoi les Webtoons ces bandes dessinées sur smartphones enthousiasment autant*. Le Monde Paris: Groupe Le Monde.

Cullingford, C. (1995). Children's attitudes to holidays overseas. *Tourism Management, 16*(2), 121–127. doi:10.1016/0261-5177(94)00022-3

Di Pietro, L., Edvarsson, B., Reynoso, J., Renzi, M. F., Toni, M., & Mugion, R. G. (2018). A scaling up framework for innovative service ecosystems: Lessons from Eataly and KidZania. *Journal of Service Management, 29*(1), 146–175.

Foley, J. (1985). *Oral-formulaic theory and research: An introduction and annotated bibliography*. New York, NY: Garland Publishing.

Fox, D., Gouthro, M. B., Morakabati, Y., & Brackstone, J. (2014). *Doing events research. From theory to practice*. Abingdon: Routledge.

Getz, D., & Page, S. J. (2020). *Event Studies. Theory, research and policy for planned events* (4th ed.). London: Routledge.

Hammond, M., & Wellington, J. (2013). *Research methods. The key concepts*. Abingdon: Routledge.

Hertzman, E., Anderson, D., & Rowley, S. (2008). Edutainment heritage tourist attractions: A portrait of visitors' experiences at Storyeum. *Museum Management and Curatorship, 23*(2), 155–175. doi:10.1080/09647770802012227

Hixson, E. (2014). The impact of young people's participation in events: Developing a model of social event impact. *International Journal of Event and Festival Management, 5*(3), 198–218. doi:10.1108/IJEFM-09-2013-0026

Instagram. (2022). Travel journals hashtag, Menlo Park: Meta platforms. Retrieved from instagram.com/explore/tags/traveljournals. Accessed on October 9, 2022.

James, A., & Prout, A. (2003). *Constructing and reconstructing childhood: Contemporary issues in the sociological study of childhood.* New York, NY: Routledge.

Jobst, N. (2022). *Webtoon industry size South Korea.* New York, NY: Statista.

Kamble, Z. (2022). Reflections of a qualitative researcher: Structuring a qualitative research methodology. An illustration from PhD thesis. In, Okumus, F., Rasoolimanesh, S. M., & Jahani, S. (Eds.), *Contemporary research methods in hospitality and tourism.* Emerald Publishing Limited: London.

Katz, C. (2004). *Growing up global: Economic restructuring and children's everyday lives.* Minneapolis, MN: University of Minnesota Press.

Lego. (2022). *Kids Included: Enabling meaningful child participation within companies in a digital era.* KidsKnowBest and The LEGO Group: Billund. Retrieved from https://www.kidsincluded.report/. Accessed on September 22, 2022.

Mallen, C., & Adams, L. (2013). *Event management in sport, recreation and tourism: Theoretical and practical dimensions* (3rd ed.). Abingdon: Routledge.

Mansfield, C. (2018, June). Cultural capital in place-making. *Journal of Hospitality & Tourism, 16*(1), 1–17.

Mansfield, C. (2022). *An Exeter Waytale Webtoon.* Totnes: Travel Writers Online.

Mansfield, C., & Potočnik Topler, J. (2021). Building the Ethnopôle: Eliciting and sharing Ethnobotanical knowledge in tourism development. *Annals for Istrian and Mediterranean Studies – History & Sociology, 31*(2), 197–208. doi:10.19233/ASHS.2021.13

Mansfield, C., & Potočnik Topler, J. (2023). *Travel writing for tourism and city branding. Urban place writing methodologies.* Abingdon: Routledge.

McKay, J. (2002). Storytelling – A celebration. *Arts Professional.* Retrieved from artsprofessional.co.uk. Accessed on August 19, 2022.

Oswald, A. (2011). *Memorial.* London: Faber & Faber. Retrieved from poetryarchive.org/explore/?key=oswald. Accessed on August 19, 2022.

Panodyssey. (2022). Creative room European Alliance. Asnières-sur-Seine: Panodyssey holding. Retrieved from panodyssey.com/en. Accessed on October 9, 2022.

Poria, Y., & Timothy, D. J. (2014). Where are the children in tourism research? *Annals of Tourism Research, 47*, 93–95. doi:10.1016/j.annals.2014.03.002

Poris, M. (2006). Understanding what fun means to today's kids. *Young Consumers, 7*(1), 14–22.

Radic, A. (2017). Towards an understanding of a child's cruise experience. *Current Issues in Tourism, 22*, 237–252.

Richards, G., & Palmer, R. (2010). *Eventful cities. Cultural management and urban revalidation.* London: Butlerworth-Heinemann.

Séraphin, H. (2021). COVID-19 and the acknowledgement of children as stakeholders of the tourism industry. *Anatolia, 32*(1), 152–156 doi:10.1080/13032917.2020.1856690

Séraphin, H., & Green, S. (2019). The significance of the contribution of children to conceptualising and branding the smart destination of the future. *International Journal of Tourism Cities, 5*(4), 544–559.

Séraphin, H., Platania, M., Spencer, P., & Modica, G. (2018). Events and tourism development within a local community. The Case of Winchester (UK). *Sustainability*, *10*(10). doi:10.3390/su10103728

Séraphin, H., & Vo-Than, T. (2020). Investigating the application of the principles for responsible management education to resort mini-clubs. *International Journal of Management in Education*. doi:10.1016/j.ijme.2020.100377

SFS. (2022). *Find a storyteller*. Poole: The Society for Storytelling. Retrieved from sfs. org.uk. Accessed on September 3, 2022.

Sundhall, J. (2017). A political space for children? The age order and children's right to participation. *Social Inclusion*, *5*(3), 164–171.

Tagg, B., & Wang, S. (2016). Globalisation, commercialisation, and learning to play at KidZania Kuala Lumpur. *International Journal of Play*, *5*(2), 141–158.

Wall, J. (2008). Human rights in light of childhood. *The International Journal of Children's Rights*, 16, 523–543.

Wall, J. (2010). *Ethics in light of childhood*. Washington, DC: Georgetown University Press.

Wall, J. (2019). From childhood studies to childism: Reconstructing the scholarly and social imaginations. *Children's Geographies*, *20*(3), 257–270. doi:10.1080/14733285. 2019.1668912

Yeoman, I., Robertson, M., Ali-Knight, J., Drummond, S., & McMahon-Beattie, U. (2012). *Festival and events management*. Abingdon: Routledge.

Appendix

Appendix 1: List of Events in Winchester

	Event	Type	When	Year
1	Taste of Wickham	Food & drink	September	2020
2	Winchester guitar festival	Music	October	2020
3	Hyde900	History & arts	October	2020
4	Winchester film festival	Film	November	2020
5	The cheese & chilli festival	Food & drink	August	2020
6	Winchester poetry festival	Literature	October	2020
7	Winchester bonfire & fireworks	Entertainment	November	2020
8	Wine festival Winchester	Food & drink	November	2020
9	Winchester heritage open days	History & arts	September	2020
10	Harvest festival	Food & drink	October	2020
11	Winchester comedy festival	Comedy	September	2020
12	Winchester design festival	Arts	October	2020

(Continued)

Event	Type	When	Year
13 Winchester Christmas lights switch on	Christmas in Winchester	November	2020
14 Christmas market	Christmas in Winchester	November	2020
15 Christmas ice rink	Christmas in Winchester	November	2020
16 Christmas lantern parade	Christmas in Winchester	November	2020
17 Film screening for LGBT month	Film	February	2020
18 Winchester comedy gala	Comedy	March	2020
19 Children of Winchester festival	Children	February	2020
20 Winchester beer & cider festival	Food & drink	March	2020
21 Winchester fashion week	Fashion	April	2020
22 Hampshire pride	Entertainment	April	2020
23 The grange festival	Music	June	2020
24 Winchester chamber music festival	Music	April	2020
25 Stone festival	Arts	June	2020
26 Winchester & country music festival	Music	May	2020
27 Alreshford music festival	Music	June	2020
28 Winchester Mayfest	Arts	May	2020
29 Winchester Ukelele festival	Music	May	2020
30 Winchester cocktail week	Food & drink	June	2020
31 Winchestival	Music & comedy	June	2020
32 Hampshire festival	Food & drink	June	2020
33 Winchester Criterium & Cyclefest	Sports	June	2020
34 Hat fair	Arts	July	2020
35 Winchester school of art degree show	Arts	June	2020
36 Wickham festival	Music	August	2020
37 Writers' weekend Winchester	Literature	July	2020
38 Boomtown	Music	August	2020

Source: The Author.

Appendix 2: Events Which Are no Longer Running in Winchester

Coffee festival	Food & drink	2019
Worthys festivals	Music	2019
Ginchester fete	Food & drink	2019
Winchester & country music festival	Music	2019
Winchester writers' festival	Literature	2019
Wooly hat fair	Arts	2018
10 × 10 new writing festival	Literature	2018
Winchester jazz festival	Music	2018
Winchester community games	Sports	2018
Illumination of festival of flowers	Arts	2018
Graze festival	Music	2018
Eastern bunny hop	Children	2017
SC4M American music festival	Music	2017
Southern cathedrals festival	Music	2017
Winscifest	Science	2017
Armed force day	Culture	2017
Cascade	Arts	2016

Source: The Authors.

Section 3
Planning and Delivering Events: A Practical Guideline

Chapter 8

7 Steps to the Perfect Children's Event

Chris Powell

Abstract

Events feed our desire to connect, celebrate and share experiences. Visiting or taking part in Children's events forms part of many a child's upbringing. They are part of family life. All well-planned events share the same core principals whatever their size or type. Children's events are no different. Events designed with children in mind require no less time or effort. The audience may well be young but don't be fooled into thinking that they are any less demanding! Your event needs to work on many levels to please this audience and their parents and or guardians. While the process of planning a Children's events is the same as that aimed at adults, they are more difficult to deliver because of the requirements of the legislation designed to safeguard and protect children, while at events. The legislation and best practice guidance is all designed to ensure children attending events are kept safe, free from harm and if they, for example, get lost, there is a procedure in place to reunite parents and children. This chapter is specifically about events where children are the primary audience, either specifically or because of the nature the event programme children often attend with their parents. It will give you an overview of the seven steps event managers take to ensure they deliver successful and safe children's events.

Keywords: 7 steps; event planning; children; experience; performance; guideline

Introduction

Events feed our desire to connect, celebrate and share experiences. They are part of who we are. Events organised by friends and family and delivered by a range of organisations such as schools and clubs have always been attended by children too. Visiting or taking part in events are often part of a child's upbringing. Events are complex projects and likened to directing a live stage show, but without the

Events Management for the Infant and Youth Market, 121–137
Copyright © 2023 Chris Powell
Published under exclusive licence by Emerald Publishing Limited
doi:10.1108/978-1-80455-690-020231016

dress rehearsals, safety nets and once started, no second chances. Creating successful and memorable children's events is however no easy task. Children and their parents and guardians are just as demanding as their adult contemporaries. All well-planned events share the same core principals whatever their size or type. Children's events are no different. While the process of planning children's events is the same as that aimed at adults, they are more difficult to deliver because of the requirements of the legislation designed to safeguard and protect children, while at events. The legislation and best practice guidance is all designed to ensure children attending events are kept safe, free from harm and if they, for example, get lost, there is a procedure in place to reunite parents and children.

This chapter is specifically about events where children are the primary audience. It will give you an overview of the seven steps event managers take to ensure they deliver successful children's events. The advice shared relates specifically to the larger public events and not to invitation style family events such as birthday parties and children's workshops.

In general, there are two types of children's events:

(1) Specifically targeting children: children only (plus their parents)
(2) An event not specifically targeted at children but because of its nature and programme children often attend with their parents.

Purpose: Creating Events Children Want to Attend?

Believing you have a great idea for a children's event is one thing, finding a receptive and enthusiastic audience in sufficient numbers is another thing altogether. Developing the type of event that children and of course their parents want to attend requires you to do some pre-event market research. It is an essential part of the event planning process.

The way to tackle pre-event market research is as follows:

• Create a new document, write a couple of sentences about the event idea, give it a working title and outline timeframe.
• Conduct an online market analysis using the keywords somebody looking for this type of event might use.
• Conduct a survey using an existing mailing list. You are seeking to get a sense of what they think of your event idea and gleam information on timings, location, content and acceptable entrance fees (if applicable). Surveying children is however difficult and often yields unhelpful answers.

So, What Should You Be Looking for?

• Any relevant emerging trends/new activities making waves or any current conversations, concerns or social chatter you can pick up on.

- Who might the event idea appeal too? Who will benefit and enjoy attending your event? Are they known to you or if not, where will they come from and what is the best way to reach them. The objective of this exercise is to create an exact customer profile (your target audience) and establish how you are going promote your event to them.
- Your research may uncover other people or organisations (schools, clubs, uniformed organisations, children's and young people's service providers) interested in your plans. A conversation with them could reveal a potential partnership, access to an expert, funding or a joint promotional campaign.
- Are competitors already running similar events and potentially targeting the same audience? Should you compete with them? Does the idea need tweaking to avoid clashing with them?
- Operational factors. Are there any specific permissions or licences required for a children's event or legislation that dictates how the event is delivered.
- Establish the potential costs involved in planning and delivering the event. Gather estimates for hiring a venue and equipment, contracting entertainment, equipment, costs of licences fees, specialist expertise (creche providers), event day staff, creating promotional material, catering etc. Do include a 5–10% contingency figure. If appropriate, also make some conservative guesstimates of any potential revenue sources and forecasts. As with all types of events it's important to know exactly what you could be getting into financially. My rule of thumb: overestimate costs and underestimate incomes.

Your pre-event market analysis seeks to provide you with compelling evidence (or not) that what you are planning is worth investing time, effort and money in. In other words, it is a smart idea and ultimately more likely to be successful. With your research completed and evidence to support your idea and a complete picture of what you are getting involved in, you can now complete an event brief.

Event Briefs

Your event brief should cover the following:

- Background information about the event's organiser – experience and relevant expertise
- Target audience
- Principal purpose
- Proposed event timelines and dates
- Outline thoughts on the programme
- Any 'must happens'
- Outline budget
- Detail all permissions, licences and legislation that need to be addressed and indicate any processing timeframes (application to successful completion).
- Success criteria

Your finished event brief should be agreed and signed off by all interested parties.

Designing and Programming Must Attend Children's Event

With your event brief to hand it's now time to use your research findings to design and programme your event. In the design stage you are looking to create a visual image of your event. It's look, style, feel and possibly give it a theme. The event programme is the schedule of activities the children are going to take part in, listen to or watch. It is constructed much like a play, scene by scene and is the most important component of any event because it is the reason why your audience are there. It can make or break a children's event.

It's crucial your event design and programme must be entirely target audience led and inspired (children in the agreed age group).

Generating Event Design and Programming Ideas

To get the ideas ball-rolling I would look for five to eight people with creative flair and a range of different experiences to participate in an event brainstorming session. Remember, creativity works best when you and your colleagues keep an open mind, are brave and ignore the constraints of practicality and cost. The objective of the brainstorming meeting is to uncover ideas that resonate and inspire everyone.

To help add some direction to the process let's have a look at what child-friendly events look like. There will be areas for highchairs, baby-changing and breast-feeding areas, buggy and slings park, supervised play areas, a creche and a range of age-appropriate children's activities and entertainment. These events provide healthy child-friendly food options (allergies noted on offerings), children's priority toilets (marked accordingly) accessible toilets, supervised entrances and exits, a booking system for onsite creches, easy access to fresh, tested and approved water and a wristband service for children and parents to use. All activities will also be run by suitably qualified staff so ensuring a professionally run event, for the children and parents alike.

At your brainstorming meeting you are looking to generate a list of activities, entertainment and things; to take part in that will help deliver strong take-away memories.

Design and Programming Ideas

- Marquees, temporary structures, bespoke stage sets and backdrops
- Lighting to create atmosphere
- Outdoor lounges, child-friendly chill-out areas, creches, supervised play areas with equipment
- Relatable children's stories

- A shareable moment, message, activity, picture moment
- Photographs, illustrations, animations, video
- Entertainment (on stage) or mix and mingle
- Gifts and giveaways
- Age-appropriate circus skills and funfair rides
- Music, live or recorded
- Themed decorations and props
- Games, competitions and have a go taster session
- Things to do, learn, make activities
- Mass participatory activities
- Child-friendly eating options

Engaging Children at Events

Children are easily distracted. Therefore, any planned activities need to be delivered with a high degree of energy and audience engagement. This will help to make the activities fun and memorable.

Event Timings for Children's Events

The length of your event will depend on the age of the children you are targeting.

(1) 1–2 years old: 1 to 1½ hours is enough and which fits around normal child care routines of feeding and naps. Sensible start times will be mid-morning.
(2) 3–7 years old: up to 2 hours
(3) 8–11 years old: 2–3 hours
(4) Certain larger family festivals aim to meet both the needs of parents and children in equal measure. These events often run all day and over a weekend. While they do attract a wide range of children, entry conditions always state that any ticket holder can only enter the festival with a parent, legal guardian or nominated guardian of a certain age.

Of note, children's events will have shorter activity sessions and schedule breaks more often.

On the whole, weekends are best for children-centred events, but as they get older after-school events work too, if they have a very definite end time.

Evaluating Your Brainstormed Event Ideas

Having brainstormed and noted a variety of ideas, it's time to sift through them: reducing your long list of ideas to a shorter list the event team really like and best fits the original design brief.

With your ideas to hand, it's now necessary to make a more reasoned assessment of the relative merits of each suggestion.

I recommend checking each idea against the following five-stage event idea evaluation process.

(1) Do the ideas help deliver the why: the organisational need for wanting to organise the event in the first place? (Strategic)
(2) Do the suggested programme ideas deliver an impactful, relevant and fun series of activities and contain a high degree of engagement?
(3) Will the targeted children like and enjoy what you are planning? (Marketing). Try testing your ideas out on a sample group of children and parents. Do they like them, understand what they are coming to and consider it to be a valuable and useful use of their time?
(4) Can you afford it (financial)? Having got estimates for key programme and design items, do you think you are going to be able secure an appropriately sized budget to run the event in the way you want to.
(5) Does your team have the skills to plan and deliver the event confidently. Do you need to train team members or recruit an expert in these types of children events to help you?

With a list of evaluated ideas agreed, it is now time to start planning your event.

Planning a Children's Event – Making It Happen

Now you have a clear idea of your event design and programme, it's time to start planning it. The event planning process for a children's event is the same whether you have just a few children or 100's attending your event.

As your audience is children, you are legally required to keep them safe and free from harm. To do this, you will need to comply with a range of legislation and best practice guidance. The specific requirements will vary depending on whether children are accompanied by a parent or are left under the supervision of event workers or volunteers.

Event Planning Team

Like any event you'll need a team of people to help make it happen. This team will usually be comprised of work colleagues, committee members, event partners, volunteers and subject matter experts (there to fill any gaps in understanding or skills). This team must have regular event planning meetings, which should be purposeful and productive occasions designed to solve problems, stimulate ideas and generate action.

Event Project Planning

Events are projects. They have a beginning, middle and end. Like any other project, there will be a comprehensive and sequential (and often parallel) series of actions with start and finish dates. Each action will need a description, realistic timescales, a named responsible person and a section to indicate its status, i.e. completed, on track, not started and or urgent. Every task on the plan will require discussion and decision. A useful suggestion is to include milestone dates in the plan. The meeting of these milestones is often critical to the overall success of the event.

The event planners' job is to fixate about the detail and drive the process forward by injecting continuous urgency: making sure actions are completed and deadlines met. Creating an event project plan is not a one-off exercise. They are active documents that require regular review and must be adapted to changing circumstances. You can use project management software or more conventional spreadsheets to help you plan your event.

The Money: Event Planning Budgets

All events require time, effort and money. If you want to create a great looking and memorable children's event, you will need a suitably sized budget. A big bold event aim will often require a big budget. The size of the budget has to be determined with the events objectives and aspirations in mind. The budget describes your event in monetary terms.

As you begin the budgetary process, there are five things to do in advance of setting the final budget:

(1) Establish everything and everybody that has associated costs.
(2) Agree any 'must have' items. You can also have lists of 'like to haves' if revenues are higher than projections or the budget permits.
(3) Agree what the events' financial strategy is going to be. Your options are too break-even: make a profit (if so, how much): accept a loss (up to (x) % and or spend the budget.
(4) Do your Research. Investigate the market, search and analyse your supplier options and connect with other event professionals. There's a lot to be learnt from others who have already been there and made the mistakes for you!
(5) Do also look for genuine in-kind opportunities to reduce your expenditure.

As you gather quotes for externally and internally sourced items (things or time), enter the figures into a spreadsheet. Standard event spreadsheets are laid out as follows:

* item
* description
* quantity
* estimate
* actual
* variance

It is also wise to build in a 5–10% contingency fund for unforeseen expenditure. You must conduct regular budget reviews as part of your planning meetings.

Revenue: Can You Make Any Money From Children's Events?

Children's events can be monetised. Indeed, all the larger children's festivals will charge an entrance fee. If your content is good enough, people will pay. Your realistic revenue sources are ticket sales and upsells, selling trade and catering pitches, charging for onsite activities or selling merchandise. Gaining sponsorship for a children's event is possible but unlikely.

Searching and Selecting the Right Contractors

There is every chance you will need to hire contractors to supply you with, for example, stages, audio-visual equipment, lighting, stewards, toilets, entertainers, marquees etc. They must be competent contractors. I recommend all your prospective contractors compete a competent contractor checklist.

The checklist is to establish their competence and experience by asking for their risk assessments, health and safety policies, relevant references, contact details, relevant qualifications and to request sight of all their current insurance policies. Competent contractors are fully acquainted with such requests and will provide the information readily. Whilst you might think this is a little over the top, consider the consequential loss of money and reputation if you don't undertake some basic checks and then there was an accident.

Planning a Safe Children's Event: General Safety Requirements for all Events

Event managers of any kind of event have a legal duty to protect the health, safety and welfare of those people attending events as well as employees, contractors and sub-contractors working at events. Employees (event teams), event venues (event spaces) and contractors have similar responsibilities to protect those who may be affected by their work. For example, a venue must ensure that the building, fire extinguishers, fire escapes, safety procedures etc. are working and properly maintained and meet all current building regulations.

In terms of event health and safety, all event managers need to understand and comply with a range of Acts, legislation, regulations, Approved Codes of Practice and guidance. They also have a duty under the auspices of the Management of the Health and Safety at Work Act 1999 (United Kingdom) to carry out risk-assessed work. In essence, an event risk assessment is a careful, suitable and sufficient examination of what at your event (place of work) could cause harm. Event risk assessments should be completed by a competent person and deal with all reasonable, foreseeable and significant hazards. They must be recorded, reviewed and dynamically revised at your event, if required. The risk assessment would document not only all general hazards on site, but it would also make in this case, specific references to all children's activities and to those hazards associated with having children onsite.

As with any kind of event, safe events require a designated and competent event and or safety manager, trained staff, a method of communicating with your staff and the audience, an appropriate number of emergency exit routes leading to safe places, fire precautions and fire-fighting systems. You will need expertly installed electrical systems, stages, barriers, seating, catering, toilets, information and help points and security.

For larger children's events where you could have 1,500 people on site at any one time: two things are possible.

(1) You may or rather should write an event management plan (i.e. covers all the safety and organisational aspects of your event in great detail) outlining the following:

- An evaluation of your event and venue
- The services
- The infrastructure
- The way you intend to manage your event
- What you intend to do in certain situations

(2) You may be required to attend a safety advisory group. These types of meetings are usually coordinated by the local authority in which your event site is located. These meetings are attended by the emergency services and council officers who will want to discuss and advise you on the content of your event management plan.

The goal of the plan is to demonstrate exactly how you intend to keep everyone safe at your event and create a defendable position. For large events you may wish to consider employing a qualified safety coordinator to help you maintain, apply and coordinate a site safety plan.

Keeping Children Safe and Free From Harm: Specific Requirements

In addition to the above requirements, event managers, whether the event is entirely for children or children are likely to attend, need to comply with a range of legislation and best practice. The legal requirements around children fall into two categories, those relating to all children and those relating to children performing at events.

The Children and Young Persons Act 1933, updated in 1963, 1969 and 2008, consolidates all the child protection legislation.

The Working to Safeguard Children (2018) Act – In essence the act says everyone who works with children has a responsibility for keeping them safe, knowing how to identify any concerns, sharing information and taking prompt action. Safeguarding means looking out for the safety and welfare of children.

Children's event managers will therefore deploy several safeguarding policies to keep children safe and free from harm at events and ensure everyone on site is aware of it. What this means on an event site is several things. You must:

(1) Understand the process and organisations you should report to if you are concerned about a child at your event.
(2) Know the contact details of:

- your local multi-agency safeguarding hub, local safeguarding partnership and or the child protection team (local authority) and their out-of-hours numbers
- your events local police force
- the National Society for the Protection of Cruelty to Children anonymous support and advice phone line.

(3) Know what to do if a child makes a disclosure to you in a conversation on an event site. These conversations need to be conducted by trained safeguarding staff.
(4) Have in the interest of protecting, you and your staff a process for managing allegations against event staff. This process will outline how you handle these.

As well as having a safeguarding policy, you also should have the following:

- Lost/found child policy. The policy will include what you will do with a missing/found child, what records you will keep, where will they be held (a child-friendly location) while waiting to be recovered by their legal guardians. It will detail who will be responsible for them while lost (appropriately checked, qualified and have been Disclosure and Barring Service checked and cleared to work with children) and what to check when returning a lost child to their legal guardian. It is important to remember that as soon as a lost child enters your system, you are now legally responsible for them until they are safely returned to their legal guardian or handed over to the authorities.
- Create a team code of conduct. The code ensures that everyone directly working with or are designated key staff or team leaders know what to do, should they be in a situation where they have to deal with a child. They need to have read the code of conduct and indicate so, by a signature when signing on to work at the event. If possible, you might want to consider offering some training to all key staff on how to approach and speak to children.
- Photographs and videoing. Always a difficult one to manage but you should be clear how the images will be used and where they will be used. Where appropriate, parental permission should be sought.
- If you are likely to have early teenagers on site (the event is not ticketed and there are no entrance checks), do consider how you will deal with those who have missed their transport home, got separated from friends and have no money.

- Designated and clearly visible meeting points can be very helpful on an event site. Again, they need to properly supervise with qualified staff. A pick-up point where parents can wait is also a useful addition to a large event or festival.

Creches and Stay-and-Play Areas

At larger events or where you are keen to attract working parents, then the provision of a creche at the event is a good idea. These services should be provided by a professional.

Creche providers will:

(1) Be registered with the Office for Standards in Education (Ofsted). Registered creches or other day care providers understand their responsibilities and obligations. They will complete all the necessary paperwork on your behalf. The registration requirements vary across the United Kingdom and Europe. Please check your local requirements.
(2) Have to ensure all those working in event creches will be Disclosure and Barring Service checked as part of the Ofsted registration process.
(3) Be fully insured, risk assessed and compliant with all the appropriate regulations and best practice.
(4) Have a booking service to mitigate against queues forming and improve the experience. Parents can therefore plan their day better knowing what and when they have a creche booking.

Of note, creche providers can also provide stay-and-play areas which means effectively parents can watch their children play in a supervised play area.

A final point here is if event organisers are going to provide a lost and found service, they should ensure their event insurance policy states – Lost and Found service.

Event Specific Legislation for Children Performing at Events

There are also requirements relating to children performing at events rather just participating in activities or workshops on site.

The child performance licensing system run by local authorities can issue child performance licences when a child is performing at music events, theatre and dance festivals. The licences are intended to keep children safe and free from harm in entertainment settings. They are issued in certain circumstances and have to be applied for. Applicants will be successful if they can demonstrate they meet all required safeguarding and protection practices. These licences must be applied for at least 21 days before the performance.

Body of Persons Approval (BOPA) is used when there are many young performers in the programme. A BOPA is awarded to an organisation instead of an individual child performance licence.

Licenced chaperones are needed when no parents or suitably qualified persons can be found to accompany the child performers. Again, local authorities will issue these.

It is wise when planning children's events to make speaking to your local licencing officer one of your first priorities. They can advise you on exactly what you will need to do and how to manage the process to a successful conclusion.

Places – Creating the Great Event Spaces

Finding the right venue for your children's event or making the best use of your own is an important decision. The right venue and the way it is laid out, really does set the tone and sense of occasion of your event.

The process for finding a venue for a children's event will be the same as any event. The caveat to this will be that some venues are just safer spaces for children to be in. They are less likely to come to harm.

Your venue search criteria will involve the following:

(1) Location: city centre, iconic, unusual, in the countryside
(2) Geographical location: number and quality of access links to the event site
(3) Size of space required to include infrastructure and bespoke installations
(4) Numbers visiting/Event size
(5) Parking capacities and any temporary parking options
(6) Timing and duration of event
(7) Blank canvas venue or already themed
(8) Catering: in-house or can use own
(9) Budget: agree a price range you can afford to go up to.

Using the above as your venue search criteria, conduct an online search or instruct a venue finding agency. The search can often reveal a long list of potential venues which through further research can be reduced to a short list of ones, which you want to arrange a site visit. Once on site you will conduct a thorough site evaluation to decide which venue best fits your criteria and ask for a quote. You would then contract your chosen venue and then get to know the site and its operating staff.

In making your final choice you will seek to ensure your chosen venue is a good fit with your organisation, the audience profile and the programme of activities. It also needs to come in around budget.

Designing Your Event Site

With your venue contracted it is now time to think about how you will lay out your event site. The intention of all event planners when creating their event site plan is to create a space that feels comfortably full, vibrant and alive. In order to do that they will need to consider

- Audience safety: location of entrance and exits, evacuation routes, event capacity
- Creating an arena where audiences can enjoy the entertainment (see and hear it), be able to move around the site easily and has good entry/exit access options.
- The location of traders, entertainment, activities and infrastructure and make sure there is enough space to queue, e.g. in front of a catering unit.
- Accessing and servicing areas for site contractors to refill, clean or restock infrastructure.

Specific site planning considerations for children's events include:

- The distance from the car park to main children's facilities
- Creating easy routes for those with buggies to access children's facilities
- Ensure toilets are ideally located at or near the creche/stay-and-play areas and are signed as children's only toilets
- Locate key children's facilities to be away from high noise areas and slightly away from busy, high footfall event thorough fares
- The location of fresh water drinking points

The plan should be drawn to scale and therefore requires accurate activity, equipment and infrastructure measurements.

As part of the site design process, you would also be considering what sort of external and internal event signage you will need across the site indicating the location of all key facilities. This means signs relating to travelling to the event site, parking and finding your way in and around the site. It is helpful to have colour or design coordinated signs at all event site cross-sections and off the main thoroughfares.

Promotion: How to Design Super Effective Event Promotional Campaigns

Your event maybe the next big thing in the world of children's events, but if your promotion misses the mark, your event will fail. The aim of all your promotional activities must be to make your target audience aware of your event; get them wanting to know more and encouraging them to take action: to register interest, buy tickets or sign up.

For your promotional plans to work, it is vital that you have a very clear idea of who your target audience is and how best to promote to them. You will need to create compelling messages to attend statements, use a mix of media, have an optimised and keyword-rich web page (on a website or social media platform) and a budget to help the process along.

All events should have an event promotional plan, and typically it has nine stages:

(1) Set some targets: how many children would you like to attend or wish to engage with.

(2) Conduct an internal promotional audit: can you currently reach your target audience? If not, what do you need to secure access to them?

(3) Audience: decide who they are, their age, gender, interests and create a profile

(4) Content: entertainment profiles, previews, videos, messages (for children and their parents) website landing page or chosen social media site to include 'calls to action': reserve your ticket or buy now messages.

(5) Media: best 'audience' fit, on/offline media, email, cost

(6) Event promotional budget: design time, print cost, media hire, media updates. It is recommended that you allocate 15%–20% of the event budget to promotion.

(7) Test and edit it: edit $x3$ (be brutal), review key content and visuals, proofread it and then test it out. What do a representative audience think?

(8) Timeline and activity plan with critical dates

(9) Implement and monitor: analyse which campaign delivers people (tickets sold) and do more of it and stop anything that does not deliver results

Promotional activities aimed at children do tend to involve bright bold colours and age-appropriate images and graphics. If you are using a website or a page on a social media platform and want to be found via organic search, your site needs to be keyword-optimised and have a great meta description.

For ticketed events, organisers will need to source a ticketing platform that takes payment, issues tickets and provides a system for scanning them on arrival. The site used will have to display your tickets' full terms and conditions, one of which must be, that any ticket holder under the age of 18 cannot enter the event without a parent, legal guardian or nominated guardian. It is wise to remember that legally a person remains a child up to the day they become 18 years old.

Production: Delivering Your Event

Producing children's events is like directing a play: it is built scene by scene. There is a necessary and logical order to delivering an event and getting it right is important. Essentially, you need to break down your event day into its component parts and work out what needs to happen first, second, third and so on.

The best way to manage the delivery of an event is to create an event operational plan or function sheet. An event operational plan is a sequenced list of tasks to be completed on or before the event day. The plan is a full chronological running order of everything that needs to happen detailing the time it needs to happen, where it needs to happen, who (contractors/supplier) is going make it happen and which member of the events team is responsible for making it happen.

In compiling the operational plan, consider the following.

(1) When do you need everyone on site and in what order? This includes the event day management team, contractors, event day staffing team, programme activities and the audience or participants.

(2) Agreeing times of ticketing, registration or entrance opening times. With opening times agreed, you can then work backwards from this time and calculate how long you will need to get everything and everyone in place. A word of warning setting up an event will always take longer than you expect.

(3) Implementing the event site plan: as your contractors and event team arrive to help you set up, do make sure you have your site plan to hand and that everyone is following it. A copy of the site plan should form part of your operation plan and be sent to key staff, the venue and all contractors prior to the event.

At this stage of the event delivery process, you will also:

(1) Recruit an event day team to help you set up, run and breakdown your event. This will include identifying tasks, any skills, qualifications and or experience (of running similar events) they need and the numbers of people you require. You would then recruit, interview, select or reject them and then contract and induct them. Once you have your event day team in place, it is wise to establish a family tree to show them where they fit in and to identify who they report too.

(2) Send out contractor, entertainment and staff member joining instructions before event day outlining what you expect them to do on arrival and while on site. In the case of your core event team, you would send them a full event briefing pack beforehand. On event day you will ask them to sign in, provide a mobile number and indicate they have read and understood the contents of the briefing pack and children's code of conduct.

(3) Ensure you contact all of the key players at your event and double-check the details with them.

(4) Consider your contingency plans. What if a key team member, headline act or contractor does not turn up or the weather turns nasty? What would your plan B look like.

(5) Collate a contacts list of everyone and all staff on site.

(6) Create a list of any VIPs, their arrival times and locations and who will be responsible for them.

(7) Complete your final site plan and circulate to all those arriving to work or provide a service or entertainment.

(8) Welfare information. These should be very detailed with the objective of ensuring parents and children really understand what they are coming to and what is expected of them. These should be on the event webpage and or sent on ticket purchase.

They would outline what there is to do and where to find things out. You may remind them what to wear, spares to bring, favourite snacks (just in case) clothing for sun (sunscreen / lightweight clothing) and rain (waterproofs and wellies), wet wipes, water and spare water container for filling up on site and a copy of the event programme so they don't miss anything. Included in the welfare information will also be advice about looking after yourself, some dos and don'ts when onsite (potentially older children) and what to do in certain circumstances. Ultimately, how to have a great and safe time at this event.

(9) Parent-friendly site plan. A good suggestion is to create a more simplified version of the site plan indicating all the main children's activities and facilities. A parent-friendly site plan should be available on the events website and in a downloadable format. It's advisable to also have some hard copies available in key locations.

During Event Set-Up

While it is important to ensure everyone's safety during the set-up phase of your event, you do also need to pay special attention to kiddie traps. What I mean by this is that children will always find the gaps in fencing, open doors to walk through and things to swing on. It is therefore vitally important to remind staff and contractors to lock, remove or secure these opportunities. You would also remind all your event team to check any potential 'kiddie traps' as part of their event stewarding duties.

People – It's What Makes Successful Children's Events

It's event day: the culmination of all those meetings, conversations, debates, phone calls and emails. The successful conclusion of your event; lots of happy children and parents is likely to have been a team effort, driven forward by you, the event manager. Your performance, as the event manager, during the build-up to event day and on the day itself, will be a crucial factor in ensuring the day is memorable for all the right reasons.

It's Show Time!

The role of the event manager on event day is twofold:

Role 1: to manage the practicalities of running an event: which means

- managing the set-up
- solving problems and making quick decisions
- running the programme to time
- implementing all safety plans and assessments and or reacting to a safety incident and taking remedial actions and documenting them.
- You will need to keep control, calm and diffuse difficult situations

- keep event visitors informed about the programme and any helpful information.

Role 2: to manage your various event day teams: which means

- briefing your event day team
- ensuring they sign in and have read briefing pack and code of conduct
- Keep communicating, talking, leading and motivating your teams
- making sure your teams are your eyes and ears on the ground – watching how audiences use the site and reporting back to you

And, of course, to … deliver an outstanding event!

Conclusion

Everybody loves a great event. It's an important part of family life for many. Events are unique, complex and above all planned occasions. Events designed with children in mind require no less time or effort. The audience may well be young but don't be fooled into thinking that they are any less demanding! Your event needs to work on many levels to please this audience and their parents and or guardians. While the process is the same for an event aimed at adults, children's event organisers must have robust safeguarding policies and procedures in place. They must also pay particular attention to anything and anybody that could cause harm to them at events.

The future? In my opinion I see no end to our desire to be together, be entertained and to celebrate occasions. As long as events and festivals remain safe places, children and their parents and guardians will continue to attend them. Above all else remember that having children at events is a lovely thing, and to know that you put smiles on their faces and created a memorable moment is a wonderful and rewarding feeling!

Sources of Information

A guide to the health safety and welfare at outdoor events. Retrieved from https://www.thepurpleguide.co.uk/index.php

Disclosure and Barring Service: The Home Office. Retrieved from https://www.gov.uk/government/organisations/disclosure-and-barring-service

Learning, development and care standards for children under 5. Retrieved from https://www.gov.uk/government/publications/early-years-foundation-stage-framework–2

Licensing Act 2003. Retrieved from www.legislation.gov.uk

National Society for the Prevention of Cruelty to Children (NSPCC). Retrieved from www.nspcc.org.uk

Nipperbout. Retrieved from www.nipperbout.com

The Children (Performance and Activities) (England) Regulations 2014. Secondary legislation. Retrieved from https://www.legislation.gov.uk/uksi/2014/3309/contents/made

Chapter 9

Venue Considerations When Planning Child Centric Events

Emma Delaney

Abstract

Events that are designed around the needs of children are particularly challenging to plan and thus choosing the right venue to stage such an event is a substantial task. Venue considerations for such events includes location, access and nearby amenities, capacity and flow, facilities, catering, decor as well as safeguarding. Given that event managers can now choose from purpose-built event spaces, hotels, academic, sporting and unique venues, the decision is even more complex. This chapter provides a comprehensive assessment of key venue considerations for event managers when planning child-centric events and outlines the typical characteristics of a range of venues, as relevant to organising events for family audiences.

Keywords: Venue; planning; childism; events; design; children

Introduction

Choosing an appropriate venue is a crucial stage of event management and having the 'right' venue is critical to the event's success. As the backdrop to all activities, the venue will make a notable contribution to the theme and ambience of the event and as many of its facilities will be used by attendees, it will have a significant impact on their experience. Delivering successful events for children or families requires careful management and evidence shows that a lack of planning can create much disappointment with events that have claimed to be family-friendly (Foster & Robinson, 2010). As such, finding a suitable venue for a child-centric event, one that is designed around the specific needs and wants of children above other potential attendees, is an important and substantial task.

In recent years, the number of event venues has increased exponentially (Nolan, 2018) as visitor attractions, religious buildings and sporting complexes, among others, have diversified to make their venues available for private hire.

Events Management for the Infant and Youth Market, 139–151

Copyright © 2023 Emma Delaney

Published under exclusive licence by Emerald Publishing Limited

doi:10.1108/978-1-80455-690-020231017

Thus, event managers now have an increasing list of viable spaces to use as the location for each of their events. Consequently, when planning child-centric events, an event manager's list of venue factors is extensive and finding the right venue has become a considerable challenge. This chapter presents a comprehensive review of these factors as relevant to the organisation of events with a family audience. The chapter also outlines the types of venues available to hire with an assessment of their typical characteristics, particularly in relation to organising events that children will attend. As such, this chapter provides a detailed and practical assessment of key venue considerations for event managers, when planning child-centric events. Currently, there is limited inclusion of this topic in the array of event management literature; additionally it is missing from venue-focussed event texts from Nolan (2018) and Berners (2019). As such, this chapter fills a gap in the literature and begins to address this important subject.

Child-Centric Events

Many events are aimed at families or permit the attendance of children, but this chapter focusses on events that are child-centric as these stakeholders have particularly needs and interests (Séraphin & Green, 2019). Evidence suggests that children prefer to attend events that are performance- or sports-based and involve participation (Foster & Robinson, 2010) plus smaller, community events can be hugely important to a younger audience (Beech, Kaiser, & Kaspar, 2014). Such events can be hugely enjoyable for all members of a family unit, as attending events together increases interaction between family members, helps parents understand their children and creates positive emotions and strong bonds between family members (Liu & Draper, 2022). Additionally, the satisfaction of children will influence parents and carers (Séraphin & Green, 2019), and parents gain satisfaction particularly if the event uses leisure activities that will be intellectually or physically stimulating to children's development (Foster & Robinson, 2010). Events can be valuable for developing children's problem-solving and social skills and in particular can help them to learn how to get along with others (Liu & Draper, 2022).

Across the globe, many societies are now very child-centric and as such the role of children within the community is given much consideration which means that children are major decision-makers within the family group when decisions are made about attending events (Foster & Robinson, 2010). As a distinct and important stakeholder group, event managers need to understand children's particular needs and preferences, and these should be taken into account when planning events (Séraphin & Green, 2019). Ultimately, an event which satisfies children will in turn satisfy their guardians or parents; however, many events and by association, many venues, fail to live up to claims of being family-friendly (Foster & Robinson, 2010) and this may be caused by a poor choice of venue. Choosing a suitable venue for a specific event is a challenge, and given the extensive number of event venues now available, this is potentially a very complex task that requires careful planning (Nolan, 2018). Selecting a venue that will make a suitable backdrop to a child-centric event can be even more challenging as there is much to consider, as this chapter will demonstrate.

Venue Requirements for Child-Centric Events

Event managers have a huge number of potentially suitable venues to choose from in which to stage events; therefore, evaluating venues can be a very time-consuming process as, even for a short and straightforward event, the role of the venue is going to be significant. Choosing an appropriate space for any event includes assessing many variables, but to ensure the venue works well for a child-centric event, the list of variables increases (Pielichaty, Els, Reed, & Mawer, 2016). Firstly, in order to start looking for a venue, it helps if the event manager can estimate the time of year that the event will take place (season or month), an estimation of the number of attendees, the rough outline of the event programme and the budget available as this information will immediately help to narrow down the list of potential venues. Much of the initial search for a venue can be done online. Venue websites can be hugely informative, providing event managers with information on capacity, flow and layout, the availability of furniture and power and catering options. It is often possible to download a brochure as well as take part in a virtual walk around the site. Venue websites are repositories for information such as a technical specification which gives details about available facilities as well as photographs of previous events and testimonials from past clients. Technical specifications (often abbreviated to tech specs) can be quite challenging to understand, even for the most experienced event manager. However, very few venues provide detailed information that relates to the use of the venue for a child-centric event. For example, capacities will be based on adult activities (standing buffets, seated meetings etc.) Ultimately, a site visit of potential sites is essential before making a final choice but evaluating the venue's location, access, facilities, capacity, catering availability, staff and price are an important starting point to create a shortlist (Berners, 2019), and this must be done in relation to the needs of the audience, which in this case will be children and their families or carers.

Location, Access and Local Amenities

Even though the destination for an event may be predetermined (e.g. a specific town or region), this may still leave the event manager with a large number of viable venues to choose from. Thus, the shortlisting process can begin by assessing their locations in relation to on-site and local amenities. It is likely to be very important that families do not have to travel far to attend the event and so it can help to assess venues based on their drop-off and parking facilities at or near the venue as well as local transport provision and the availability of taxis. Many venues are located in areas that are well served by local transport and road networks. Sometimes this is a result of urban development, around historical venues, for example. And sometimes this is by design, as is the case with a number of purpose-built venues that have been located in areas that already have such infrastructure in place (Delaney, 2023). A number of large, international exhibition centres, for example, have been purposely built on sites that are near to motorways, principal railway stations and even international airports. Few venues have, by modern standards, adequate parking spaces and although some venues have their own car parks, these are not necessarily going to be reserved for (or even made available to) event attendees. As such, this is an important question to ask the venue if this information is unclear on their website and it may be important to note how many parent/child spaces are allocated, if any. Additionally, the environs of the venue must be carefully assessed. For example, a venue on a busy road, near a river or with a water feature near the entrance may prove high risk for children.

Access to UK venues has significantly improved in the twenty-first century, and many older buildings have been modified to provide greater ease of access for people with limited mobility or those with prams or buggies through the introduction of lifts and ramps as well as disabled toilets and baby-change facilities (Nolan, 2018). However, some historical venues, including some hotels, visitor attractions and theatres, for example, are unable to alter the infrastructure of the building which means that they may have restricted access and limited facilities. This should be considered as part of the venue selection process as well as the width of entrances to rooms to ensure items such as prams will comfortably fit. Amenities in the vicinity of the venue may be important too, and it can help to assess the number and variety of family-friendly restaurants, hotels, shops, visitor attractions and places of interest nearby. This may be particularly important if the event is short in nature, and families are going to build a day out around the event. Or, conversely, if the event is long and families may wish to stay overnight nearby either before or after the event. Many venues are residential, which means that as well as having function rooms they also offer bedrooms which may be made available to event attendees. Hotels are the obvious example of a residential venue, but a good number of academic, unusual and sporting venues also have accommodation on site. If families are likely to want accommodation, then it will be vital to check on the number and availability of family rooms within a small radius of the event venue. Therefore, in order for a venue to be appropriate for a child-centric event, access for prams (either for children or younger siblings) and the availability of nearby facilities for the whole family must be considered.

Capacity and Flow

Having a rough idea of how many people will attend the event is helpful at the start of the search as the venue's capacity is always going to be key to its suitability to the event. Therefore, when undertaking an initial search, note the venue's overall size as well as the breakdown of the various room capacities. Most venue websites and brochures will give a full breakdown of these capacities as they will vary according to the nature of the room usage and the furniture, equipment and staging being used. For example, an empty room of around 350 square metres may hold 400 people for a reception during which everyone will be mainly standing and chatting. However, if the same room were to be set up with tables and chairs for dinner (known as banquet style), the capacity of the room will be significantly reduced to, perhaps, around 250 people. Naturally, room set-ups that require a lot of chairs and tabling will have smaller capacities than rooms used for dancing, standing or looking at exhibition panels. It is important to note that venue capacities are often worked out based on strict health and safety regulations (Nolan, 2018) and as such, all children will count and even babies that will remain in prams or in the arms of a parent or guardian will still be counted. Few venues calculate capacities based on child-centric events; thus it may be prudent to shortlist venues with large capacities to allow extra space for prams, buggies and the movement of children within rooms.

Another key consideration is if an event requires the fluid movement of a high number of children and parents, from room to room, for example, they will need to be monitored for bottlenecks and overcrowding which can lead to children becoming separated from their families. It is possible to get a fair assessment of the number, size and location of rooms by looking at the venue's floor plan and noting whether or not these rooms are close to each other or even on the same floor. A site visit will determine the number and location of lifts and width of hallways which could be important if there will be a lot of families with prams or buggies in attendance. Most venues can provide scaled floor plans for rooms that are event spaces and suggest how they might be set up. These are also useful for judging the proximity of tables and chairs to the stage which is useful when assessing sightlines for both adults and children of different ages. It is also important to check on room proximity to toilets, baby-change facilities, catering points and the main entrance and assessing how easy or difficult it might be for an adult to move from room to room and supervise their children in the process.

Safeguarding

The National Society for the Prevention of Cruelty to Children (NSPCC) state

> Every organisation has a duty to safeguard children and young people in their care. This includes making sure that all children who attend your events and activities are kept safe, whether they are regular or one-off.
>
> (NSPCC, 2022)

Further NSPCC (2022) guidance confirms that an event organiser should consider interaction between other event attendees, event staff and children. As such, it is prudent to assume the possibility of children coming into contact with unknown adults at the event such as venue staff (receptionists, porters, cleaners, venue managers etc.). Additionally, at child-centric events, it can be very useful for event staff to have access to a private room. A separate space in which lost children can be looked after can be valuable and it is particularly useful if this is a quiet room close to the heart of the event. Unless the event that is going to make full use of all available rooms on site, it is unlikely that the event organiser will have exclusive use of the venue. There may be several other events taking place in parallel, and of course the venue may also be in use in relation to its primary function (e.g. a museum may have private event spaces within a building which is otherwise open to the public). Therefore, it is important to discuss safeguarding with the venue management. Additionally, it is important to look at the entrance to the venue and the internal layout of rooms. If the venue has one main entrance, this will probably have to be shared with other users. Similarly, it is common in venues to share lifts, toilets, restaurants and other facilities with other users of the building. As such, safeguarding of children must be considered early on in the venue selection process, and if total privacy is essential to the event, then these considerations must be made early on. Ultimately, it is essential to ensure provision for lost children at the venue which can be managed by appropriately trained professionals (Pielichaty et al., 2016). This does usually mean that Disclosure and Barring Service (DBS) checks will be required for staff as part of event preparation (Ryan, 2021).

Facilities, Catering, Decor and Theming

It is important to assess what other facilities the venue has and can make available to an event and its attendees such as the number of tables and chairs on site. Additionally, the availability of booster seats, highchairs and low-rise tables may be an important consideration. Although the catering elements of the event may be discussed and finalised sometime after the venue has been booked, it is a good idea to weigh up the catering options at each venue as part of the initial assessment. This can be a surprisingly complex process and it is worth investigating whether the venue has its own catering team which is common (Berners, 2019). In-house catering is a standard practise at many venues such as hospitality providers and common at a good number of academic, sporting and unusual venues and usually, if the venue has a catering team on site, the event manager is going to be obliged to use them for the provision of all refreshments at the event. Although there is usually room to negotiate with the team on catering charges, this is going to be restricted by the fact that once the venue has been chosen, the choice of caterer is nil. An early discussion to assess the venue's experience of catering for children will be important, and considerations such as child menus and facilities for heating milk and baby food may form part of the discussion. There are a growing number of suppliers to the events industry, in the form of specialised catering as well as the provision of decorations, theming and props, and the venue should be able to make appropriate recommendations based on their previous encounters with suppliers.

As well as the overall size of the venue and individual room capacities, it is important to assess the architecture, design and layout of buildings. Modern-day and purpose-built venues are typically less adorned and more likely to have well-proportioned and regular-shaped internal rooms. Large or neutral spaces which provide a completely blank canvas for an event can facilitate the adaptation of the room to any given theme. The design of the venue itself will influence not only the experience of the audience but also their emotions, and therefore, the theme of the event should be carefully matched to an appropriate venue (Ferdinand & Kitchin, 2017). For example, a historical venue may have creaking doors, dark corridors with nooks and crannies that enhance ghostly themed events while a famous sporting venue may be filled with competition memorabilia that imbue a sense of glorious determination that will complement a celebratory or a competitive event. Some venues, such as the Sydney Opera House, have such a distinctive design and façade that the image of the venue is instantly recognisable the world over. In terms of child-centric events, evidence suggests that they should be creatively and innovatively themed (Liu & Draper, 2022), and unusual and historic venues may be full of quirky features and require little theming. However, they can have strict rules against the use of decorations, covering floors and walls, poor lighting and limited temperature control (Matthews, 2017). Some venues may have items of furniture that cannot be removed as well as fireplaces, arches and columns which may be attractive but not suitable for family events. Conversely, transforming a bland venue into a meaningful and enticing event space for children could be more appropriate but overall could cost more money. On balance, many visitor attractions make excellent locations for events as typically their day-to-day operations are designed around families. For example, museums and theme parks target families and ensure that their facilities (access, toilets, furniture, food, exhibitions, rides) are suitable for children. Consequently, public and private events held in these venues can be very successful for family events. Nonetheless, to effectively plan a child-centred event, there is much to be considered when shortlisting potential venues and these variables are illustrated in Table 1.

Types of Event Venues

The number of venues that have been principally designed to host events is increasing globally (Delaney, 2023). Additionally, many non-purpose-built venues have diversified and can be privately hired for events. As such, there are essentially five types of venues that can be used to host events; purpose-built event venues, hospitality providers, academic institutions, sporting venues and unique venues and these are illustrated in Fig. 1 with examples of each.

Every venue will be unique, however each type of venue may share certain characteristics that can have a significant impact on how the venue is used as the setting for an event (Nolan, 2020) and these attributes should be incorporated into event design (An, Kim, & Hur, 2021). Thus, assessing the commonly shared characteristics of each venue type can be a time saver when reducing hundreds of potential venues into a shortlist.

Table 1. Key Venue Considerations for Child-Centric Events.

Location, Access and Local Amenities	• Distance to attend the event • Drop-off and parking facilities • Local transport provision • Availability of taxis • Environs (e.g., proximity to traffic or water) • Lifts and ramps at venue • Disabled toilets and baby change facilities • Width of entrances to rooms • Number and variety of family-friendly restaurants, hotels, shops, visitor attractions and places of interest nearby • Number and availability of family rooms within a small radius of the event venue.
Capacity and Flow	• Venue's overall size • Number, capacity and location of rooms • Number and location of lifts • Width of hallways • Sightlines for adults and children • Room proximity to toilets, baby change facilities, catering points and the main entrance
Safeguarding	• Availability of a lost child/quiet room
Facilities, Catering, Decor and Theming	• Number of tables and chairs • Availability of booster seats, highchairs and low-rise tables • Catering options (e.g. child menus) • Facilities for heating milk/baby food • Architecture and design of buildings • Rules on decoration and theming, lighting and temperature control

Source: The author.

Purpose-Built Venues

Purpose-built conference and exhibition centres offer many benefits to event planners as they have been designed to facilitate the set-up, running and break down of large and complex events (Matthews, 2017). As such, they usually have service roads and large dock doors big enough to allow large pieces of equipment or vehicles inside. Floor loading limits and ceiling heights will typically be greater than in any other type of venue, and there will be a number of entrances and exits. Exhibition halls in particular will be huge and empty spaces which provide a

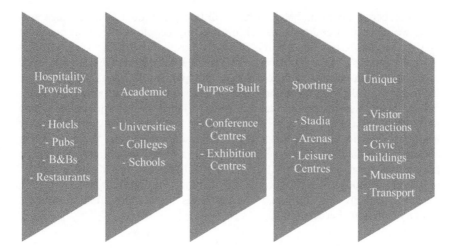

Fig. 1. Types of Event Venues (Adapted from Nolan, 2018). *Source:*
The author.

completely blank canvas for each event and sound, lighting and temperature control as well as the flow of delegates can be well managed in these spaces (Nolan, 2018). Additionally, communal facilities in purpose-built event venues have been typically well designed for event attendees with plenty of step-free entrances, lifts, toilets and baby-change facilities. However, these are usually shared between conference and exhibition halls (and therefore between events). Thus, these are not always the best choice of venue for child-centric events as shared facilities may not be ideal and there is also a high cost to theme these spaces including the standard carpeting required to cover their exposed floors (Davidson & Hyde, 2014).

Accommodation Providers

Hotels are perhaps the most popular venues with meeting planners around the world due to their ease of use and functionality (Quinn, 2013). Hotels, bed and breakfasts (B&Bs), pubs, inns, restaurants and cafes will typically have a fully operational catering facility on site, and venues with onsite accommodation can suit a variety of events. However, although many hospitality venues have separate function rooms, which can sometimes be hired for free for fully catered events, there can be a disparity between the capacity of the function space and the number of bedrooms at the venue. As a result, some hotels can accommodate large events but can only provide bedrooms for some of the attendees and may have a limited number of family rooms.

A number of hotels and some B&Bs will have additional facilities, such as a pool, which may of course be useful in attracting people to the event but these may or may not be open to children. Similarly, hospitality providers can be found in rural locations as well as town and city venues and therefore they can suit, or be unsuitable for, a number of different types of child-centric events, depending on the location of the target audience and the availability of transport to the destination. Many historic inns and taverns have survived for centuries and continue to operate today as pubs with facilities for many types of small events. They may not seem like an obvious choice for child-based events, but they are worth considering as they typically have private function rooms which can frequently be hired at no charge providing the food service facilities will be well used or that the on-site accommodation will be occupied by overnighting event attendees. Meeting space is effectively sold at a loss, to fill bedrooms and therefore fulfil the venue's primary function (Berners, 2019).

Unique Venues

One of the benefits of using historical and unusual venues is that they can often be full of original features and still convey a sense of power or excitement and their appeal lies in their ability to impress adults and children alike. Matthews (2017, p. 172) refers to unique venues as ritualised spaces which have retained 'a certain mystique' and as such, their features can influence the ambiance of an event. However, one must be mindful that historical venues can have many drawbacks as mentioned earlier in this chapter; additionally they can have limited AV facilities, restricted access for equipment and limited parking (Beech et al., 2014). Additionally, many of these venues can only be hired in the evening and for short periods of time or only in the daytime (e.g. cinemas and theatres), thus limiting their appeal for certain types of events.

A number of unusual venues, such as museums, will have very strict rules to protect their artefacts and exhibits. This may prevent the event manager from moving existing equipment or furniture and there may be restrictions as to what can put on floors and walls. The capacities of some unusual venues may be quite generous in total but many are designed to move small numbers of people around the site quickly, such as in-visitor attractions, and therefore these spaces may not work for events that are going to incorporate lots of performance, sports or participation which tend to be popular types of events with children and parents (Foster & Robinson, 2010).

Sporting Venues

In general, sporting venues have much to offer event managers due to their extensive facilities (Berners, 2019). While the outdoor seating and pitch area of the stadium provide a generous capacity for large-scale music concerts or activities, many sporting venues have a plethora of smaller rooms used for match-day hospitality and these are suited to small events. Generally, these spaces are not used outside of sporting competitions and tournaments and therefore any revenue generated through private events is extra and as such it may be possible to negotiate excellent rates for hiring the facilities (Nolan, 2018). Typically sporting venues have strong transport links owing to their suburban locations and generous onsite facilities such as toilets and lifts. Although the availability of these venues may be a little restricted, there will usually be plenty of scope to host events outside of competition time and around training sessions. Nonetheless, such venues can lack ambience for events held on non-match days when the larger venues lack the atmosphere and frisson created by thousands of fans, and using arenas and stadia can be a challenge in terms of creating memorable events (Matthews, 2017). Thus, they make viable spaces for a variety of child-centric events but the pros and cons of sporting venues must be weighed up.

Academic Venues

There are more than 150 universities operating in the United Kingdom alone (Statista, 2022), which primarily offer higher education, but typically they also have a specialist events team dedicated to promoting the use of their campuses to event planners. A number of academic venues have invested heavily in their facilities in recent years in a direct attempt to attract event planners (Nolan, 2020) and academic venues can be very suited to many types of events. Most educational establishments will be made up of a large number of lecture halls and seminar rooms all equipped with lecterns, microphones, projectors and screens. Campuses are generally well designed to support the flow of people and have excellent on-site catering, transport links and parking. Once again, as many of these venues would otherwise go unused out of term time, they can offer competitive hire charges. Primary and secondary schools are likely to be very secure properties that have the furniture and facilities for children and as such they can be ideal for child-centric events. However, they may lack the wow factor for families who already spend much of their time in such buildings. Additionally, it is worth noting that while universities may be somewhat more interesting and may boast of their ample, onsite and very reasonably priced accommodation for event guests to use, these are likely to be mostly if not all single rooms. Table 1 illustrates some suggestions of appropriate venues for child-centric events which are all UK venues with 'Fantastic for Families' accreditation from the Family Arts Campaign. This organisation is supported by Arts Council England and recognises organisations that are committed to providing exemplary experiences for families (Family Arts Campaign, 2022) (Table 2).

Conclusion

Many events marketed to families have been described as 'disappointing' due to a lack of consideration of the particular needs of children when planning the event and choosing the venue. The venue will play a substantial role in any event and typically, attendees will form an opinion of the suitability of the venue in terms of

Table 2. Venues With 'Fantastic for Families' Accreditation.

	Name of Venue	Location	Website
Hospitality Providers	Tapton Hall	Sheffield	https://taptonhall.com/about.html
Academic Venues	Royal Welsh College of Music and Drama	Cardiff	https://www.rwcmd.ac.uk/who-we-are/hire-us
Purpose-Built Venues	Bournemouth International Centre	Bournemouth	https://www.bic.co.uk/conferencing/our-spaces
Sporting Venues	Mountbatten	Portsmouth	https://www.bhliveactive.org.uk/centres/mountbatten-leisure-centre/
Unique Venues	Courtyard, Hereford	Hereford	https://www.courtyard.org.uk/venue-hire/

Source: The author (Adapted from Family Arts Campaign, 2022).

its location, access and facilities. This chapter has demonstrated that venue selection should involve assessing these attributes as well as the venue's capacity, catering options decor and safeguarding options. In particular, when assessing venue suitability, event mangers should consider the availability of parent/child parking bays, baby change facilities, the width of hallways and availability of lifts, sightlines for children and the number of booster seats, highchairs and low-rise tables. Additionally, it is prudent to check on rules for decorating and theming venues, facilities for heating milk and baby food and the proximity of the venue to family-friendly restaurants, attractions and accommodation providers.

Many event spaces claim to be suitable for a range of events, and this chapter has discussed typical challenges of choosing to host an event in a purpose-built, academic, sporting or unusual venue or in a venue that is primarily a provider of hospitality. These can include a lack of sole use of the venue, high costs, restrictions on decor and theming, and limited ambience. Thus, this chapter demonstrates that to effectively plan a child-centric event, time and thought must be devoted to a thorough assessment of venues in order to find a suitable space that works for the audience.

References

An, J., Kim, H., & Hur, D. (2021). Keeping the competitive edge of a convention and exhibition center in MICE environment: Identification of event attributes for long-run success. *Sustainability*, *13*. doi:10.3390/su13095030

Beech, J. G., Kaiser, S., & Kaspar, R. (2014). *The business of events management.* Harlow: Pearson.

Berners, P. (2019). *The practical guide to managing event venues.* London: Routledge.

Davidson, R., & Hyde, A. (2014). *Winning meetings & events for your venue.* Oxford: Goodfellows.

Delaney, E. (2023). The role of DMOs in business events. In C. Arcodia (Ed.), *The Routledge handbook of business events.* Abingdon: Routledge.

Family Arts Campaign. (2022). Your directory for fantastic arts providers, venues & organisations! Retrieved from https://www.familyarts.co.uk/fantastic-for-families/. Accessed on August 13, 2022.

Ferdinand, N., & Kitchin, P. (2017). *Events management: An international approach* (2nd ed.). London: SAGE.

Foster, K., & Robinson, P. (2010). A critical analysis of the motivational factors that influence event attendance in family groups. *Event Management, 14,* 107–125.

Liu, Y., & Draper, J. (2022). The influence of attending festivals with children on family quality of life, subjective well-being & event experience. *Event Management, 26,* 25–40.

Matthews, D. (2017). *Special event production; the process* (2nd ed.). London: Routledge.

National Society for the Prevention of Cruelty to Children (NSPCC). (2022). Safeguarding children & child protection. Retrieved from https://learning.nspcc.org.uk/safeguarding-child-protection. Accessed on August 12, 2022.

Nolan, E. (2018). *Working with venues for events; A practical guide.* London: Routledge.

Nolan, E. (2020). The supply and design of different types of venues for business events. *International Journal of Tourism Cities, 6*(4), 691–710.

Pielichaty, H., Els, G., Reed, I., & Mawer, V. (2016). *Events project management.* London: Routledge.

Quinn, B. (2013). *Key concepts in event management.* London: SAGE.

Ryan, W. G. (2021). *Managing international events.* Abingdon: Routledge.

Séraphin, H., & Green, S. (2019). The significance of the contribution of children to conceptualising the destination of the future. *International Journal of Tourism Cities, 5*(4), 544–559.

Statista. (2022). Number of universities & higher education institutions in the United Kingdom from 2010/11 to 2018/19. Retrieved from https://www.statista.com/statistics/915603/universities-in-the-united-kingdom-uk/#:~:text=There%20were%20164%20universities%20&,with%20the%20previous%20academic%20year. Accessed on September 8, 2022.

Chapter 10

Sports Events and Children: ReesLeisure Management Approach

Abi Knapton

Abstract

This chapter explores some of the key operational steps and marketing activity required to organise a children's sports events based on the experience of event management company ReesLeisure. The chapter highlights the importance of conducting research pre-event, creating robust event aims, developing a target market, marketing the event correctly, working with competent suppliers, hiring the correct number of staff and having the vital paperwork and policies in place. It explores some of the barriers and challenges that organisers face and have to work through when organising events for children.

Keywords: Sports events; children; ReesLeisure; system management; successful experience; event operations

Introduction

ReesLeisure (RL) is a sports events management company based in Hampshire. RL has designed, built and operated some of the South's largest sporting events such as the ABP Southampton Marathon, Winchester Half Marathon, Southampton Sporterium and TryTri Events. Sport events can directly impact the quality of life of people living in the host communities; this can lead to positive or negative outcomes, and if the event is continuous and sustained, the outcomes can be named as 'legacies' in a local area (Taks, Chalip, & Green, 2015). RL aims to provide great competition for serious athletes, fun for youngsters and families, and provides the right environment for those new to sport to thrive. They also offer sponsorship opportunities for brands and businesses enabling them to reach thousands of people. RL works closely with the communities in the area and helps charities raise money for their individual causes. At each RL event, there are a range of ages and abilities taking part from 2 to 82, and no matter if it is

Events Management for the Infant and Youth Market, 153–167

Copyright © 2023 Abi Knapton

Published under exclusive licence by Emerald Publishing Limited

doi:10.1108/978-1-80455-690-020231018

someone's first event or their 50th, RL aims to supply everyone with a welcoming event environment.

This chapter is about the management of children's events particularly in the sports event sector. RL currently operates the ABP Southampton Fun Run, Winchester Children's Triathlon, Southampton Sporterium (Cycling) Youth Races and Family Ride. These events run alongside, and are an off shoot of, the already established adult races, and they aim to involve a whole family in the event weekend. This chapter will cover some of the key operational steps required to deliver a children's event from the experience of RL. Also, marketing and event messaging tactics RL has used and other experiences RL has had as a sports event organiser. Steps from this chapter can be used to aid a new event's organiser looking to organise a children's event.

Aims and Target Audience

Before starting the process of organising an event, the type of event, target participation group and achievable aims of the event have to be decided. The type of event organised will depend on the desired event location in the country. It is beneficial for the organiser to conduct extensive research in the proposed area. For example, are there already events with a similar design taking place in the area? This could be positive or negative for the event suggestion. Is there a need or want in the local area? Speak to sports clubs, schools, residents, local council and key local influencers to gauge interest and potential support. What is the age of the local community, and are there enough young people and children to make the event viable?

Research into the potential event location will then help develop the demographic of the event participants so attendees can be targeted and thus a target market created.

The target market and the communities in the event location must see value in supporting the event (Booth, 2010); hence, aims need to be established. These could include:

- Promoting a healthy lifestyle and the importance of exercise at a younger age
- Involving local youth sports clubs to take part in an event
- Providing youth sports competition in a local area where competition may be lacking or needs further additions
- New challenges for children to participate in
- Involving the community, boosting local community spirit
- Team-building

The Southampton Sporterium (Fig. 1) has been used as an example.

What (Event Type) – The event is a set of criterium races in Southampton City Centre where riders compete for a set amount of time on a lapped closed road circuit. Youth Riders aged 8–16 take part against people of the same category (age and gender). The Southampton Sporterium is part of a regional race series

Fig. 1.　Southampton Sporterium Youth Races.

affiliated with British Cycling. Riders collect points throughout the year of racing to move up the rankings which opens up further competition opportunities for the rider.

It was discovered that there was a lack of large city centre cycle road races where riders are competing on closed city streets within the region and nationally. With existing connections in the city of Southampton with the organisation of the ABP Southampton Marathon, the Sporterium was a beneficial addition to the Southampton events calendar and allows more opportunities for involvement in sports events, especially for young people and children.

Who (Participants) – Cycle clubs with a large youth membership within the South region; riders must be a British Cycling member.

Aims

- Showcase youth racing within Southampton and across the region
- Involvement of national and local cycle clubs for healthy competition
- Engage with local community groups
- Showcase local talent
- Encourage spectators to visit
- Boost local economy through participants using local accommodation and spending in restaurants, cafes and bars

Event Messaging

As there is such a spread of sporting ability amongst children, it can be challenging for event organisers to find the correct balance between a competitive event and a welcoming first-time event.

Many children that take part have no event experience but want to give their first triathlon or running event a go. For these children, RL is extremely warm and welcoming, ensuring that children feel comfortable and understand the rules and layout of the event. One way RL does this is by offering a team lane option in their triathlons where children can choose to swim with three friends or family members. As this is the first section of their triathlon, having the team lane option can ease them in and make the starting experience less daunting by starting with family and friends.

Conversely, RL has younger and older children who compete throughout the year, are part of sports clubs who train regularly, may have parents that participate in the certain sport already and have parents that are pushing them to do more. For these children to be interested in and want to attend RL events, RL must enable them access to the correct level of competition. A sector of the older children in this category, especially those in their early teens are often looking for adult events to achieve that level of competition. However, they may be prevented and restricted by Sport Governing Body rules and regulations. Therefore, RL ensures that they supply these children with a challenge and allows them to succeed while making sure the event is a safe, child-friendly space which adheres to rules and guidance.

RL has found that taking part in events can help children develop positive planning and preparation habits from an early age. When taking part in the triathlon, children must switch between swimming, cycling and running with minimal support from their parents. This helps to teach them key organisational life skills as they have to plan out and prep everything for each section of the event. Even if they are supported by their parents pre-event, on the day, management of their race is completely down to the child. For the organiser, this is where pre-event instructional videos within event marketing may be helpful to prepare children.

Supporting Parents

Ultimately, parents are putting their trust in the event organiser to keep their child safe. It is crucial for event information and timings to be clear and for contact details of the event organiser to be easily accessible. If the information provided is clear and there are good channels of communication, parents are going to find it easier to put their trust in the organiser and sign their child up.

Venue

Without a venue there is no event and finding a suitable venue for a children's event can have more challenges due to the extra safety measures and features that need to be included. There are options with choosing a venue, and based on the experience, RL would opt for private sites that are hireable or public areas of a city. It is great when RL can have an event that allows an element of participation for children. The event can then advertise to and involve the whole family. However, this isn't always possible and RL needs to gauge, as organisers, whether it is feasible and safe to also have children competing at the event.

The Winchester Triathlon is conducted at a school in Winchester. Some of the route for competing adult triathletes is within and around the school, but there is an element of the route on open, public roads. However, for the children, the event can be conducted entirely within the school boundary; they do not have to leave the site or compete on any open roads which is an ideal situation. As organisers, RL wants to duplicate this layout to other venues and locations as it is a method that works. However, when visiting other venues, RL has found that having a children's event isn't always feasible due to the logistics and layouts of the site.

Site visits are crucial when identifying potential sites so that the organiser can get a feel for the venue and how the participants and spectators will flow through the site. It is beneficial to create a set of criteria of what is needed, as this allows the organiser to easily compare one site to the other and identify the best event venue (Greenwell, Danzey-Bussell, & Shonk, 2019).

Specific criteria to think about includes:

- Access to the site by car and public transport
- Is there a car park on site and is the car park in close proximity to the event registration and start
- Available indoor and outdoor space in the case of adverse weather
- Changing facilities and number of toilets – extra toilets may need to be ordered to the event site.
- Space for spectators in key areas such as start and finish as this is a children's event there are likely to be more spectators per participant
- Route planning – how many signs are needed
- Exit and entry points

Many events that RL organises are in city centres on public sites and roads with no event boundary or fencing. Therefore, for the children's element of the event, RL has to make sure that children are contained safely within the event site. This is the case for the ABP Southampton Fun Run. During the event RL works closely with infrastructure suppliers and extra barriers are built to create designated, safe waiting areas for children participating. These areas are often marked with bright coloured branding and flags, so they are easily identified by the children and parents.

Event Management Plan

A successful event must have a sound event management plan covering all organisational and safety aspects.

This includes but is not limited to:

- Detailed Event Risk Assessment – It outlines all hazards at the event within the main site and on any routes and aid stations
- Staff Organisational Chart – How is the hierarchy of staff on event day structured?
- Waste Management Plan – How will you manage the disposal of waste on site? How many items of waste will need disposing of? Will you need to hire external waste management systems? How could you make the event more sustainable?
- Adverse Weather Plans – It is the policy of RL to monitor the weather forecasts for two weeks prior to an event and ensure that appropriate contingency plans are written and in place for all weather conditions. Should these forecasts predict hazardous weather, then the appropriate actions will be taken in order to prepare the site. If dangerous or severe weather is forecast, then the event will be cancelled or postponed. Should the conditions on site become inclement without warning, then the appropriate action will be taken as detailed in the contingency plan.
- Site Plan
- Lost Child Policy – Paramount at all events but particularly important at a children's event is a Lost Child Policy

Lost Child Policy

LOST Child – A carer/parent/guardian who has lost their child.
   FOUND Child – A child who has lost their carer/parent/guardian.
   All events must have a designated Lost Child Point which is always staffed by a Disclosure and Barring Service (DBS) checked member of the events team.
   The RL Lost Child Policy is as follows:
   Procedure for dealing with a carer that has lost their child – LOST CHILD.

Initial Steps

- Inform event control immediately in coded language
- Always refer to a lost child as a LOST MOSES
- Take Carer to Lost Children Point (staffed by DBS checked member of the events team)
- Gain description of the child and complete section 1 of Lost Children sheet (Table 1)
- Explain to carer what is being done to help
- Do not make rash promises

Initiating a Search

- Inform event control and give description
- Event control to alert all staff in relevant areas, giving description
- At least one staff member to remain at Lost Children Point with carer

Table 1. Description of Missing Child (to Be Logged With Event Control).

Name
Gender
Age
Build
Height
Hair colour
Hair style
Eye colour
Distinguishing features (moles, scars, glasses)
Contact number
Called at
Clothing: Top, bottom, footwear
Medical concerns
Any other information
Name of person reporting
Time of report

Source: The author.

If Child Is Located

- Inform event control
- Confirm identity of child
- Inform carer that child has been found
- Escort child to the carer
- Confirm ID of carer
- Complete section two of Control Sheet and file in event folder for six months (Table 2)
- If the child is unwilling to reunite with the carer, inform Event Control and do not release child. Contact police if necessary

Table 2. Reunited Confirmation.

Reunited with
Relation to child
Contact number
ID checked?
Event control signed off?
All staff stood down (time)

Source: The author.

If Child Is Not Located

- If after 10 minutes, the child is not located Project Manager to contact the police
- Please note that the length of time for this is to be assessed on an individual basis (for example, can be longer for a competent 15-year-old etc.)
- Inform carer of actions being taken
- Staff and volunteers to continue search
- One staff member to remain with carer until child located or police take control of situation
  Procedure for dealing with a child that has lost their carer – FOUND CHILD.

Initial Steps

- Inform event control in coded language of the potential lost child
- Always refer to a found child as a FOUND MOSES
- Report location and description of child to Event Control

Approaching the Child

- Get down to the child's height, smile and introduce yourself
- Do not give the child any food or drink
- Avoid physical contact unless to prevent potential harm

Gaining Information

- Ask simple questions to identify/locate carer, e.g. where did you last see them? What are their names? What are they wearing?

If Carer Located

- Do not release to anyone under 18
- Inform event control of reunion
- Confirm ID of carer
- Complete section two of Control Sheet and file in event folder for six months (Table 2)
- If the child is unwilling to reunite with the carer, inform Event Control and do not release child
- Contact police if necessary

If Carer Not Located

- Confirm with control and give description of child
- Take child to designated Lost Child Point (with two DBS checked members of staff)
- Complete section one of Control Sheet
- Control to make PA announcement (Do NOT release child's identity)
- Child to remain at designated place with two staff members, one of the same gender (both DBS checked)
- Inform child of actions being taken

- If carer not found after 20 minutes, contact police
- Event control to explain all information gained. Please note that the length of time for this is to be assessed on an individual basis (for example, can be longer for a competent 15-year-old etc.)

For this policy to be in place successfully, all core event staff must be briefed effectively on relevant policies pre-event. All information will need to be safely secured for six months by the core events team; this is in case it needs to be further investigated by the police and so that a record is kept by the event.

The NSPCC Child Protection in Sport Unit (CPSU) has developed a document on the safeguarding of children at different sporting events; this ranges from small scale, less formal events to large international children's events. It mentions such measures as having a lead member of staff for safeguarding at the event, the safe recruitment of volunteers and the layout of the event site (NSPCC, 2017). Below are examples of some of the measures RL have in place at events to safeguard children and young people. All participants, no matter their age, are allocated a race number which is linked to all of their details. This is beneficial in a Found Child situation as event control are able to find the child's name and details along with their emergency contact who can then be reached.

At the ABP Southampton Fun Run, the accompanying parent/guardian to each child is given a coloured wrist band with a number matching the child's unique race number. Children are only released from the enclosed Finish Distribution area to the parent/guardian with the matching number on their wristband. No child is released to anyone under the age of 18, and marshals are positioned at the entry/exit point ensuring that children are released to the correct person.

Registration Systems

RL uses a secure online registration system to collect data and key information for all event participants. For children, it is extremely important to ensure that this information is completed and correct. Registration reports of all key information are downloadable from the online system and these can be secured in event control for the prompt finding of necessary information on event day. The online registration form itself must be filled out by a child's parent/guardian and this applies to anyone under the age of 18. This is RL policy across all events, and it ensures that the correct information is given to us.

Certain key information that we collect is as follows.

- Emergency contact details, name and phone number of a responsible parent/guardian above the age of 18. This person must not be taking part in the event themselves in the case of an emergency or a found child situation
- Social media and photo permission. Parents/guardians must sign a waiver/agreement to whether or not they give permission for photos of their child at the event to be used in potential future marketing material.

- Clear and strict age limits must be in place and visible on the event registration form, this is not only for a child's safety but also to ensure that events abide by Sporting National Governing Body rules such as UK Athletics and British Cycling (age limit advice can be found on their website for each race discipline and type)

Event Day Timings and Set-Up

As expected, children often take longer to do a certain task than adults do. This being the case, RL always allows plenty of time for set-up on the event morning and, if possible, conduct as much of the set-up the day before. This means that RL has more time on event day to ensure that all children are correctly briefed as they need more support and guidance than adults. Also, this allows families to walk around the site and route pre-event to gauge where everything is before they compete. This is encouraged by the events team on the day, where safe, as it makes the children a lot more comfortable and avoids confusion.

During briefings, when explaining rules and regulations to children, RL makes sure that the regulations are simplified enough for children to understand and are delivered in an enthusiastic way, and this is a good way to support children (Vaillancourt & Cameron, 2021). Conversely, RL still makes sure children understand the importance of following rules and regulations for their own health and safety. The message has to come across as serious, so they know the importance but friendly so that they are not scared or discouraged. This again is a careful balance for the event organiser to make sure that the right person is delivering the instructions.

RL often finds that colour coordinating areas with flags and branding is easier for children to understand and simplifies the race. For example, at the RL children's triathlon, there are blue flags for the pool, yellow flags for the cycle and red flags in transition. This also makes it easier for RL to explain in event briefings.

Marshal Support

It is key to have plenty of marshal support at an event; at all levels of sport, volunteers are crucial and central to development (Hoy, Cuskelly, Auld, Kappelides, & Misener, 2019) At a children's event, due to the nature of the participants and event they are marshalling, marshals must be helpful, friendly and approachable at all times. The organiser must also make sure they are briefed in all event information and any relevant safeguarding policies and understand the importance of these.

On a run route or cycle route, marshals should be placed at all turnings on the course and roughly every 10m apart from each other, this is so children can always see a marshal ahead of them for reassurance and to direct them the right way. Where possible, it is beneficial to have marshals in teams of two so if there is a problem on the course one marshal can be helping the situation with the other still supporting the other participants on the route.

Other key support staff would include lead bikes and sweeper bikes and sweeper walkers to walk at the back with any younger or slower participants.

Suppliers, Contractors and Consultants

The RL events team are always supported by a proficient team of existing suppliers, contractors and consultants to aid with the operational side of the events. It is crucial that suppliers meet budget requirements and environmental targets. RL has tendered, commissioned and worked with suppliers and contractors with a wealth of event experience on a national scale.

Health and Safety

RL works with an event health and safety consultancy to investigate and oversee the overall health and safety of the event; this is especially important for events involving children.

All event suppliers must submit a risk assessment method statement (RAMS) and their public liability insurance pre-event. Depending on the supplier, further documentation is required relevant to the work carried out. For example, wind loading or competency certificates/cards. The safety consultants will also inspect the event management plan.

The health and safety consultancy will also provide a health and safety officer for the events to oversee all infrastructure and site build and rectify any issues during this process. The health and safety consultant will report any problems to the event manager and will send a report post event which can be used for continuous event improvement.

Infrastructure

The event site and any route infrastructure at the event are always supplied and built by a competent supplier. RL makes sure a detailed production schedule is created. For this supplier, RL has a loading/storage yard within close proximity to the event site. This area keeps all loading vehicles for the event and any extra infrastructure and barriers. This area is secured and fenced off to the public to aid their safety and the security of the equipment. Depending on the size of an event, this may not be necessary, but it is always important to have an area designated for event equipment to be stored so participants, spectators and staff are all safe at the event.

Medical

It is crucial to have competent medical support at an event, at RL events they are responsible for:

- Overseeing the event medical planning, provision and review
- Creating and delivering the event medical plan.

- Collating a relevant summary of medical activity
- Provision of medical personnel
- Operating a clinical support line which can be utilised by any event medical personnel to seek advice, input, shared decision-making or referral of patients
- Facilitating a documented and governed model for input into decisions to refer patients to a NHS facility and/or discharge of patients who have been unwell
- The clinical leadership of the event medical provision and specialist medical input into the event planning and management process.

Event Control

The event control room is a controlled environment with a few management personnel, control room assistants and the medical team. Their role is to deal with any problems arisen on the course or event village effectively and efficiently.

A clear structure of communications is implemented at RL events to ensure relevant and accurate information is being relayed to event control via radio communications. Radio logs are recorded as well as traffic and medical operators collecting their own logs for reference post event.

Briefings are given to all volunteers on radio to ensure that they are comfortable using the radio system and are informed of necessary communication channels.

Sustainability

Sustainability is a topical subject not just in the current climate, but it has become a key concept in event management (Allen et al., 2022). Therefore, as organisers RL needs to keep up with trends and discussions to make sure the event is reaching the required sustainability standards where it can. This isn't just for adult events, there are things that can be in place at children's events to hit sustainability standards, as follows:

- RL has recently been using recyclable water pouches at events and in their production, 82% less plastic is used than in conventional PET bottles (Drinq, 2017)
- Extra food left over from the event (including bananas) is donated to local food banks post event.
- Participants are given a free swim hat at triathlons which they are encouraged to reuse
- Many event vehicles are either hybrid or electric models
- Branding and signage reused at each event

Marketing Tactics

There are many ways that an event can be promoted and targeted. For children's events, organisers spend more time marketing to parents than the children taking

Fig. 2. ABP Southampton Fun Run.

part as ultimately, they will be the ones making the final decision to participate. Targeting parents that are already interested in sports, part of a running or cycling club or have taken part in RL events already is much more likely to encourage and enter their children in events too. Therefore, a key tactic for RL is to promote and market their children's events to adult participants already signed up. RL uses the messaging of making the event a family day out where everyone can take part in something. Many children who compete in the triathlon have parents competing the same day. A lot of ABP Fun Run (Fig. 2) participants run with their mum or dad who has done one of the longer distances and many Youth Sporterium Riders are part of the same cycle club as their parent!

Working With Schools

For the ABP Southampton Fun Run, RL has previously run a 'Schools Challenge' within Southampton. Prizes were awarded on the event day to the school that had the largest percentage of their pupils competing and for the fastest child in each year group across all schools. Visits were made by the events team to the schools throughout the year to encourage as many children to take part. The idea of a reward and competing against other schools was a huge motivation for children to take part. Partnering with schools is a great way to tap into the local parent community, many of whom may also be involved with other local sports clubs, work for local charities or work for big corporations for potential sponsorship conversations. This is particularly advantageous for new events in an area to make the much needed connections and develop a network.

Furthermore, word of mouth among parents within school communities and sports clubs is a great way to spread news of new events and for parents to speak of their experiences at an event. However, this can either help or hinder an event. If parents feel their child has had a great experience at an event, they can positively spread this news to others in the community. However, bad experiences will also spread through the school community which will have damaging effects on the event reputation.

In order to capture feedback on event experience, RL sends out post-event emails with a link to review events on 'RaceCheck'; this can then be analysed and collated to find common trends at the event to make improvements for the following year.

Medal Discounts

Separate to marketing the actual event, when organising an event in a city RL wants to be a positive influence and benefits the city where possible. In Southampton, RL organises a Medal Discount Scheme where local businesses offer discounts to medal holders from the event. These offers and businesses are then promoted on pre-event emails, social media and a designated 'Medal Discounts' page on the event website. This has proven to be extremely beneficial to both parties involved as it encouraged runners to stay in the area after the race to take advantage of the discounts thus filling seats and tables in the local facilities. For children's events it is great to get child-friendly brands and businesses involved in a scheme similar to this, as not only will families appreciate the offered discounts but the scheme also promotes the brand straight to the target audience. For example, RL has previously had a Go Ape offer discount for all medal holders.

Conclusion

Overall, managing a children's event can come not only with its challenges but also with its benefits. Young people and children are being given a chance to access an event, achieve a new goal and reach new challenges. Important things to consider are the size and amenities of a venue, the calibre of staff and ensuring you have the right policies in place for everybody's safety.

The future of children's events is definitely expanding, new venues are opening, better training is in place to ensure that the events are safe for children, and more opportunities for children to take part in sport from an early age are developing. Organisers must ensure they watch current trends to stay visible in the event marketplace; with more event, there is further competition.

RL plans to continue developing their offering of children's events; it is beneficial to provide opportunities for children to participate and challenge themselves. Ultimately, the joy and excitement that many children have when they cross the line or start their first race is a contagious feeling and provides a feeling of positive fulfilment for all those involved.

References

Allen, J., Harris, R., Jago, L., Tantrai, A., Jonson, P., & D'Arcy, E. (2022). *Festival and special events management* (Essentials ed., 1st ed.). Milton: John Wiley & Sons.

Booth, A. (2010). Developing the event concept. In P. Robinson, D. Wale, & G. Dickson (Eds.), *Events management* (pp. 19–31). Wallingford: CABI.

Drinq. (2017). A new standard for environmentally friendly water consumption during sport. Retrieved from http://drinq-water.de/en/. Accessed on October 27, 2022.

Greenwell, T., Danzey-Bussell, L., & Shonk, D. (2019). *Managing sports events* (2nd ed.). Champaign: Human Kinetics.

Hoy, R., Cuskelly, G., Auld, C., Kappelides, P., & Misener, K. (2019). *Sport volunteering* (1st ed.). London: Routledge.

NSPCC. (2017). Safe sport events, activities and competitions. Retrieved from https://thecpsu.org.uk/media/328759/safe-sport-events-activities-competitions-update-apr-2017.pdf. Accessed on October 19, 2022.

Taks, M., Chalip, L., & Green, C. (2015). Impacts and strategic outcomes from non-mega sport events for local communities. *European Sports Management Quarterly*, *15*(1), 1–6. [Online]. Retrieved from https://www.tandfonline.com/doi/abs/10.1080/16184742.2014.995116?journalCode=resm20. Accessed on December 5, 2022.

Vaillancourt, R., & Cameron, J. (2021). Health literacy for children and families. *Themed Issues: Drugs in Paediatrics, Pregnancy and Lactation*, *88*(10), 4328–4336. [Online]. Retrieved from https://bpspubs.onlinelibrary.wiley.com/doi/abs/10.1111/bcp.14948. Accessed on December 5, 2022.

Section 4
Case Studies

Chapter 11

Children at Weddings: How to Manage Parents and Children Before, During and After the Wedding

Marie Haverly

Abstract

When celebrating with newly-weds on their wedding day, many would imagine the best way to enjoy the day at its best would be to invite and include all members of the family, including the youngest. However, unlike adult guests who will usually happily enjoy the food and drink offered alongside any entertainment, children can be trickier to keep safe and happy all day long as their boredom threshold may well be lower than their adult counterparts and their needs more complex. There has long been a difficult debate over whether children bring unwanted stress to wedding plans or actually enhance the fun and celebration wished for. This chapter discusses all sides of an emotive argument of whether children should be invited to weddings and wedding receptions and how we might ensure their presence is enjoyable for all including the young person themselves.

Keywords: Children; parents; wedding; adult only; childism; childcare

Introduction

Weddings are known as a time of celebration, a chance to welcome family and friends to a carefully chosen venue to wish the happy couple well, eating and drinking into the night whilst dancing to favourite music and enjoying time with those you love and cherish. However, aside from these essentials, this idealist vision of what form the entire wedding celebration takes can vary greatly from one couple to the next, and many soon to be newly-weds will have a good idea of what their 'perfect day' looks like and here begins the planning journey. Alongside the usual plans, a wedding requires various aspects to be considered such as a suitable venue, catering for all the guests, entertainment, a celebrant and decorations for the day. Couples will spend

Events Management for the Infant and Youth Market, 171–179

Copyright © 2023 Marie Haverly

Published under exclusive licence by Emerald Publishing Limited

doi:10.1108/978-1-80455-690-020231019

much of their time making sure that their guests have a wonderful time, and this can be tricky to navigate as there are so many different factors to consider. A lot of effort tends to go into thinking about how well fed and watered these guests will be, where they will sit, how they will be entertained and any special gifts the couple wish to offer. Caring for guests at your wedding should be a priority, bored and restless guests can wander or bring negativity to the day. There are many ways you can ensure this does not happen such as introducing entertainers during the drinks reception and plenty of activities for your guests to enjoy; alongside this keeping the day flowing is crucial and many couples will devote time to plan everything well so this is achieved. Many venues are usually very experienced at knowing what works best for your guests within their premises, for example, they may suggest the ideal time to serve food or what drinks packages to ensure everyone has a good mix of soft drinks and alcohol to accompany dinner. They will guide on ideal numbers and timings for the day alongside offering links to suppliers and stakeholders who play an important part of any special day.

With all of this in mind it would seem that many weddings are planned to perfection, guests' expectations are managed and everyone is set to have a good time. However, experienced wedding planners will confirm that one area that is often overlooked is the provision or management of children and young people attending such an auspicious occasion. Inviting or excluding children from your invitations can be an emotive decision to make, one that may well meet with frustration and disappointment from family and friends although inviting them shouldn't just be a given, an expectation that they will be part of the day isn't always a certainty and couples would do well to think about this option carefully before rushing to confirm arrangements (Stafford, Faulkner, & Scott, 2020). Of course, if the couple have their own children already, then it would be expected that they will be an important part of the day; however, this does not mean that the couple will want everyone else's children to attend.

The decision to invite children can be based on many factors, it may be based on budget or space available to the couple, where they may wish to ensure adult guests take priority and therefore children of friends or family may take up valuable room. It is important to remember here that the value and priorities of any wedding will vary from person to person and also to the child itself – having a right to participate within an event that matters to them can and should be considered if the couple wish to take a holistic approach to their wedding invi-tation list (Canosa, Graham, & Simmons, 2022). The couple ultimately know what is important to them and this may be very different from their friends or family, yet this is something the couple should hold in mind when making important choices for their big day – after all it is their day, and they should hold dear what they consider to be important and vital for their own personal cele-brations. Whilst they may wish to take into account others' opinions and thoughts (and there is usually an abundance of advice to consider), they would need to remain emotionally strong to keep control of their plans and base their informed decisions on discussions and choices made together (Haverly, 2022).

Child-Free Wedding

The decision not to invite children, as has been mentioned, can be based on financial burden, space available or suitability of the day. For example, if your wedding is going to be held in a small, bespoke venue, then you may be limited on space and therefore eliminating children from your guest list will mean you can invite all your adult family and friends. Another example might be if you are restricted on budget or your wedding isn't suitable for children, then this decision may be an easier one to make; there are also venues that are adult only so this would force your hand when deciding on who to invite. Some couples feel by not inviting children – they almost give permission to their friends and family to let their hair down, have a relaxed time whilst their children are safely tucked up in bed. Many parents rarely get the chance to enjoy child-free time, so this is a good opportunity to do just this, have fun as a couple and remove the worry of managing and caring for their children whilst trying to enjoy the day. Another benefit to not including children is you will only have to cater for adults, no additional menus for the younger guests or having to ensure everything is child-friendly such as entertainment or location (ponds, rivers and ancient buildings or artefacts can be quite a concern to many couples where children are in attendance). Couples who are yet to start a family may also make the obvious choice to have a child-free wedding as they do not feel the desire to share with younger guests as they are not parents themselves, or they may just decide to have close-family children only rather than open the doors to everyone. Choosing to not invite children can be met with a negative or an ambivalent response from guests, parents may feel that their children are unwanted or rejected (especially if they are close to the couple, this can feel quite disappointing) and the couple making this decision may find themselves having to explain many times and justify their decision not to have younger guests. There can be a debate to whether justification should be demanded upon, if the couple decide to invite adults only. This should be respected perhaps and not challenged; however, those wanting to bring their children to the event may require a further discussion as to why they are not wanted to ease their concerns. This can cause concerns for the parents as they reach out to childcare whilst they attend the wedding themselves, however where this is family this can cause concerns as much of the family may well be attending the actual wedding thus resulting in childcare options being unavailable. There can be a cost involved when hiring a childminder or babysitter which the parents will have to face, and this might not be positively approached and could result in the parents not attending the wedding at all or on some occasions, turning up with their children anyway and hoping they can be catered for last minute.

Inviting Children and Including Them Fully

Choosing to invite children and embrace all this will entail is a decision that many couples make without too much consideration; many couples cannot imagine a wedding without every member of their family or loved ones sharing the day with them. Alongside this we could consider that empowering children to participate and have some control over their environment and experiences can positively contribute to their development and engagement with the activity presented (Canosa et al., 2022); therefore, a wedding might be a good platform to allow for their interaction and contribution when considering entertainment and structure for the day.

If your venue is sizeable and accommodating for larger numbers of guests, then this is an ideal choice, one that is usually made by couples with their own family or being close to nieces and nephews or friends' children. Similarly, if you have the budget to invite a larger number of guests and not have to exclude younger guests, then you will have chance to really enjoy having all age groups at your special day, which can add such a varied and wonderful atmosphere to the day. One area couples should consider however is how to entertain and keep children safe and occupied during what can be a very long day; younger guests can have shorter attention spans and therefore may not wish to stand around for photos or listen to an hour of speeches. Younger children and babies may find keeping quiet during the ceremony a challenge, and therefore this should be considered as part of all wedding plans so that every eventuality is considered so the day does not hold any cause for concern for the couple, guests or parents. Some ways to care for and occupy children are listed below; any experienced wedding or event planner will urge all couples to carefully consider options for this; not providing anyone to care for, entertain or manage children during the wedding day can result in these children getting bored and finding their own entertainment and perhaps causing damage or disruption as well as putting themselves at danger on occasion, a situation everyone would want to avoid at all costs. An assumption some couples can make is that parents will take care of their own children during the day, this is often something that fails to happen as parents catch up with friends and family they perhaps haven't seen in a while or they feel safe in the knowledge that they are surrounded by family who will no doubt jointly take care of or watch out for any children whilst attending the wedding. Often at weddings children will wander unaccompanied in the pursuit of excitement and exploration at this enjoyable event where everyone is excited. Another option for some couples and parents turn to is to provide lots of sugary treats to appease the younger guests. This can result in over-excited and over-stimulated children who then of course may suffer the post-sugar crash and cause disruption and upset to those around them as well as feeling pretty rotten themselves. A wedding planner would advise that when inviting children to a wedding, providing suitable and paid for care and entertainment is a guaranteed way to ensure children are safe, comfortable and relaxed all day. Having a professional company or registered childcare provider will allow parents and guests to relax knowing their children are cared for but also able to enjoy the day at its best without worry.

Some options for caring for children:

(1) Ask your venue if they have a babysitting or childcare service – this could be in a room or as part of the venue space. Ideal for very young children who

will need to sleep during the day, do always make sure these options are insured, trained and of course child-safe and can provide options such as warming up food or changing nappies.

(2) Hire an entertainer – a good option for slightly older children (young pre-teens and teens) where they will have a set timetable to enjoy some child-specific entertainment such as a magician or animal-petting zoos. Depending on what your venue (and budget) will allow these entertainment options will offer a chance for your younger guests to get involved in something and break up the day for them whilst the adults can catch up with other guests.

(3) Hire a nanny and/or full childcare company – these can usually cater for all age groups and offer everything from baby care to teenage games and challenges. They are usually staffed with a number of team members and will be able to offer a wide range of options all day ensuring that every young person is cared for to a level they require. This option is usually the more costly option but if your budget allows, it can be the answer to a stress-free wedding for everyone involved.

(4) Enlist the help of an older child, such as an older sibling or young adult to be in charge of childcare. Whilst this is usually a much cheaper option, such as sitting the children on a table with an older child who is 'in charge', this isn't always a suitable option as lack of training or consideration for all needs prevails and quickly the situation can become overwhelming or disjointed for all involved. Hiring a company or professional will guarantee that childcare is of a standard expected from a paid supplier, rather than relying on the good grace of a family member or friend.

What to Consider When Hiring a Childcare Company

First and foremost, you will want to ensure the company is registered, insured and safe for your child. Checking with your local authority will be a good option to see if the company or staff members are registered locally. They will also have a licence for working with children – proof of any training and proof of staffing DBS checks (Disclosure Barring Service, checking for a criminal record) which can be carried out through the government website easily. These are a must as they offer a basic understanding and reassurance that the company being hired has carried out all necessary checks and ensured their staff are safe and well trained. If you are hiring a company that are providing entertainment such as live animals and props, you will want to be sure to ask for copies of insurance and licences for this also – you can also check with your local authorities for this as well and your venue may also have copies of these if they have used them before. Always check for references also; this can be carried out as a simple internet search (however, be aware that not all online written references are true and exact, some can be added from the company owner themselves to generate good marketing options). Ask around, check if the venue staff have used them before and if so, do they recommend them at all. Ask family and friends for recommendations also and ask the company themselves if they can put you in touch with previous clients and venues so you can carry out your own research. If a company has confidence in its services and nothing to hide, then they will happily share this with you; be cautious of any companies who are reluctant to share details of venues they have been to before or if they themselves give negative comments on a venue or previous couples they have worked with – any company being negative can lead to concern as this gives a rather disappointing overview of their feelings around their business or people they work with. Also ask for copies of any contracts alongside asking for insurance certificates, ask questions around timings and costs and especially liability – you want to know what you as a client will be responsible for. For example, if you hire someone to bring some baby animals to the wedding for children to meet and pet, who will clean up after them or make good any damage? What if the animal bites or frightens a child, who will be responsible for this? Some companies will offer a disclosure or liability waiver form where parents will decide if they want their child to be involved and accept any accidents or liability in terms of damage and more. These are areas to consider carefully, and some questions you could ask of your childcare company could be:

(1) Are you insured and what cover do you have?
(2) What do I as a client need to provide?
(3) Who cleans up and tidies up the room(s) after you have finished?
(4) What are your working hours and, on the day, when can I expect you to arrive and leave?
(5) How many staff will you have working with children (there will be an Ofsted-based ratio of adult: child that you will want to be aware of to make sure children of all ages are safely cared for)?
(6) What are your emergency procedures?
(7) Where have you worked before?
(8) What are your prices and what do I get for this?
(9) Do you have staff capable of caring for children with special needs?
(10) What are your security protocols? These may be a password-protected signing in/out process where only 'safe' people can collect children from the childcare setting, for example
(11) Do staff work full time or part time at the company? What are their 'day jobs' if this is a part-time role – this might help a couple to see what experience the staff members have already

Other areas to consider when booking a company that provide professional childcare is what happens at the end of the evening, Nova Childcare (novaeventchildcare [Online]) tells me that one of the most difficult decisions for their staff to make is handing over a child to a parent who seems to be drunk or less than capable of caring for a child. There are laws in place in an official childcare setting that provide security for the child and staff where they can refuse to hand over a child to a parent who presents as drunk or under the influence of a substance; however, at a private event such as a wedding, this isn't the case which can leave staff caring for a child a dilemma as to whether to hand over a child to a parent clearly under the influence or to refuse and cause disruption without specific procedures in place. Another comment Justine from Nova mentioned was the strange requests some couples ask, such as 'do you care for dogs at the same time?' whilst companies are encouraged to have an open mind and trained for every eventuality, this might not cover all aspects. So, encouragement should be given to couples to understand the limitations to the companies being hired, and a simple conversation would eliminate any misunderstanding hopefully.

Deciding to Invite Children But Without Official Childcare

Whilst hiring an official childcare company or entertainer is ideal, not all couples wish to take this route or can afford to but there are still things you can do to help entertain younger guests and ensure the day runs smoothly and stays enjoyable for everyone. Can you speak to the venue about risk areas, for example, if they know of any parts of the premises that are dangerous, can these be shut off for the day (ponds and roads are a good example). Also perhaps ask the venue if they have a spare room where games and a TV, games console etc. can be set up for some of the children to disappear to if they are bored of the adult-based activities. Whilst these might be unsupervised, you could ask a non-drinking adult guest who is willing to help, to keep an eye on the room or perhaps ask the venue if a member of staff can be hired to keep an eye on the room. Some couples might choose to feed children before the adults, the waiting around for courses to arrive can be tiring and tedious for children so having them eat in another room or before the adults might help ease this concern. As mentioned before, sitting children at the wedding breakfast together with an older child or adult to supervise might also work; however, it would be worth discussing this with the adult or older child to make sure this is agreeable to them, managing other people's children whilst the parents let their hair down isn't everyone's idea of fun and of course these guests might not have training or experience in doing so which can cause anxiety. Whatever you decide to do, there are ways to help ensure everyone is as happy as can be. Make sure your younger guests are cared for appropriately, preferably by a professional and if you do decide to not invite children, be sure to word your invitations carefully and have your justification at the ready as this will no doubt cause some upset at some point.

Conclusion

Troubleshooting: Common problem areas:

- Your adult guests turn up with their children anyway despite being asked not to bring them
  This happens more often than anyone would imagine; guests think that 'surely there will be space, they don't eat much'; but a venue may have charged the

couple per guest and this will add a financial burden on the couple and there may not be baby space at the tables or appropriate provision for a child such as changing facilities or suitable food to offer. A couple could politely remind the guest that this is a childfree-wedding and explain briefly this might be met with an understanding guest who returns home with the child, but it may also become a little disruptive if the guest refuses to take the children home. If this happens, then all the couple can do is speak to the venue and ask for support in finding them space, keep communication clear and aim to include the child where possible whilst ensuring the parents are aware that they need to care for the child as there are not options for this elsewhere.

- Parents refuse to attend unless their children can attend
  This can be such an upsetting situation; however, the couple should stay strong in their decision, inviting some children and not others can also bring about upset and negative emotions in some guests. The couple can explain again their reasons for not inviting children, they could offer some babysitting type options if they know of any and reiterate that they would like the adult guests to attend but if they decide not to, then all the couple can do is respect their decision.

- Parents state they will leave early to collect children from their childcare setting
  Perhaps, the couple could consider adapting the schedule if the wedding party guests need to leave early or a significant number of guests will be leaving for this reason. They might hold their wedding a little earlier or at a time that might suit an early finish if wished.

- Children are bored at a wedding where there is no childcare provision
  Children who are bored or over-stimulated at weddings are a frequent problem at many events; not having anyone to care for the younger guests can mean they are left to their own devices for hours on end and this can lead to frustration and upset. Parents could consider bringing their own babysitter to the wedding, and they could speak to the venue or a local hotel and have them set up in a room to help – perhaps a group of parents could book something between them and spread the cost of such. They could also consider bringing plenty of healthy snacks and toys to help keep children occupied, perhaps have someone on standby at home that could collect or take in the children at bedtime so parents can head back to the party.

- Wording invitations appropriately
  Careful wording of your invites can be key to alleviating concerns or upset at the first instance, and something like the following could be considered:

'Whilst we adore our extended families and their children, we have decided to have an adult only wedding due to space and provisions at the venue we have chosen'

'We understand that you may wish to bring your children and they are most welcome, however we are unable to provide childcare on the day so please ensure you bring plenty of food and entertainment for your little ones, so they enjoy the day fully'

'We are delighted to welcome guests of all ages and will be providing a professional childcare company – please send us your requirements for the day so we can make sure your children are cared for properly all day'

'We have decided to hold a child-free wedding, we would love our friends and family to enjoy a drink and relaxed day and can happily provide local childcare options for you to book as you wish'.

References

Canosa, A., Graham, A., & Simmons, C. (2022). Progressing children's rights and participation: Utilising rights-informed resources to guide policy and practice. *Australian Journal of Social Sciences*, *57*(2), 473–758.

Haverly, M. (2022). *The practical guide to wedding planning*. London: Routledge.

Nova Childcare. Retrieved from www.novaeventchildcare.co.uk. Accessed on December 20, 22.

Stafford, L., Faulkner, S., & Scott, A. (2020). It's the best day of your life: Dominant discourses in brides' wedding planning. *Communication Studies*, *71*(2), 226–243.

Chapter 12

Creating Unique Workshops and Events for Children: The Case of Birdhouse Studio

Sarah Green

Abstract

This chapter tells the story of an intense but rewarding five years of running events for children in Hampshire in the south of England, UK, from 2015 to 2020. Whilst there will be a wealth of theory and academic models presented within this book, here the focus is primarily practical with lessons learnt from direct, and sometimes hard-earned experience. There are of course many formal options for becoming a primary school teacher or trained event host, for example, but we took a more lean and pragmatic approach to designing our off-curriculum activities and events.

Keywords: Workshop; events for children; unique selling point; case study; Birdhouse Studio; entrepreneurship

Introduction

The purpose of this chapter is to provide an account of what happened, to share lessons learnt and provide guidelines for setting up and running a business for children. The business discussed here was based in Winchester, Hampshire. Winchester is a prosperous and designated heritage city that is situated within a district covering 250 square miles, with more than 39,000 of the 118,000 district residents living within the town itself (Winchester City Council, 2022). House prices are among the highest in the region and there are over 46 primary schools in the district of Winchester (Snobe.co.uk, 2022) and hence a large amount of children in this age group. Organised after-school activities have been muted as having positive outcomes, both academically and in terms of well-being (Simpkins, 2015). Whilst such programmes appear to be a financial challenge for families on poorer incomes, they are seen as a confidence booster and a clear requirement for parents with professional jobs (BBC.co.uk, 2010) which encompasses much of Winchester's demographic (Winchester City Council, 2022).

Events Management for the Infant and Youth Market, 181–195

Copyright © 2023 Sarah Green

Published under exclusive licence by Emerald Publishing Limited

doi:10.1108/978-1-80455-690-020231021

From a methodological point of view, this chapter takes an interpretive approach, based on 'thick description' (Geertz, 1973) where the aim is to describe minute details and descriptions of happenings in terms of the context and the behaviours that took place, as observed directly by the researcher. In other words, the accounts that follow help to paint a picture of realities on which conclusions and guidelines might be based.

The chapter is structured by first providing an overview of the business, its audience, how the business was initially formed and how it developed over time into a children's events and education business. Then the significance of different locations and the pros and cons of venue types are discussed. Finally, lessons learnt are presented before recommendations for planning children's events are outlined.

Birdhouse Studio

The Birdhouse Studio was situated within the somewhat affluent community of Winchester in the south of England. The concept was to bring a fresh approach to design for a broad audience and to bring together learning from arts and crafts, commercial advertising and brand design. To some extent this was a passion project, as I had always wanted a shop and studio and felt I had a lot of design knowledge to share. It provided a platform for experimentation and for me to create things that people had not seen before, whether that was prints, greetings cards, jewellery or the formulation of unique workshops.

The satisfaction gained from creating something and then someone walk in off the street to then purchase it was very fulfilling. Customers would come back frequently, often to request for something to be personalised, or would send their relatives in to purchase things from their birthday wish list, often bringing their young children who loved all the colours and visual imagery.

The business offering consisted of several strands including a brand consultancy (design studio), a retail offering featuring design work by myself and affiliated brands/artists, homewares and curated vintage items by brands with a similar aesthetic and a series of related educational workshops for adults and children. All of these were established within the core brand values of the company: to be original and fun, to brighten someone's day, to show how everyone can be creative, to be friendly and approachable and to inspire. These goals align well with the overall benefits of children's clubs being noted as learning, socialising, interacting with others and creating memories and souvenirs.

Initially the setting for these events was a self-contained and owner-managed creative design studio and shop (more about that to follow), but as the business grew, this expanded into events taking place at 12 primary schools within the region as well as frequent parties at children's own homes and other rented venues such as church halls/theatre venues/libraries.

The retail venue was designed to be a place where people could come and essentially hang out, have a coffee and browse and chat about all things design. In terms of productivity, this sometimes backfired as people would stay for a long time telling their stories. Making the design studio open and visible, as opposed to a hidden office, was also a popular move with visitors wanting to peek at work in progress. This work included brand design work for small businesses and free-lancers, as such commissioned work was in demand in an area that was dense with over 90 thousand businesses (Hampshire 2050 State of the Economy, 2020).

The Format of Workshop Events

Some workshops were one-offs: jewellery/floristry/crochet for both adults and children and took place in the space at the rear of the premises. To enable these events involved creating bespoke promotional adverts and managing bookings as well as arranging for any external class leaders and even refreshments on the day.

Many of the workshops for children had three stages, a warm-up activity, the main event and then an extra option, with fun art and design activities throughout. All were designed exclusively for this purpose with an aim of being totally original and sometimes aligning with cultural events such as the London Marathon, Easter or Diwali. These lasted between 1.5 and 2 hours and were mostly in classes of a maximum of 15 children, as smaller classes are known to increase engagement and attention Blatchford, Bassett, and Brown (2011).

The Relevance of Venue

The original plan was not to take such children's events 'on the road' but to host everything in the shop and studio space. This worked well for the adult workshops where the attendees were pleased to be out and about and could make their own way there but presented different challenges with children. The workshop space at the rear was fairly limited to comfortably accommodate approximately 14 persons, so anything larger than this required a different venue. Parking was problematic as the space was on a main road so even dropping off and particularly picking up young children could be a challenge at busy times, and this was therefore not ideal.

Another key factor was that many of our workshops for children needed to be at a time and place to involve minimal travel. Had we decided to try and run weekday workshops in the studio, this would have meant arranging transport for the children, thus taking up valuable time and resource, aside from the health and safety issues. The key reason for this is because many parents were working and could not interrupt their day to shuffle children around, so the logical approach on weekdays was to offer this in the school settings so children could simply leave their class and arrive at our hired classroom. This came with benefits and challenges as outlined below.

The exception was birthday parties and Christmas parties, with the former taking place sometimes at the studio, sometimes at the child's home and sometimes at a hired venue by the parent, and the latter involving bringing together a fairly large number of children – approximately 100 at a venue we hired for the purpose.

The Pros and Cons of Venue Type

We found that no venue is perfect and that you must be flexible in the way you organise events depending on the venue. The Table 1 below shows some of the pros and cons of each type of venue that we experienced.

There were various benefits and challenges of each venue choice.

Using Your Own (Studio) Space

Since our brand was all about a clear aesthetic proposition of fun and colour, it was important for us to be able to create spaces that reflected this as much as possible. We could really go to town on decoration and customising for work-shops or parties with examples of work hanging from the ceilings, sketches on the walls and appropriate lighting settings. In rented venues this was much more difficult as these were sometimes shabby, very neutral in decor and palette and had other elements such as a heavy black curtain, piles of wooden box props or other non-moveable equipment in the environs. This was particularly the case with some church hall type of venues.

It was also a real benefit to be able to set the space up the night before and sometimes not fully clear it until the following day.

Bringing the parents and children into the environment through the front shop area also meant they would have sight of fun-related items that were for sale, and this was a temptation for both parents waiting and children excitedly arriving and leaving, providing us with frequent cross-selling opportunities – essentially, they could take a part of the experience home with them.

It was comforting to know what we could and could not do in terms of making noise, as we had used the venue so many times before often several times per week.

The downsides of using our space were that it was quite small, so we had to restrict numbers for workshops and parties; a shame when we were charging per child. Likewise, there was little space for children to burn off energy, which is much recommended when planning any children's event!

A somewhat unexpected challenge was that we often had trouble getting families to leave. They enjoyed the environs so much (as catching up with each other) that they tended to stay way past the event finishing time, which meant we were obliged at times to politely ask them to leave – a particular challenge when another workshop was happening on the same day.

Above all we found the children really enjoyed our setting and were fairly respectful and well-mannered as they were coming into somewhere exciting and new with plenty of precious looking things around.

Table 1. A Table of Pros and Cons of Each Type of Venue.

Venue	Pros	Cons	Notes
Owned studio space	The look and feel (branding) is under your total control.	Size – always the same limitations on capacity.	Behaviour tends to be quite good as new environs.
	No time limitations to exit other than your own.	Tidying up – all down to you.	
	'Free' to rent (other than usual rental) They visit your space, so you have a sense of control.	Need to be strict with exit times as cannot use venue hire time as a reason.	
	Chances to upsell other services.	Parking issues and not outdoor space (in this example).	
	Noise etc could be easier to manage as you know the venue well.		
(After) school classroom	Very convenient for the children.	Tended to be cluttered classrooms.	Behaviour could be difficult as children excitable after the long day and in school mode.
	No travel worries.	No set-up time.	
	Almost guaranteed audience.	Little chance to brand the space.	
	Additional support from venue	Rushed tidy up time.	
		Interference from school staff.	
		Tired children as no gap between the workshop and their school day.	
Child's home (parties)	Lovely environments that are familiar to the children.	The power dynamic – you are in the parent's home, and they would affect the timings etc.	Behaviour variable as children very comfortable in own home and more

Table 1. *(Continued)*

Venue	Pros	Cons	Notes
	Venue at no cost to us.		scope to run in and out.
		Often eating at same table as the artwork and more food involved.	
	Parents tended to handle toileting etc.		
	Health and safety primarily down to the parents.	Other family members distracting the children.	
	Parent tidies much up.		
	Outdoor space.		
Hired venue	Scale can match attendees.	Timing tends to be very strict.	Equal playing field – a 'neutral' venue for us and the parents.
	Less cleaning.	So you are paying for set-up/set-down time.	Children excitable as all new.
	Flexible according to workshop theme.	Little chance to create brand impact unless considerable time spent.	
	Outdoor space.		
	Often with a kitchen area and other facilities such as a lobby.	More health and safety concerns.	
		Tends to be expensive.	
		More work to plan the use of that particular space: (Electricity, tables etc).	

Source: The Author.

Using School Classrooms

The main benefits of workshops taking place at the school venue related to convenience. As mentioned, there was no need for travel, and we had an almost guaranteed list of attendees for each workshop. Pick-ups by parents were usually prompt as they had other places to be, and we could therefore tidy up and exit usually within 15 minutes of the workshop ending.

There were, however, more challenges at these settings. We would have little to no set-up time as the classroom would just have been vacated of other children. The rooms could be stuffy and dirty after a day's use. These rooms were typically cluttered with other school items and there was little to no opportunity to brand the space to look and feel like our brand.

Some school class teachers were quick to vacate the space for us, whilst others remained, or came and went and this would at times be quite a distraction when we were trying to create a different experience for the children.

As the children had literally just dashed from their school day, we found them to be either extremely energetic after having to behave all day, or weary and hungry so we had to 'reset' them which we did manage to do. Since they knew the environment extremely well, and to some extent we were the visitor, the behaviour of the children would vary.

At the Child's Home

Parties or events at the child's home were a whole different ball game. The environments were typically lovely, very creative and comfortable homes, and often the parent(s) had gone to considerable effort to set the table and the whole scene on the same theme we had agreed. The 'venue' did not cost us anything and certain practical aspects such as use of the bathroom were not our responsibility so we could concentrate on our topics.

However, the typical immediate access to outdoor space (the garden) was both a benefit and also a challenge, in that the children were more inclined to jump down as they saw fit and the group was more dispersed during an activity. We also found the parents friends and family tended to stay for the duration (sometimes with a beer or two!) and at times we politely had to ask them to be quieter so we could work with the children!

Perhaps the most curious part was a subtle change in power dynamic – you were at the mercy of the parent, in their environment and they would sometimes switch the order of activities at their whim, or indeed completely ignore our class leaders all together. Since families tended to stay on, it could be difficult to exit these events at times as there was no official ending apparently.

Using a Hired Venue

A more 'official' route for running your children's event can be through hiring a venue designed for the purpose. For us these varied from somewhat old and tatty church halls to community centres, to theatre venues and more state-of-the-art modern facilities such as purpose-built events rooms in our contemporary library wing. All of these come with a price of course, and it can vary greatly.

The good news is that you can select the size of venue to suit your event, so when we had a small summer holiday workshop, we hired a classroom at the library fit for 20 children, but when we held a Christmas party for over 100 children, we managed to upscale to theatre space. The important thing here was not too have too much space, as the atmosphere can be compromised, and it is not safe to have children wandering around a large area. We also found that venues with 'safe' outdoor space were useful in summer and those with plenty of cloakroom options were really needed in the winter. It is amazing how much space a pile of children's coats can take up!

Hired venues usually need to be left exactly as you leave them, but this is good practice anyway when running a children's event – although it can eat onto your hire time considerably, so make a tidy-up plan.

There is certainly less option to customise the space however, and for most themes you need to 'go big' and decorate broadly to make any kind of an impact. For our Christmas disco in a large venue (and a tower with a high ceiling), we bought metres of snow scene wall hangings which took some time to assemble but did have an impact. Placing a foil curtain over the main internal door and a red-carpet offcut leading up to the entrance did however help to create the festive atmosphere we were looking for.

Venue Hire Checklist

For us, the checklist when choosing a venue to hire included:

(1) General location – close to the community?
(2) Outdoor space – if needed and does it have boundaries?
(3) Size in relation to expected number of attendees
(4) Price per hour (remember set-up and set-down time)
(5) Parking and safe dispatch of children
(6) Lobby area (very useful for keeping buggies and chattering parents out of main event)
(7) Kitchen area (especially if attached to main room)
(8) Bathrooms
(9) Lighting – does it provide options?
(10) Light/windows – can these be covered if necessary?
(11) Other clutter – is this an issue?
(12) Seating and tables – where needed
(13) Noise – any limitations?
(14) Arrivals and entry/key issues
(15) Coats storage area
(16) Breakout space, should it be needed?

There are benefits to reviewing 'what works' and taking a pragmatist approach to understanding experiences can shed light on the meanings of our actions (Dewey, 2008). Whilst every single situation in our business taught us a lot about how to successfully manage a children's event and the necessary factors such as venue size and location, budgeting, risk assessment and health and safety; some other key factors that we discovered/implemented are summarised in the table below as five key realities.

- Parents/carers will compare your offering directly with previous experiences
- Treat the children like mini adults
- Manage the time closely
- It's not the children, it's the parents!
- Make it personal

Parents/Carers Will Compare Your Offering Directly With Previous Experiences

It may seem obvious that when choosing whether to send their child to your event, parents/carers will weigh this up directly against previous events their children have attended. Putting it bluntly, they will primarily be thinking about time versus price. If your business is anything like mine, we really think we had something special to offer over and above a 'typical' event such as chains of activity centres/ swimming parties/after school clubs. This meant we charged a little more for our activities (approx. 15–20%) than the typical offering. This was problematic for the parents to some extent in that, until they (and their child) had experienced our event, it was hard to know what was coming and why it was better. Additionally, they would always compare their spend with other perhaps inferior activities and even babysitting services, as this was certainly seen as a childcare option for many.

This is where the marketing materials and the initial communications with the parent/carer are so important. It is necessary to detail all the special features of the event you are offering as well as presenting this in a way that will be attractive to both parent and child. The old advertising adage of 'pester power' rings true here, as children will see the vision and not worry about the cost. So, all communications were designed to charm the young recipient. These were typically created initially as a teaser piece to gain interest and awareness and then followed up with more detail about the event offered. The wording was simple to appeal to the child and 'calls to action' (next steps for the viewer to take such as booking) were clear.

I have seen many parents/carers initially seem to object, or be unsure about, the more premium level of offering (and price point), but later the same parents/ carers raving to us and other families, and anyone who will listen about the experience and how much their child loved it.

The plus side of this is that I have also had parents/carers phoning, desperate to book an event before any of their peers, so that they can be the first and original.

HOT TIP: Do not underestimate the apparent importance of being the first parent to do something new and exciting for their child before other children in the class/peer group!

Treat the Children like Mini Adults

This does not mean to provide alcohol or late nights, but through experience, we found that children engage well when they think a topic or theme is something usually only reserved for adults. It is known that children should be empowered and included in the shaping of offerings (Seraphin & Green, 2019) rather than simply being on the receiving end.

Through our style of communications, they also felt that we respected them and appreciated a more equal relationship with us than they were used to perhaps at school or elsewhere. If you try to think for a moment back to perhaps a school trip or other special event when you were young, you too may remember these boundaries shifting at that time and you may hold those memories dear. A simple example is that I remember we were allowed to address the activity leaders by their first names on school camp. So in essence, it is about trying to communicate with them on their level.

Some examples of how we implemented this are below:

(1) Party Invitations: we created these for children to hand to their friends – these were delivered to the birthday child's home with the child's name on the front of the envelope rather than the parent/carer and included stickers saying, 'private and confidential', 'not for grown-ups' etc.
(2) Enabling the child to make a choice: within workshops, each child had a varied choice of materials rather than simply being treated all the same.
(3) Workshop topics: there are numerous examples of where a workshop topic was formulated that might usually be the domain of adults – for example:

- Tattoo creation
- Street art
- Mobile phone case design
- Logo/brand design
- 'Mocktail' creation
- Architecture
- Branding projects

These are topics that might be considered in the domain of the adult and the children relished this. Any staff at events were addressed by their first names and other features at events themselves helped to provide a more aspirational mature vibe and were extremely well received. Examples include:

- A VIP area for older children at the Christmas parties where they could have table service and wristband-only entry. This was still visible as part of the main event but made the older children feel special.
- A red carpet and rope barriers on approaching the parties.
- Nail bars and 'tattoo' bars (usually the reserve of teenagers or adults)

HOT TIP: If you are choosing more grown-up themes, be prepared to justify these to the parents and ensure themes are still treated in a light-hearted way – you are not trying to turn the children into adults or poison their young minds.

Manage the Time Really Closely

- Juggling arrivals
  Children will invariably arrive to your workshop at slightly different times and in different moods. There will also possibly be a time of trying to organise coats, bags and snacks, so be wary of this by having a plan to implement during this potentially chaotic time. We found some children arrived promptly and smoothly and were ready to be occupied whilst others ran in energetically later and fussed with their coats and therefore this dual situation required managing. Our solution was a ten-minute arrivals window (as from experience this worked for workshops which were primarily after-school and on-site) during which the children may undertake a simple but fun worksheet activity. This was not a critical part of the workshop and therefore was not a problem if missed or partially completed by the latecomers. This was also the munching window so that children could focus on their snack. We found the children could not wait to see what was on the sheet each week!
- Keeping pace and focus
  In our workshops, the children sometimes worked at different paces – some would impatiently or skilfully whizz through an activity whilst others worked at a detailed level very slowly. It is up to you to manage the pace of this as they will not! After introducing a topic (they will only pay attention for a few minutes) and kicking it off, we checked the clock continuously. We always gave a five-minute warning that they needed to add any final parts and rang a bell/ beeper at the end. For us a selection of coloured musical bells worked brilliantly and each week a child was chosen to ring it. They found this incredibly exciting.
  Another important aspect of keeping pace was staying ahead of material needs. In essence this meant putting the right number of materials in front of the child just in time, so they neither raced ahead nor ran out of resources and became preoccupied with the task of find more. Naturally in this context we mean craft materials, but for you this could simply mean organising your sports or musical equipment to align with your workshop plan. A small challenge here related to choice (as mentioned above), as letting the children choose their own colours and types of materials can add substantial time to your workshop.

Getting Around Early Finishers/Bored Children

Invariably there will be children at any activity or workshop who finish their task/ game early.

For this, we had two solutions:

(1) We always had a simpler second optional activity on the same theme lined-up (and for those who did not complete they could take this home).
(2) We engaged the children with a small organisational activity in relation to tidying up – for example, collecting up materials. This always worked and saved us some effort too!

Wrapping Up

The time it takes to close an event should not be underestimated. For us, working with children as young as 5, this could sometimes be a hefty task. Depending on the nature and location of your event, there may be very little to tidy up and organise or a great deal.

Running an arts and crafts business meant this aspect could be quite a burden due to the wealth of materials used during a workshop/party. At venues we rented this that came with the added pressure of leaving the venue before your rental time was up, and ensuring you left it exactly as you found it (see venue types above).

Children are messy. The quicker you accept that the quicker you can put in place plans to facilitate a smooth exit process. If I am honest this was never easy, and the burden was always a challenge. However, some of the ways we approached this part of time management was as follows:

(1) Give the children plenty of warning that the session is wrapping up
(2) Support those children who are reluctant to cease their activity by distracting them
(3) Tidy as you go (essential!)
(4) Engage the children in tidying as much as possible – they love an individual responsibility – but police this so that they are not snatching materials from other children, for example
(5) Organise coats and bags by intervening and holding them up if necessary to save the scrummage
(6) For larger events label/colour code coats and bags
(7) Involve the parents where applicable as they can spot their own child's baggage easily
(8) Decide how to manage children whose parents are late and be prepared for this as there will always be at least one!
(9) Decide on your plan for parents who don't wish to leave

It's Not the Children, It's the Parents!

Naturally events for children are centred around the children first, after all they are the audience, but we found that the parents frequently also needed to be considered. We did find that the greater the event, the higher the parent expectations, so for each party (where children would often return a second or third time), we had to ensure we invented something new and fresh to ensure the parents felt they were getting a 'special' level of service.

As aforementioned, in certain environments, particularly at their homes, or a venue they had rented, the parents sometimes liked to try and take charge, so our staff became adept at gently managing the timings and activities to stay on task and on time.

Another feature we felt was important for our business was that the children should be free to experiment with their creativity and maybe even 'go wrong' as the experience was as important as the outcome. As the parents were not in the workshops, they did not always see it that way, and judged value for money on the completion and finishing of the items the children had made and brought home. We sometimes had a child who had a great time exploring ideas in class, only for the parent to say, 'is that all you did?'. Similarly with goody bags, should you choose to offer these after your event, the parents are measuring these against the quality of the event so be wary of your approach to these. Goody bags tend to be expensive to produce but leave a lasting impact on perceptions of your event from the parent perspective.

Be prepared for all eventualities when it comes to parents staying for the whole event or leaving and picking up later. We tended to see either, parents who would not leave (and literally some would sit beside their child undertaking the activity for them!) and those who arrived late and picked up late. If you know parents are going to be staying, you may want to consider providing refreshments – you could of course charge for this.

In every workshop there would typically be one parent who was late, sometimes by as much as 30 minutes, for example. So be prepared to cover your bases here with reference to good and ethical management of parent contact data and you may also like to put in place a late pick-up policy of some kind. Of course, it goes without saying that your recording and management of all contact data should comply with GDPR (data protection) rules. It is also very wise to check that data are up to date if you have reoccurring events, as parents do not always inform you of changes.

Finally, be wary of children being taken home by other parents when you have not been informed. This can cause confusion and leave you needing to cross-check, which can somewhat spoil the happy end to your fun event.

Make It Personal

One of the key strengths of our business, that all our customers loved, was personalisation. Children love to see their own name or other features at their event, and parents love to see their children featured in this way. Some of the ways we undertook this for our events included:

Personalising every name (including those of attendees and child host) on the
    event invites
Letting the child host choose the invite colour and imagery
Offering a good choice of workshop activity/theme
In workshops – personalising the names and design of place mats
Personalising any paper templates, the children used (e.g. 'Mimi's self-portrait')
Letting children choose from a range of different skin tones for their self-portrait
    collages
Providing a very large choice of craft materials so they could individualise their
    work
Providing a range of colours of paper wristband to choose from (these were useful
    for arrivals, queue management and groupings).
Customising goody bags

Conclusion

Whilst it is essential to ensure you cover the practical aspects of events for children including health and safety/safeguarding, GDPR, risk assessment, parking and venue location/size, we found other factors really made a difference to a successful and memorable event. These included being able to customise the space, pre-empting the needs and behaviours of parents/carers, treating the children more like mini-adults (where appropriate) and personalising the offering as much as possible.

We found that it is essential to stay one step ahead of the children when managing a party or workshop, to recognise that children have different attention spans and being able to accommodate this in various ways. Staying true to your brand values and ensuring these are communicated in every aspect of your event also helps the customer to understand your offering, to want to come again and to recommend you to others.

References

BBC News. (2010) After-school clubs too expensive, poll suggests. Retrieved from
    bbc.co.uk/news/education-11110060. Accessed on November 20, 2022.
Blatchford, P., Bassett, P., & Brown, P. (2011). Examining the effect of class size on
    classroom engagement and teacher–pupil interaction: Differences in relation to
    pupil prior attainment and primary vs. secondary schools. *Learning and Instruction, 21*, 6.
Dewey, J. (2008). Human nature and conduct. In J. Boydston & G. Murphy (Eds.),
    The middle works of John Dewey, 1899–1924 (Vol. 14, pp. 1–227). Carbondale, IL:
    Southern Illinois University Press. (Original work published 1922).
Geertz, C. (1973). Thick description: Toward an interpretive theory of culture.
    Interpretation of cultures. New York, NY: Basic Books.

Hampshire 2050 State of the Economy. (2020). Retrieved from https://documents. hants.gov.uk/hampshire2050/h2050-stateofeconomyreport.pdf. Accessed on November 20, 2022.

Seraphin, H., & Green, S. (2019). The significance of the contribution of children to conceptualising the destination of the future. *International Journal of Tourism Cities*, *5*(4), 544–599.

Simpkins, S. D. (2015). When and how does participating in an organized after-school activity matter? *Applied Developmental Science*, *19*(3), 121–126.

Snobe.co.uk. (2022). Retrieved from snobe.co.uk/best-primary-schools/Hampshire/. Accessed on November 20, 2022.

Winchester City Council. (2022). Retrieved from winchester.gov.uk/data/facts-and-figures-about-the-winchester-district/. Accessed on November 25, 2022.

Chapter 13

Organising Events With Children With Disabilities at ANPRAS (Mauritius): Insights and Implications

Vanessa G. B. Gowreesunkar and Shem Wambugu Maingi

Abstract

Children with disabilities are integral part of the society, but they often confront challenges due to barriers that people throw in their way. As a result, their participations in public events are often limited. Despite several treaties and conventions, children with disabilities still face discrimination that spreads into all spheres of life and not much is done to empower them to become resilient. According to the UNICEF Report (2020), children with disabilities are stigmatised and they are often isolated without having a possibility to participate in events and activities of the schools. While the government sector undoubtedly provides the basic support and facilities to them, the rest is often left in the hands of private sectors and NGOs. As a result, it is important to recognise and acknowledge NGO's effort in empowering children with disabilities and integrating them in the society. The African Network for Policy, Research and Advocacy for Sustainability (ANPRAS), an NGO affiliated with the African Union and headquartered in Mauritius never neglected this segment of the society while organising its flagship activities and annual event. Unlike Dowse, Powell, and Weed (2018) who argue that children are mostly undermined as community members, the current study seeks to demonstrate that children have a voice at ANPRAS and those with disability have a louder one. In fact, children with disabilities are gifted with talents and they may live a normal life if they are accepted by the society and if appropriate support is given. Methodologically, the chapter is built on secondary data from documents archived at ANPRAS office. The chapter closes with a concluding note on few implications related to the participation of children with disabilities in public events and ANPRAS activities.

Events Management for the Infant and Youth Market, 197–207
Copyright © 2023 Vanessa G. B. Gowreesunkar and Shem Wambugu Maingi
Published under exclusive licence by Emerald Publishing Limited
doi:10.1108/978-1-80455-690-020231023

Introduction

The African Network for Policy, Research and Advocacy for Sustainability (ANPRAS) is an established non-governmental organization (NGO) located in the island of Mauritius. With over a decade of experience in the field of sustainability, its main purpose is to engage into community-based actions for sustainable development and to bring about positive changes in the life of the local people. ANPRAS has been spearheading many activities which are directed towards the achievements of the United Nations Sustainable Development Goals (SDGs) and the African Union Agenda 2063. Several of those activities engage children, as this segment of the population has attracted significant attention in terms of their role as agent of change in the society (see Canosa, Graham, & Wilson, 2020; Norwood et al., 2019; Séraphin & Gowreesunkar, 2020). Children with disabilities are integral part of any society. However, they confront additional challenges as a result of their impairments and the many barriers that society throws in their way (Cheng & Monroe, 2012; Franklin & Sloper, 2007). Despite several treaties and conventions on children with disabilities (see Mahadew & Mootooveeren, 2020), they still face discrimination that spreads into all spheres of life and not much is done to empower them to become resilient. Children with disabilities are rather viewed as a problem to be 'fixed', with the focus on their disability and a medical response, rather than on their abilities and potential (UNICEF Report, 2020). Likewise, Murphy and Carborone (2008) observe that children with disabilities are stigmatised, and they are often isolated without having a possibility to participate in events and activities of the schools. This point is also confirmed in the UNICEF Report; children with disabilities are isolated from social activities and participation in their communities – a problem exacerbated by transport means and buildings that remain inaccessible, as well as the stigma that surrounds disability (UNICEF Report, 2020). International efforts to promote the social and emotional well-being of children with disabilities through participation in recreational sports and physical activities are therefore highly recommended by UNICEF (Murphy & Carborone, 2008).

Likewise, it would seem that many countries rely on NGOs to cater for children with disabilities (Mahadew & Mootooveeren, 2020; Maingi & Gowreesunkar, 2022). As a result, it is important to recognise and acknowledge NGO's effort in empowering children with disabilities and integrating them in the society. ANPRAS, as an NGO affiliated with the African Union, follows this guiding philosophy of inclusiveness. ANPRAS considers children with disabilities while organising events and this goes in line with SDG 10 (reduced inequalities) which targets at empowering and promoting the social, economic and political inclusion of all irrespective of age, sex, disability, race, ethnicity, origin, religion or economic or other status. The previous study of Gowreesunkar, Maingi, and Mohanty (2022) on children's activities at ANPRAS clearly demonstrates that children occupy a leading position in civic actions despite being seen as the most vulnerable human population. However, the study did not take into account children with disabilities. In response, this chapter chooses to focus on children with disabilities. Unlike Dowse et al. (2018) who argue that children are mostly undermined as community members, the current study seeks to demonstrate that children have a voice and those with disability have a louder one. In fact, children with disabilities are endowed with gifted talents. Jane Constance is a living example for Mauritius. Visually impaired since birth, she was designated UNESCO Artist for Peace in September 2017, in light of her commitment to promoting and raising public awareness on inclusion and empowerment of persons with disabilities in societies (UNESCO, 2017). In light of the above discussion, this chapter will provide a brief account of ANPRAS's sustainability activities through children with disabilities. In so doing, the chapter will unveil challenges faced by them while identifying factors that make children with disabilities more vulnerable and less resilient. Methodologically, the chapter sources from secondary data from documents archived at ANPRAS office. The chapter closes with a concluding note on few implications related to the participation of children with disabilities in ANPRAS activities.

Status of Children Rights in Mauritius

The island of Mauritius has a population of approximately 1,266,030, of which around 279,782 are children of under 15 years old (Statistics Mauritius, 2022). Being a welfare state as well as state party to almost all international human rights instruments, Mauritius tries its best to ensure that children with disability are able to enjoy the right to education irrespective of any ground of discrimination (Mahadew & Mootooveeren, 2020). The protection and promotion of the right to education of all children including those with disabilities is vital in Mauritius (Ombudsman Ombudsperson Report, 2019). As a result, Mauritius is party to the Convention on the Rights of the Child (CRC) since 1990 (Bunwaree & Kasenally, 2007). It is interesting to note that 'disability' per se is a prohibited ground for discrimination as set out in Article 2 of the CRC (CRC Report, 2015). Hence, the CRC is one amongst the few Conventions where the definition of 'discrimination' includes 'disability' as a ground. The right to education is provided at Articles 28 and 29 (1) (a) of the Convention restating the duties of States which include the need to make educational and vocational information and guidance available and accessible to all children. The implemented Child Protection Act mostly aimed to help children vulnerable to violence was followed by a monitoring committee established directly under the Ministry of gender equality and family welfare. With changes in the government in recent years, Mauritius has begun to focus more on the status of children's rights in the country (Mahadew & Mootooveeren, 2020). Having already ratified the Convention in 1990 with the first two of the optional protocols, the island started working on the better application of these protocols and the addition of extra protocols to increase the standards of children's rights. Like all children, those with disabilities are also concerned with the right to education (UNICEF, 2020). The international and regional instruments to which Mauritius is party binds to protect and promote human rights including the right to education of children with special needs. Likewise, these children require special care and attention, along with schools equipped with the proper facilities. For instance, State secondary schools are already equipped with ramps and toilets for students with disabilities (Mahadew & Mootooveeren, 2020). Likewise, the Ombudsperson for Children Act 2003 in Mauritius was enacted to provide for the establishment of an office of Ombudsperson for Children. The Ombudsperson as a statutory and independent body advocates for children's rights; advises the Minister and other public bodies and institutions on matters relating to promotion and protection of children's rights. Since the establishment of the Office of the Ombudsperson for Children in 2004, children with disabilities have been given due consideration by the Ombudsperson and investigators who work in close collaboration with NGOs offering services and care to these children. The Ombudsperson intervenes in the field of access to education, leisure, special care, social security and support to parents having a child with a disability. Children with disabilities benefit from the support services offered by the Ministry of Social Security, National Solidarity and Sustainable Development and the support of the Ombudsperson for Children (Mahadew & Mootooveeren, 2020).

Insight on ANPRAS Activities

ANPRAS is an elected member of the Economic, Social and Cultural Council (ECOSOCC) of the African Union. Since its existence in 2008, ANPRAS spearheaded various environmental and sustainability projects which are in line with the aspirations of the African Union Agenda for 2063 (Gowreesunkar & Chintaram, 2014). The organisation's flagship activities like LDI Mauritius, the Earth-Hour, the Earth Day, the Africa Day, the World Environment Day, the International Woman Day and Green Award have been important milestones. ANPRAS is also actively involved with a number of international organisations, namely Common Ground Publishers, Earth Hour Global, Earth Day Network, Global Alliance for Climate Smart Agriculture, Organisation of African Youth and the LDI. The guiding philosophy of ANPRAS is 'a small step in philanthropy, a significant step in sustainability' (source: www.anpras.org). Similar to Prashad (2015), ANPRAS members also consider children as the reflection of God and they believe that children with disability are gifted differently. The benefits of physical activity are universal for all children, including those with disabilities (Murphy & Carborone, 2008). As a result, organising events with children at ANPRAS has always been both challenging and exciting. The participation of children with disabilities in sports and recreational activities are encouraged at ANPRAS. This promotes inclusion, minimises deconditioning, optimises physical functioning and enhances overall well-being, a point shared by many researchers (Mahadew & Mootooveeren, 2020; Murphy & Carborone, 2008). ANPRAS follows the philosophy of UNICEF – the organisation also aims to end isolation and ensure that they participate in everyday community life. Activities are geared towards making children with disabilities survive, thrive, learn and are protected from violence, abuse and exploitation, and have the opportunity to actively contribute to their communities.

Activities With Children With Disabilities at ANPRAS

An estimated 200 million children worldwide experience various forms of disability (Peek & Stough, 2010). Disability is a broad term that is not consistently defined, and it is mostly seen by society from a negative angle (Murphy & Carborone, 2008). Children with disabilities are often viewed as a problem to be 'fixed', with the focus on their disability and a medical response, rather than on their abilities and potential (UNICEF Report, 2020). In the study of Mahadew and Mootooveeren (2020), children with disabilities have been seen as 'unfortunate' because of their inability to enjoy material and social benefits of modern society like others. The exclusion of children with disabilities from a country's social system is in fact due of the country's failure in catering for their needs and integrating them in the society. This point is also captured in the study of Franklin and Sloper (2007) who argue that the most disabling attitudes faced by children with physical or sensory impairments is the assumption that they do not have a view to express, and they cannot participate in social activities along with children without disabilities. To prove this theory wrong, ANPRAS has always encouraged children with disabilities to join flagship activities such as Earth Hour and Earth Day (Gowreesunkar & Maingi, 2021). The primary goals for increasing physical activity in children with disabilities are to reverse deconditioning secondary to impaired mobility, optimise physical functioning and enhance overall well-being (Murphy & Carborone, 2008).

According to the International Union for the Conservation of Nature and the Children and Nature Network, there is a pressing need to involve children in sustainability initiatives, a philosophy deeply entrenched in ANPRAS's aspiration. Likewise, research reveals that when children are engaged in sustainability endeavours at schools (for example, environmental conservation, protection of the ocean, energy saving, gardening and tress planting among others), it promotes their physical and mental health and cognitive performance (Kuo, Barnes, & Jordan, 2019; Otto & Pensini, 2017; Tillman, Tobin, Avison, & Gililand, 2018; Séraphin, Gowreesunkar & Canosa, 2021). As a result, ANPRAS's main concern is how to integrate children with disabilities in its activities. Inclusion of children with disabilities aligns with the SDG 10 of the United Nations which is about reducing inequality.

According to the population census of 2011 in Mauritius, the disability prevalence of the age group, under 10 years, was 0.8% for both male and female while for the age group, 10–19 years, it was 1.3% for both sexes (Government of Mauritius Population Census Report, 2011). ANPRAS works to ensure the best possible support for every child living with a disability and as such gives possibility to integrate them in its sustainability activities.

The Earth Hour and Earth Day Activities

The Earth Hour is a national event where children participate in sustainability actions such as planting trees, gardening, flowering of the environment and composting among others. The annual hosting is held at historical places and

ANPRAS chooses children as ambassadors to disseminate sustainability messages. The Earth Hour activity is organised yearly and ANPRAS team works in collaboration with several schools to implement the sustainability action plan.

The Earth Hour event comprises switching off the light and use candle in order to show solidarity towards energy saving. On that occasion, children are invited to spread sustainability messages through poems and songs, and back home, they also collaborate with their parents and have candle light dinner. In the case of children with disabilities, the same kind of activities are proposed to them. Children with disabilities suffer physical challenges. As such, they understand the importance of sustainability more than normal children who often do not value resources surrounding them. Few examples of activities that have been conducted by children with disabilities at ANPRAS are songs and painting by children on wheelchair. The objective is to sensitise and educate the mass on the importance of sustainability issues and popularise the SDGs. At ANPRAS, children with disabilities also have the same voice as children without disabilities. Since parents did not give permission to take pictures of the children, no visual documents are available to support the statement.

The World Clean-up Day is a global clean-up event organised by LDI aiming to make the world a cleaner place and raise awareness of the harms of mismanaged waste through clean-up and campaigns in participating countries across the world. On World Clean-up Day (commemorated on 21 September) millions of people in over 150 countries stand up against global waste pollution by cleaning up communities, parks, forests and beaches. ANPRAS, being the focal point for the LDI, annually organises several clean-up campaigns across the island with the collaboration of schools and NGOs. The key objectives are:

- To sensitise the population against illegal dumping;
- To advocate for cleaning and embellishment of the environment;
- To raise awareness about sustainable consumption and climate change;
- To report the trash points to local authorities for effective clean-up and monitoring.

The aim of World Clean-up Day is not only to pick up waste but to also raise awareness that children with disability play a significant role in tackling global climate crisis. Children without and with disabilities are engaged as they are seen as agent of change. The campaign usually attracts over hundreds of children. For every clean-up activity organised, children with disability are accompanied by parents and teachers. Parents' and teachers' level of interest and awareness about disability issues often affect how they appeal to their children as environmental 'agents of transition' (Walker, 2017), and having parents, teachers and other role models who show an interest in nature can predispose others to take an interest in nature themselves and later work for its protection (Chawla & Cushing, 2007). As such, briefing of the activity usually takes place with parents and teachers and participating children. A meeting is also separately organised so as to sensitise participants without disability on the importance of respecting children with disability. This is to raise awareness for the rights of children with disabilities, helping to increase public acceptance for the inclusion of children with disabilities.

Children with disability are given the freedom to engage in any part of the event and in some cases, they join children without disability. This helps in developing understanding of this vulnerable segment of the society and a sense of community is also nourished, and a sense of place is cultivated. On the positive side, this also enhances the event experience for kids that may have allergies or developmental concerns that would previously impact their ability to participate equally with their peers. Children are future citizens of a nation, and their adequate development is utmost priority of the country.

Raising Disability Awareness Through Events

Disability awareness is an important step in establishing inclusion for people with disability. Fears and discomfort about interacting with people with disability is mainly due to the lack of knowledge, uncertainties and stereotypes about children with disabilities. Promoting disability awareness is therefore important to recognise and remove social and workplace barriers to create more inclusive environments for all who have dealt with discrimination because of disability. Many countries are now increasingly engaging in events that raise awareness on people with disability, as learning more about disability is essential in improving equal opportunities for disabled people. As example, the Paralympic School Day (PSD) is a sports-focussed disability awareness and education programme that offers an avenue for raising awareness and changing attitudes towards people with disabilities in New York (McKay, 2013). Through the PSD programme, students look at their feelings, beliefs and behaviours, and begin to question the impact their dispositions have on other people. PSD activities challenge the idealised notion of 'normal' against which people with disabilities are often compared. Through the PSD programme, students are able to identify common assumptions they may have about peers with disabilities and can test these assumptions during the activity stations. Disability awareness campaign also occupies an important place in university event's agenda. In recent years, college and university campuses have also sought a stronger understanding of the needs of students with disabilities, and the ways to offer support to this traditionally underserved student population (Roth, Pure, Rabinowitz, & Kaufman-Scarborough, 2018). The study of Ison et al. (2010) demonstrates that organising events on disability awareness aim to increase knowledge and acceptance of disability. The study evaluated a disability awareness programme for students aged 9–11 in Australia. It was found that disability awareness events, such as Disability Awareness Day, which is the world's largest voluntary-led disability exhibition, were impactful as people with no disability are exposed to people with disability and the former gets a chance to develop deeper understanding of challenges and implications of living a life disability. These kinds of events indeed give significant information and arouse some forms of empathy which are required to better understand people living with a disability. Similar to the case study of Ison et al. (2010) in Australia, the

ANPRAS case study in Mauritius shows that children with disabilities can be empowered to become resilient and less vulnerable, if they are actively engaged in events and activities. Their confidence level can be boosted and networking with other children with and without disabilities during the event provides moral support. Based on the fact that children are leaders of tomorrow and that sustainability is possibly the most important issue in the twenty-first century (Edgell & Swanson, 2018), it is indeed imperative to engage children without disabilities with children with disabilities in order for the former to acquire the necessary moral and social values.

Conclusion

The content of this chapter has broadened understanding of the contributions of children with disabilities in the attainment of ANPRAS's goals which is sustainability actions in line with the SDGs and the African Union Agenda 2063. Evidences provided throughout the chapter (though limited) show that children with disabilities have potential. All they need is appropriate infrastructure and support. Investment and collaboration of the government and all concerned stakeholders is one amongst the main solutions to meet the challenges faced in ensuring that children with disabilities have access to school through meaningful participation. A change in the mindset of the community at large should be fostered, especially, regarding the inclusion of children with disabilities in national activities along with the other children. For instance, during the Earth Hour event, children with disabilities were surrounded by the community at large while being accompanied by teachers and parents. Training should also be provided to parents of children with disabilities to ease communication between parents and their children as well as support and encourage them in upbringing their children and ensuring that the latter have access to quality education. Inclusive education is recommended since it is economically effective and efficient because rather than taking resources out of the regular system to educate groups of students with specific needs, all of the resources stay in the system.

In the context of Mauritius, it should be reiterated that children with disabilities are part of its 1.3 million inhabitants. When children with disabilities are denied their right to participate in activities, this subsequently leads to a chain of lifelong impacts ranging from learning, achievement to employment opportunities which will consequently prevent them in their potential economic, social and human development. By excluding them, Mauritius loses valuable human resources and talents that could have contributed a lot in the economic development of the island (Mahadew & Mootooveeren, 2020). As cited at the beginning of the chapter, Jane Constance is a perfect example to illustrate how children with disability have hidden talent (UNESCO, 2017). Jane Constance is visually impaired since birth, and she was designated UNESCO Artist for Peace in September 2017 in light of her commitment to promoting and raising public awareness on inclusion and empowerment of persons with disabilities in societies. Jane was supported by the Global Rainbow Foundation, an NGO based in

Mauritius. As Jane is growing up, she continues to give her support for the inclusion of people with disabilities and for the fight against discrimination of people with disabilities in cultural, social and economic fields. This example suggests that when barriers to the inclusion of children with disabilities are removed and such children are empowered, the whole community benefits.

ANPRAS has provided anecdotal evidences on how children with disability can also transform a society by moving their steps towards sustainability, a philosophy in line with ANPRAS motto – a small step in sustainability, a significant step in philanthropy! The ANPRAS case study shows that children with disabilities can be empowered to become resilient and less vulnerable, if they are actively engaged in events and activities. Their confidence level can be boosted and networking with other children with and without disabilities during the event provides moral support. Based on the fact that children are leaders of tomorrow and that sustainability is possibly the most important issue in the twenty-first century (Edgell & Swanson, 2018), it is indeed imperative to engage children without disabilities with children with disabilities in order for the former to acquire the necessary moral and social values. ANPRAS advocates for sustainability and by including children with disabilities in its programmes, it not only meets some of the SDGs but also demonstrates that children with disabilities can be empowered to be change agents in society. All children, including those with disabilities, have the right to participate in an event and organisers need to cater for their needs so that they feel inclusive of the society. This point also goes in line with SDG 10 on reduced inequality. Unlike the study of Dowse et al. (2018) who put forward that children are invisible and undermined community members, ANPRAS activities have shown that children including those with disabilities occupy a leading position in the local context. In order to design effective interventions for children with disabilities, future research needs to recognise how families, schools, communities and societies shape the environment around children with disabilities as well as the types of adversity that they face while participating in events and activities. In particular, it is important to understand what makes these children vulnerable and how they can be made more resilient.

References

Bunwaree, S., & Kasenally, R. (2007). Rights and development in Mauritius- A reader: Ossrea Mauritius. Chapter 107–110.

Canosa, A., Graham, A., & Wilson, E. (2020). Growing up in a tourist destination: Developing an environmental sensitivity. *Environmental Education Research*, *26*(7), 1027–1042. doi:10.1080/13504622.2020.1768224

Chawla, L., & Cushing, D. F. (2007). Education for strategic environmental behaviour. *Environmental Education Research*, *13*(4), 437–452. doi:10.1080/13504620701581539

Cheng, J.-C.-H., & Monroe, M. C. (2012). Connection to nature: Children's affective attitude toward nature. *Environment and Behavior*, *44*(1), 31–49. doi:10.1177/0013916510385082

CRC Report. (2015). *Concluding observations on the combined third to fifth periodic reports of Mauritius* (pp. 5–27). CRC/C/MUS/CO/3. February.

Dowse, S., Powell, S., & Weed, M. (2018). Mega-sporting events and children's rights and interests – Towards a better future. *Leisure Studies, 37*(1), 97–108. doi:10.1080/02614367.2017.1347698

Edgell, D. L., & Swanson, J. R. (2018). *Tourism policy and planning: Yesterday, today, and tomorrow.* New York, NY: Routledge.

Franklin, A., & Sloper, P. (2007). Participation of disabled children and young people in decision making related to social care. Social Policy Research Unit. University of York.

Government of Mauritius Population Census Report. (2011). *Housing and population census 2011-analytical report on disability.* Retrieved from http://statsmauritius.govmu.org/English/CensusandSurveys/Documents/2011HousingPopCensus/2011%20Census%20Disability%20Report.pdf. Accessed on January 30, 2019.

Gowreesunkar, V., & Chintaram, G. (2014). Engaging locals for sustainable tourism in Mauritius – The STORSA initiatives. In *Multi Stakeholder Magazine for Sustainable Development Goal 2015.* Samoa. Stakeholder Forum. Retrieved from https://stakeholderforum.org/about/

Gowreesunkar, V., Mohanty, P., & Maingi, S. (2022). *Children as ambassadors in sustainability initiatives of ANPRAS.* Emerald Publishing Limited. Retrieved from https://books.emeraldinsight.com/page/detail/?K=9781801176576

Ison, N., McIntyre, S., Rothery, S., Smithers-Sheedy, H., Goldsmith, S., Parsonage, S., & Foy, L. (2010). 'Just like you': A disability awareness programme for children that enhanced knowledge, attitudes and acceptance: Pilot study findings. *Developmental Neurorehabilitation, 13*(5), 360–368.

Kuo, M., Barnes, M., & Jordan, C. (2019). Do experiences with nature promote learning? Converging evidence of a cause-and-effect relationship. *Frontiers in Psychology, 10*, 305. doi:10.3389/fpsyg.2019.00305

Mahadew, A., & Mootooveeren, K. (2020). The right to education for children with disabilities in Mauritius: An assessment of the status of education. *International Journal of Law, Humanities and Social Science, 4*(3), 56–78. ISSN: 2521-0793.

Maingi, S., & Gowreesunkar, V. (2022). *Child rights and inclusive sustainable tourism development in East Africa: Case of Kenya: Children and sustainable and responsible tourism.* Emerald Publishing Limited. ISBN: 9781801176576. Retrieved from https://books.emeraldinsight.com/page/detail/?K=9781801176576

McKay, C. (2013). A disability awareness and education program. *ALAESTRA, 14*.

Murphy, N., & Carborone, P. (2008). Promoting the participation of children with disabilities in sports, recreation, and physical activities. *American academy of Pediatrics, 121*(5), 1057–1061.

Norwood, M. F., Lakhani, A., Fullagar, S., Maujean, A., Downes, M., Byrne, J., ... Kendall, E. (2019). A narrative and systematic review of the behavioural, cognitive and emotional effects of passive nature exposure on young people: Evidence for prescribing change. *Landscape and Urban Planning, 189*, 71–79.

Ombudsperson Report. (2019). *Annual report 2017–2018, Case 1: Advocating the right to education of children with multiple disabilities.* Retrieved from http://oco.govmu.org/English/News/Pages/Annual-Report-2017-2018.aspx

Otto, S., & Pensini, P. (2017). Nature-based environmental education of children: Environmental knowledge and connectedness to nature, together, are related to ecological behaviour. *Global Environmental Change, 47*, 88–94. doi:10.1016/j.gloenvcha.2017.09.009

Peek, L., & Stough, L. M. (2010). Children with disabilities in the context of disaster: A social vulnerability perspective. *Child Development, 81*(4), 1260–1270.

Roth, D., Pure, T., Rabinowitz, S., & Kaufman-Scarborough, C. (2018). Disability awareness, training, and empowerment: A new paradigm for raising disability awareness on a university campus for faculty, staff, and students. *Social Inclusion, 6*(4), 116–124.

Séraphin, H., & Gowreesunkar, V. (Eds.). (2020). *Children in hospitality and tourism: Marketing and managing experiences* (Vol. 4). Berlin: Walter de Gruyter GmbH & Co KG.

Séraphin, H., Gowreesunkar, V., & Canosa, A. (2021). Destination marketing organisations: The need for a child-centred approach to diaspora tourism. *Tourism Planning and Development.* doi:10.1080/21568316.2021.1903983

Statistics Mauritius. (2022). Retrieved from statsmauritius.govmu.org/SitePages/Index.aspx

Tillmann, S., Tobin, D., Avison, W., & Gilliland, J. (2018). Mental health benefits of interactions with nature in children and teenagers: A systematic review. *Journal of Epidemiology & Community Health, 72*(10), 958–966. doi:10.1136/jech-2018-210436

UNESCO. (2017). Young Mauritian singer Jane constance named UNESCO artist for Peace. Retrieved from https://en.unesco.org/news/young-mauritian-singer-jane-constance-named-unesco-artistpeace

UNICEF. (2020). Promoting the rights of children with disabilities. Retrieved from https://www.unicefirc.org/publications/474-promoting-the-rights-of-children-with-disabilities.html

Walker, C. (2017). Tomorrow's leaders and today's agents of change? Children, sustainability education and environmental governance. *Children & Society, 31*(1), 72–83. doi:10.1111/chso.12192

Chapter 14

A Kids TEDx? Handing Over the Microphone to Children to Bring Us All Inspiration, Learning and Wonder

Jan Carlyle

Abstract

This chapter explores the potential for a rigid format of event structure that has been successful for decades to be curated by, hosted by, attended by and with speakers who are all children or young people. The chapter considers the opportunities for an event and the changes in format that need to be made to stay true to the essence of the TED format yet incorporating the creativity and brilliance of children and young people to ensure they gain the most from an event of this format.

Keywords: TEDx; kids; speakers; attendees; event; legacy

Introduction

TED stands for Technology, Entertainment and Design (TED). The conferences began in 1984 in California and now TED delivers 2–3 global events a year alongside the independently organised TEDx events, thousands of which reach across the world every year. TED have protected their globally recognised brand by using a very clear set of rules for delivering a TED talk. For the global TED conferences, speakers are invited by the TED team to deliver a talk but insist on the rules being followed, to ensure consistency, fairness and the instantly recognisable format, everyone is on the red circle to deliver their talk, there is no lectern, and the timing is extremely strict. There are very few TED talks that are delivered with notes, or prompts, speakers are encouraged to learn their talks and know it inside-out. It is extremely impressive to see the TED format delivered live in quick succession with such a high turnover of ideas. TEDx events are independently organised TED events when a curator has attended a main TED conference, they can apply to host a TEDx (where *x* = independently organised

Events Management for the Infant and Youth Market, 209–217

Copyright © 2023 Jan Carlyle

Published under exclusive licence by Emerald Publishing Limited

doi:10.1108/978-1-80455-690-020231025

TED event) in their hometown or city. The speakers are usually from the local area and may not necessarily be people that would usually speak publicly. It has to be unique talk – it can't be one they've already given; it is unique to TEDx. Each talk is filmed, edited with branding and titles and uploaded to the TEDx YouTube channel.

The golden time of 18 minutes being the maximum for a TED talk is the short talk model works for events as it only demands the audience's attention for a short period of time but is long enough to communicate an idea to a group of people. The TED rules say there should not be a lectern as 'these objects disconnect the speaker from the audience, create an overly formal atmosphere, and encourage presenters to read from their notes. Which is always boring to watch'. These are just two of the many rules and guidelines that are associated with delivering a TED talk. These guidelines for delivery actually contribute to make TED one of the most engaging platforms in the world for public speaking, listening, learning, connecting and gathering. Some of the most watched or listened to TED talks have inspired action in many people.

When we hand over the microphone to children and young people are we still being inspired, curious and learn? Let's imagine that for a minute. A whole event delivered by young people and children, hosting, speaking and organising.

TEDx From a Practitioner Perspective

For my career I produce and curate events online, hybrid and in person and have been active since 1997 in this role, I'm now run an events agency, Autumn Live. As a TEDx curator and licensee, I have been on a journey with TED. It began in 2010 when I attended my very first TEDx in Sheffield in the United Kingdom, I can still now, 13 years later, recall some of the images I saw on that day. The talks were impactful, and I still have the notes from some of the sessions. That TEDx event was curated by Herb Kim, who is still now curating TEDx events across the north of England.

I have had the privilege of being part of the team for multiple TEDx events, attended one of the main global conferences, hosted by Chris Anderson, and I've curated, held the licence for and have hosted two TEDxWinchester events. The third is taking place in 2023 at the University of Winchester for the second year in a row. The format is simple, a series of individuals, though occasionally it can be two people speaking together, speak to an audience for no more than 18 minutes, with no lectern, maybe some slides, strong image or video, or maybe props on a simple idea, one that could change the world, one that's worth spreading.

TEDX and Children

The TED format is certainly one to aspire to but does this format hold for young people and children?

We probably all have our favourite TED talk. From Shonda Rhimes 2016 talk 'My year of saying yes to everything' or Brené Brown's 2010 talk: 'The Power of vulnerability' to Sir Ken Robinson's 2006 talk: 'Do schools kill creativity'. There have been a multitude of inspiring 18-minute slots we've watched from the comfort of our own home. Most of us have probably aspired to deliver one of our own – it's one of my favourite ice breakers in a group situation 'if you were asked to do a TED talk what would it be about?' I love seeing people on social media rant about a particular topic and end with 'Thank you for coming to my TED talk'. TED often create events with a specific focus TED Global or TED Women. TED did already imagine that we could hand the microphone over to children. TEDYouth was created and was an annual event hosted by TED between 2011 and 2015 in an effort to offer a wider platform for a more diverse group of people.

TEDYouth was a day-long event for middle and high school students, with live speakers, hands-on activities and great conversations. Scientists, designers, technologists, explorers, artists, performers (and more!) shared short talks, serving both as a source of knowledge and inspiration for youth around the globe. They no longer take place and other formats that TED have created with children and young people in mind which are accessible across the world are the TED-Ed videos. They are often viewed and engage with children and young people and used in educational settings.

TED-ed are short, animated videos that are used to educate people clearly and simply on a topic, they are around 5 minutes in length. The TED-Ed project – TED's education initiative – makes short video lessons worth sharing, aimed at educators and students. Within TED-Ed's growing library of lessons, it's possible to find carefully curated educational videos, many of which are collaborations between educators and animators nominated through the TED-Ed platform. With the end of TEDYouth, TEDxYouth events started to spring up. TEDx events for young people already take place all over the world. The TEDxYouth events are some of the most creative TEDx events that exist as they are focussed on young people as the speakers. Often young people are involved with organising them and the focus is still on ideas, but incorporates imagination and fun too.

As with standard TEDx events where the organiser has to apply for a licence from TED to run the event, TEDxYouth events follow the same TEDx rules as any other TEDx, the only difference being this type of event is focussed on youth. The licence holder can be a young person or a group of young people. If the young people are under 18 they need to have an adult co-organiser, alternatively the licence may be held by a young person and an adult or a group of young people and adults. Just like the TEDx events, there are rules around naming the event, each TEDxYouth event needs to include the word: Youth and the name of the city or educational establishment, such as TEDxYouth@Winchester or TEDxYouth@KingsSchool.

Mostly people who attend TEDxYouth events are young people and TED encourages organisers to engage with young people in the programming, curating the speakers and promoting the event. The number of attendees in the room at the TEDxYouth event varies depending on the licence the organiser has as only people who have attended an official TED conference can organise an event with more than 100 people. When it comes to theming the TEDxYouth event, there must be a broad range of topics, and a diversity of speakers across disciplines –

just like the regular TEDx or TED events. A theme should not be limiting and specific, but broad and general allowing a wide range of people to engage with it and formulate their ideas worth spreading. TED don't allow you to organise a whole TEDx event around a topic i.e. TEDxYouthDESIGN or TEDxYouth-Politics. TEDxYouth events can be short at a couple of hours, up to one day in length and organisers can charge up to $100USD per ticket. They still need to reflect TEDx events and themes, which should cross many disciplines and feature diversity of speakers.

There are a number of notable TEDxYouth events that have already happened: TEDxYouth@SanDiego took place in 2013 and was organised by 45 high school students with the help of a dedicated group adult mentors.

TEDxYouth@BrookhouseSchool is organised by a passionate team of students and teachers from Brookhouse School in Nairobi, Kenya.

In Southampton TEDxYouth@Bargate took place in 2018 and 2020, each of their events had a wider range of speakers of all ages alongside one young person (under 16) speak to the whole audience of young people.

To date there have been more than 13,000 TEDx events take place held in 150 countries. As of today there are 59 TEDxYouth events planned for 2023 across the globe, though none currently In Australasia or South America.

There are some historical examples of TEDxYouth events that have taken place.

In 2012, TEDxYouth@Tokyo was organised entirely by 11–18 year-olds – everyone from the hosts to the tech team were teenagers. Attendees skateboarded, talked with TEDxYouthDay attendees from around the globe on Skype and rock climbed during breaks.

TEDxYouth@Amman's 2011 event was organised by both adults and kids – the youngest team member was just nine years old! The event was held in the Jordanian capital and was live streamed all over the world with live interpretation in both English and Arabic.

Young people can curate, host and organise TEDx events. Ishita Katyal is the youngest TEDxYouth organiser in the Asia-Pacific region. She believes success comes from wanting happiness in the present moment, and she loves to read and write in her spare time. She wrote her book, Simran's Diary, when she was 8 years old.

What are the outcomes when children or young people take on the TED format and speak at TEDxYouth or TED events. There are some excellent examples of children and young people giving talks at TEDxYouth or TED.

Most 12-year-olds love playing videogames – but Thomas Suarez taught himself how to create them. After developing iPhone apps like 'Bustin Jeiber', a whack-a-mole game, he is now using his skills to help other kids become developers. His TED talk from 2011 has been viewed over 13 million times. The youngest person to ever give a TEDx talk is Kiara Kaur from TEDxRankalaLake who, aged five spoke on Unboxing Curiosity in India on Children's Day on 14 November 2021. Not only is she one of the youngest TEDx speakers, she also holds the record for youngest non-stop book reader, having read 36 books in 105 minutes at an event hosted by the Guinness Book of Records in London. Another most watched young person is Sparsh Shaha who is a 13-year-old child prodigy, singer, song writer and rapper, born with brittle bones (130+fractures), but an unbreakable spirit. Sparsh Shah wants to show people how they can transcend every difficulty that comes their way in life and how they can start a chain reaction to be a guide for other people who want to turn their life around as well. His talk was recorded in 2017 and has over 9.8m views and counting.

TEDx and Greta Thunberg

TEDx events can be an opportunity to bring a global issue to the world and can elevate individuals to future opportunities to speak on a global stage. Alongside the inspirational young people from the previous section, one of the most well-known TEDx talks given by a young person is Greta Thunberg.

Greta Thunberg realised at a young age the lapse in what several climate experts were saying and in the actions that were being taken in society. The difference was so drastic in her opinion that she decided to take matters into her own hands. Greta, at the time of giving her talk was a 15-year-old Stockholm native. She lived at home with her parents and sister Beata, who enjoys spending her spare time riding Icelandic horses and spending time with her family's two dogs, Moses and Roxy. She loves animals and has a passion for books and science. At a young age, she became interested in the environment and convinced her family to adopt a sustainable lifestyle. This talk was given at a TEDx event using the TED conference format but independently organised by a local community. Greta's TEDx talk has been watched over 6.1 million times (YouTube [Online]). She has since gone onto give an address to global leaders at the United Nations in Glasgow on 5 November 2021 and Davos – the meeting of the World Economic Forum on 25th January 2019.

In 2020 TED took the TEDx Youth format and the TED-Ed videos and combined the two ideas into one event that took place in New York: TED-Ed weekend, which brought student leaders together from all over the globe to take over TED headquarters for a youth conference. The speakers ranged in age from 14 to 19 and were from several different countries including Japan, Russia, Turkey, India and Ireland. The event hosted 150 young people from 24 different countries. Only students who are part of the TED-Ed programme could attend, but the weekend gave them an opportunity to talk to potential mentors and meet other youth leaders from different parts of the world and build the TED-Ed community. The event featured lots of hands-on media and animation workshops, workshops on community building and talk development and plenty of opportunities for the young people to learn valuable new skills. Submissions for the talks come from the young people via video and the programme is curated by the TED-Ed team.

There are a number of combinations to consider when thinking about handing over the microphone to children. It's one thing having a TEDx event organised and curated by young people, which is going to attract young people to the audience, and it's another thing to programme speakers who are all young people and children.

This chapter would like to consider a TEDx event curated by, hosted by, attended by and hosting speakers who are all children or young people. Imagine for a moment how would a TEDx event with children be? A little bit chaotic? Loud? Disorganised? Perhaps it would not be so slick or polished as a TED event. There may be more getting up and going to the toilet, speakers and hosts may forget words and be very nervous presenting to a large group of their peers. What would their biggest fear be? And is it possible for us as experienced, adult organisers alleviate their fears? Could young people be supported by adults to deliver a world-class TEDx event.

If the TED format is going to work for young people – there are a series of practical considerations to organising events with children and young people.

Critical Review of the Organisation of TEDYouth

Consideration of the Programing

Lots of breaks and short sessions in the schedule, the short 18 minutes – which fits our attention span perfectly, would still work for young people, but often TEDx events run five or six speakers back-to-back, with the host introduction and 'thank yous' which can easily fill 90–100 minutes of sitting in the same place. Challenging for adults sometimes, but definitely a hindrance to children and young people. Children and young people will need regular food and water breaks to be able to concentrate, and there would need to be toilet breaks or noise breaks where they can talk and make as much noise as they like. Young people have a shorter attention span, six 20-minute talks back-to-back is a lot of sitting still. If we had more breaks at events this would keep engagement higher.

- Catering
  Some careful thought around the catering It would be important to keep our young people fuelled and refreshed with water, not high sugar food or drinks that could lead to sugar crash and wild behaviour. Regular breaks for food and hydration would need to impact the programming. As with all events a wide range of food accounting for dietary requirements and choice of food from a sustainable, climate-friendly source. Layout of food with quick and easy access and no queueing and waiting around would also help to the smooth running of the break times.
- Safety
  Safety is a consideration when hosting young people, a good ratio of responsible adults to young people would help and security for young people with lanyard and badging making it clear if their photos are not to be taken for general event photography. Young people, and the parents and guardians who have permitted their children to attend the event would need to give permission for photographs and if they are speaking would need to sign a consent form

that their child or young person be filmed (This is a standard TED procedure for all speakers under 18).
* Talk Content
Engaging use of video and music in the sessions would keep people's intrigue and interest.

The talks would have to be shorter to keep their engagement and the content needs to be topics and themes that children want to hear about. Things they are passionate about and feel make a difference in their world, so important the event is curated by young people. At the TEDxYouth@Bargate event, the talks delivered by the young people were approximately five and six minutes long.

* Speaker coaching
Consideration of children and young people feeling confident enough to talk and extra assistance preparing them to form their ideas and speak. Youth events still hold to the TED format but there is a potential to reduce the fear of speaking and standing alone on that huge red circle for children and young people by inviting them to speak in a small group of two or three. The majority of children and young people will not have spoken in front of an audience of 100 people or more so there would be a need to start the speaker coaching early in the process to give speakers confidence. Rehearsals that can be filmed would be useful so speakers can watch back and improve their technique.
    As with regular TEDx events, the curating team could encourage the speakers to find their own style of delivery by watching a wide range of TED talks to help with preparation.
* Scheduling
With a youth event the scheduling during the year is important, exams and revision times would need to be avoided as well as school holidays. The TEDxYouth@Bargate event in order to appeal to the schools where they were inviting young people from had to make the timings school time friendly, by starting at 11 a.m. allowing time for travel and finishing by 2 p.m. so pupils could return in time for the end of the school day.
* Appropriate Sponsors and Partners
Our young people are more ethically aware than ever; sponsor and partners for a TEDx Youth event would need to be carefully considered alongside organisations that are age-appropriate, and this would be worth sense-checking with the young people who are running the event. Some brands or organisations might be instantly rejected by young people as their values maybe different from the values of young people who are attending. There is also a list on the TED website of brands that TEDx organisers are not permitted to contact so careful consideration of partners and sponsors are critical to acceptance and success of an event.
* Interactive Spaces outside the auditorium
Introducing interactive spaces in the breaks would help young people and children – there could be a dance floor or bikes generating electricity needed to

power the event. There could be somewhere at the event to exercise and burn off that extra energy. At TEDxYouth@Bargate there was lots of interactive and engaging spaces, An Interactive A0 map to colour in or post where you were from, a mindfulness space for colouring, giant games, such as chess or jenga to encourage people to interact with each other. The event still used name tags and lanyards, but just using the first name to make it more informal.

Another aspect of this event was the use of a live drawing event artist who illustrated the talks alongside the stage. They also got the young people in the audience to get involved and encouraged people to 'draw their feelings' and express with imagery how the talk may have impacted them.

Conclusion

A TEDx event for children and young people could be curated with their brains and learning in mind, so a scheduled break or workshop for some creative activity. Interactive spaces outside the auditorium could be hands-on getting messy with graffiti art or making music – These activities could actually become part of the programming. A creative musical talk with audience engagement or a hands-on graffiti session with a speaker would increase engagement and audience participation. This interactivity if it works with children and young people to engage them, the children and young people's event could lead the way and educate the TEDx events – with a programming cross-over to adults and the established TED events.

We know children are not limited by our adult understanding, physics and thinking within the laws of gravity! Their minds can be much more free-thinking than our adult minds. Could their ideas be less limiting and more liberating than ours? Could we be more inspired because they're a child or a young person and their ideas are revolutionary and re-imagined?

One option could be a TEDx Youth or TEDx Children event that is hosted by a child, all the speakers are under the age of 16, all the attendees are children and young people, and the event is supported by adults.

The TED format works for adults, but what if we asked children and young people to re-design it completely? Would they come up with the same impactful concepts? What themes are young people and children interested – careful thought would need to be given to themes and the nature of talks. Injustice, poverty, the latest social media platform, citizenship, climate crisis, sustainable fashion and the circular economy would all be topics we might see at a TED event curated and delivered by children and young people.

This would be a very impactful TEDx event. However, as is often the way when we create a dynamic and liberating space for an event, the people who need to hear the young people and see the event and be impacted by a room full of under 16-year-olds are the over 16-year-olds – the adults. To impact adults the most and create a world stage for children and young people to shine, it would be fitting to have, as part of every TED or TEDx event, a speaker who is a child or young person, that has a much bigger impact on all the 13,000 TEDx events and the millions of people who will attend and watch online a TEDx or TED talk.

All the notes are directing towards a complete 100% programme featuring children and young people as speakers. There could be a cross-over in learning from the young people's event to the adult audience and vice-versa. It would be an interesting experiment to run a TEDx youth and a regular TEDx in the same location – with one event consisting entirely of children and young people (TEDxYouth) and another event where the audience is the adults connected to those children and young people – their parents, carers, teachers and student leaders. Then comparing the audience feedback, outcomes, actions that result from both events.

If we continue along this trajectory of 100% programming featuring children and young people, this would continue to play into the established style of TED events with different audiences (Youth, Women, Global). It is possible there is an integration across the TED brands and what if speakers who are young people and children are incorporated in every TED and TEDx event. Just like people from across the globe and women are integral to the TED events. Young people and children could be programmed alongside world leaders and creatives and disruptors. It's not just diversity of age, it's diversity of speaking and ideas.

Let's start a campaign to get children and young people with ideas worth sharing on the programme for TED events, not as a token young person, but knowing diversity of age brings diversity of thoughts and ideas and imagination and creativity.

Useful Sources

Greta Thunberg TEDx talk School strike for climate. Retrieved from https://youtu.be/EAmmUIEsN9A

Kiara Kaur TEDx talk Unboxing curiosity. Retrieved from https://youtu.be/Y1kV3NQ87FY

Number of TEDx events. Retrieved from https://www.ted.com/about/programs-initiatives

Sparsh Shaha TEDx talk. Retrieved from https://youtu.be/bC0hlK7WGcM

Thomas Suarez TEDx talk. Retrieved from https://www.ted.com/talks/thomas_suarez_a_12_year_old_app_developer?utm_campaign=tedspread&utm_medium=referral&utm_source=tedcomshare

The 9 public-speaking secrets of the World's Top Minds. Retrieved from https://www.forbes.com/sites/carminegallo/2014/03/04/9-public-speaking-lessons-from-the-worlds-greatest-ted-talks/

The TED rules. Retrieved from https://www.ted.com/participate/organize-a-local-tedx-event/tedx-organizer-guide/speakers-program/prepare-your-speaker/rehearsals#:~:text=Speakers%20may%20not%20use%20a,is%20always%20boring%20to%20watch

Conclusion

Hugues Seraphin

All chapters agree on the fact to effectively design and deliver a successful event for children and young adults, a child-centric approach must be adopted. Practically, this would translate, for instance, in time and thought to be devoted to a thorough assessment of venues to find a suitable space that works for the audience. This would also translate into the use of fun activities. Children's play is not merely a physical activity, but rather a multidimensional engagement. Such an engagement can range from low cognitive level to high cognitive level, depending on whether the child is fully concentrating in an active mental state. The involvement of infants and young adults is also considered as a transformative approach. It is therefore proposed that sustainability-related career events offer significant potential to contribute transformative, whole-person teaching pedagogy. In this line of thought, this edited book has evidenced that when well planned and implemented by social marketers and managers, events can play an important role in influencing children to change behaviours and embrace sustainable practices more easily. To achieve so, three parameters are important, namely, promoting engagement, creating awareness and achieving empowerment.

Amongst the theoretical contributions of the book, could be mentioned:

(1) A framework for understanding children's engagement in events, i.e. Cognition-Affect-Behaviour (CAB) theoretical framework
(2) The fact family events create an eco-socialised childhood that idealises events and experiences.
(3) If well planned and implemented by social marketers and managers, can play an important role in influencing children to change behaviours and embrace sustainable practices more easily.

As for the practical contributions of the book, it offers specific steps to follow to design, plan and deliver successful events for children, including the choice of venue. The experience of practitioners shared in the 'Case study' section shows why it is important to have a good understanding of how to plan events for infants and young adults, and the pitfalls to avoid.

Having said that, research on children and events management is at its maiden stage. A lot still need to be done. Section 2 of the book offers a starting point for

Events Management for the Infant and Youth Market, 219–220
Copyright © 2023 Hugues Seraphin
Published under exclusive licence by Emerald Publishing Limited
doi:10.1108/978-1-80455-690-020231027

Research and Development (R&D) of future events, and/or planning of events involving children. Chapters such as 'A kids TEDx: Handing over the microphone to children to bring us all inspiration, learning and wonder' are evidence that any event organised for adults can also be delivered for children, ensuring a suitable approach is adopted, hence the purpose of this edited book.

Index